THE POST-GLOBAL CITY

AFRICAN PERSPECTIVES

Kelly Askew, Laura Fair, and Pamila Gupta
Series Editors

The Post-Global City: Theorizing Technology Cultures in Urban Africa
Katrien Pype, Omolade Adunbi, and Michael M. J. Fischer, Editors

*The Institutionalization of Islam in Southern Senegal:
Intermarriage, Qur'anic Education, and Jihād*
Aly Dramé

*The Education Alibi: Tracing Education's Entanglements
across Contemporary Africa*
Elizabeth Cooper, Erdmute Alber, and Wandia Njoya, Editors

*The Homeowner Ideology:
Economic (F)Utility of Real Property Rights in Four African Cities*
Singumbe Muyeba

Typologies of Humor in African Literatures
Adwoa A. Opoku-Agyemang

*Between HIV Prevention and LGBTI Rights:
The Political Economy of Queer Activism in Ghana*
Ellie Gore

*Protest Arts, Gender, and Social Change: Fiction, Popular Songs,
and the Media in Hausa Society across Borders*
Ousseina D. Alidou

The Imaginative Vision of Abdilatif Abdalla's Voice of Agony
Abdilatif Abdalla, edited by Annmarie Drury

Congo Style: From Belgian Art Nouveau to African Independence
Ruth Sacks

Lagos Never Spoils: Nollywood and Nigerian City Life
Connor Ryan

A complete list of titles in the series can be found at www.press.umich.edu

The Post-Global City

Theorizing Technology Cultures
in Urban Africa

Katrien Pype, Omolade Adunbi, and Michael M. J. Fischer, Editors

University of Michigan Press
Ann Arbor

Published in the United States of America by the
University of Michigan Press
First published February 2026

A CIP catalog record for this book is available from the British Library.

Library of Congress Control Number: 2025031920
LC record available at https: lccn.loc.gov/2025031920

ISBN 978-0-472-07782-3 (hardcover : alk. paper)
ISBN 978-0-472-05782-5 (paper : alk. paper)
ISBN 978-0-472-90543-0 (open access ebook)

DOI: https://doi.org/10.3998/mpub.14600788

The University of Michigan Press's broader open access publishing program is made possible
thanks to additional funding from the University of Michigan Office of the Provost and the
generous support of contributing libraries.

Cover Image Credit: iStock. Uploaded by lasagnaforone.

The authorized representative in the EU for product safety and compliance is Easy Access
System Europe, Mustamäe tee 50, 10621 Tallinn, Estonia, gpsr.requests@easproject.com

CONTENTS

Digital materials related to this title can be found on the Fulcrum platform via the following citable URL: https://doi.org/10.3998/mpub.14600788

Omolade Adunbi is a Professor of Anthropology and Afroamerican and African Studies. He is also Professor of Law (by courtesy), Director of the African Studies Center and Faculty Associate, Program in the Environment, and Institute for Energy Solutions at the University of Michigan, Ann Arbor. He is the author of *Enclaves of Exception: Special Economic Zones and Extractive Practices in Nigeria* (Indiana University Press, 2022, honorable mention for the African Studies Association Best Book Prize in 2023 and Finalist for Best Book Prize, African Studies Association of the United Kingdom, 2024). His previous book, *Oil Wealth and Insurgency in Nigeria* (Indiana University Press, 2015) won the Royal Anthropological Society of Great Britain and Ireland's Amaury Talbot Book Prize for the best book on the anthropology of Africa in 2017. His research engages with questions of climate politics, infrastructure, energy practices, and social media culture. He is the recipient of the 2022 John Dewey Award for his long-term commitment to undergraduate education. He also received the Class of 1923 Memorial Teaching Award for excellence in teaching in 2016.

Barbara Carbon has recently started work as a part-time senior research assistant for CREST, University of Chester, where she will be working on the Centre for Living with Climate Change project conducting participatory action research in Powys and Shropshire, UK. She has been living in Powys since 2018, where she also works with adults with learning disabilities and in mental health. She is presently training as a gestalt psychotherapist at the Manchester Gestalt Centre. Over the past few years she has been a freelance artist/researcher delivering a range of different creative projects within the different sections of her community. For this she has been using her talents in music, theater, and visual art. She has been affiliated to KU Leuven since 2015, when she started her PhD research on the dialectic relationship between culture and technology, with a particular focus on water and the Inga dams. She spent thirteen months in the Democratic Republic of the Congo conducting participatory observation research in and around the dams, in a village with an artisanal dam, at water purification centers across Bakongo province, on a container ship on the Congo River, and on a Chinese fishing vessel operating on the Atlantic Ocean in Congolese waters. Holding a master of arts in social work from Liverpool Hope University, an initial teacher training degree from the University of Antwerp, and a master of arts in African languages and cultures from Ghent University, Barbara is passionate about social justice, equality, and social inclusion. She has recently been reflecting on better ways to decolonize her writing and been working on a self-reflective article to explore her journey to reach this objective.

Michael M. J. Fischer is Andrew W. Mellon Professor in the Humanities, and Professor of Anthropology and Science and Technology Studies at MIT, as well as Lecturer in Social Medicine in the Department of Global Health and Social Medicine, Harvard Medical School. He trained at Johns Hopkins, the London School of Economics, and the University of Chicago (PhD). He has taught at Chicago, Harvard, Rice, and MIT, serving as Director of the Center for Cultural Studies at Rice, and Director of the Program in Science, Technology and Society at MIT. He has done fieldwork in the Caribbean, Iran, India, Singapore and Southeast Asia. He is author of ten books, including *Anthropology in the Meantime* (2020) and *Probing Arts and Emergent Forms of Life* (2023), and is coeditor of the book series Experimental Futures at Duke University Press. He has written or cowritten articles on the arts in Rwanda, the planning of Kigali, and information technology start-ups in Nairobi.

Mohamed Ghasia is the Director of Information and Communication Technology and principal educational technologist at Mzumbe University in Tanzania. He earned his PhD in Comparative Sciences of Cultures from the University of Ghent in 2019, with a dissertation on supporting micro-learning access through the Ujuzi mobile application: a brokerage deployment model and pilot study for Tanzanian higher education institutions. His doctoral research focused on studying learners' behavioral practices regarding micro-credentials and micro-learning through the Ujuzi application he developed. Mohamed holds master's degrees in computer science from both Sheffield Hallam University (2008) in the UK and the Institute of Finance Management (2001) in Tanzania. He has since then transitioned into digital anthropology at the PhD level, blending his technical expertise with cultural insights. With over two decades of services at Mzumbe University, Mohamed has led and championed several initiatives to enhance infrastructure and improve service delivery through the application of digital technologies. His key contributions include the successful implementation of eLearning platforms, digital library services, and the provision of internet access to various university communities, particularly those in underserved areas. Since 2021, he has served as the digitalization coordinator for the World Bank–funded Higher Education for Economic Transformation project in Tanzania. In this role, he focuses on expanding and democratizing access to university services, ensuring equity for all stakeholders through the use of digital solutions. Mohamed's professional interests are rooted in digital anthropology, systems design, and deployment, with a particular focus on the integration of cultural values into technology. His research spans areas such as e-learning, mobile learning, micro-learning, micro-credentials, and educational brokerage services. His works can be found on the URL https://scholar.google.com/citations?hl=en&user=FTStNPEAAAAJ.

Vivien M. Meli is a socio-anthropologist and Senior Lecturer at the University of Dschang in Cameroon, Central Africa. He is the author of some twenty-five scientific articles published in various national and international publications. He has also coedited two books. His scientific interests are linked to the dynamics of (so-called) marginalized social categories, in this case young people, women, and Indigenous peoples, assessed on the basis of practices of rurality, urbanity, informality, transgression, and so on, in the fields of health and the environment. This includes issues of mobility on urban margins, urban-rural connections, governance, and inclusion in urban transport. The aim of this work is to identify the potential of socially disadvantaged groups to make a lasting contribution to historical social action in societies in transition. He also provides consultancy services in Africa for local, national, and international organizations. He is General Secretary of Unité de Recherche Philosophie et Sciences Sociales Appliquées at the University of Dschang, promoter of the Association Centre Africain d'Études et de Promotion Rurale, and a member of the Association Internationale des Sociologues de Langue Française.

Trisha Phippard is a medical anthropologist with expertise in the domains of global health and development communication, health-related technology cultures, and epidemic discourse and response in Africa. Following a background in the nonprofit sector and care work in Canada and South Africa, she is currently affiliated as a doctoral researcher at KU Leuven, Belgium. Her current research explores the material and symbolic aspects of biomedical technology and its role in shaping the meanings, possibilities, and practices of care in the city of Kikwit, Democratic Republic of the Congo.

Katrien Pype is associate professor in social and cultural anthropology at KU Leuven, and an honorary research fellow at the University of Birmingham (UK). She has been carrying out ethnographic research in Kinshasa since 2003. Her research interests are in popular culture, media worlds, tech creativity, and innovation. She is the author of *The Making of the Pentecostal Melodrama: Religion, Media, and Gender in Kinshasa* (Berghahn Books, 2012) and has coedited *Ageing in Sub-Saharan Africa. Spaces and Practices of Care* (Policy Press, 2016, with Jaco Hoffman) and *Cryptopolitics: Exposure, Concealment and Digital Media* (Berghahn Books, 2023, with Victoria Bernal and Daivi Rodima-Taylor). Her articles have appeared in *Journal of the Royal Anthropological Institute, Ethnos, Africa: Journal of the International Africa Institute, Anthropological Quarterly, Journal of African Cultural Studies, Visual Anthropology*, and others. She has also published a large number of book chapters. Her publications draw on research on the production of evangelizing television serials; the production of news broadcasts; the elderly's experience of a mediatized urban environment; and the expanding communication eco-system in Kinshasa. Katrien cocreated the CongoResearch-Network in 2009 (with Aldwin Roes and Rueben Loffman), which she is still coordinating (with Cai Chen now). As from 2024, she co-convenes the EASA Anthropology of Media Network (with John Postill and Lotte Hoek, and Tom MacDonald. Katrien is member of the advisory editorial boards of the journals *Africa; Journal of African Cultural Studies, African Studies Review*, and *Carrefour Congolais*. In recent years, her research interests have turned toward pressing global societal issues such as climate change and digitalization. She has co-initiated a European doctoral training network on "climate urgency"; has established together with colleagues at KU Leuven a research network on air pollution; and is the principal investigator of a collaborative project on organic pesticide production in central and eastern Africa. Her research has been supported by Flemish, British, and European funding bodies.

Nick Rahier is an anthropologist at KU Leuven and Ghent University, both in Belgium. He focuses on health, pollution, and environmental change in African urban locales and leads projects on air pollution and green pesticide production in Kenya. His forthcoming monograph explores an anthropology of viability and thermal futuring in Nakuru, Kenya. He coordinates the RESPIRA stakeholder network on air pollution in Africa and is co-developing the ThermoCultures Research Network, which will bring together scholars working on life under hotter conditions across the world.

Griet Steel is an anthropologist by training and currently works as an independent researcher on issues of sustainable development, mobility, informal economy, digital entrepreneurship, urban land, and gender. Her principal research focus is on the creative and inventive ways in which people in Africa, Latin America, and Europe, and women in particular, are developing entrepreneurial practices to deal with global challenges. Working at the crossroads of human geography, economic anthropology, and migration studies, Steel has contributed to theoretical and methodological debates on everyday practices of place-making and socioeconomic development in the context of globalization, mobility, and the digitalization of society. She has participated and coordinated several international research projects on rural-urban linkages (an FP7 research program financed by the European Union), technology and urbanity (an Odysseus research project at KU Leuven financed by FWO), women's land rights (an action research program financed by the Netherlands Ministry of Foreign Affairs), the urban land nexus (an EARF research program financed by DFID) and investment frontiers of sustainability transitions (an now-funded Aspasia project). She has extensive field experience in several Latin American countries (Bolivia, Peru, Ecuador, and Nicaragua) and extended her geographical focus to the African continent by conducting research in the city of Khartoum on urban transformations, informal entrepreneurship, and land governance. The case study in this chapter is based on ethnographic research in Khartoum that was conducted when she was working as a postdoc researcher in the Odysseus research program Technology and the Postcolonial City at KU Leuven.

Koen Stroeken is Professor in Africanist anthropology at Ghent University. He codirects the Centre for Anthropological Research on Affect and Materiality, a fluid forum for ethnographers working in the most diverse terrains and regions to discern both the inarticulate energies (affect) and the tangible effects (materiality) of culture(s) in the broadest sense. He coordinates since its inception in 2012 an interuniversity exchange with Mzumbe University in Tanzania to build academic capacity on local governance, entrepreneurship, and technology. After developing apps for social innovation, the collaboration has extended to comprise social robotics in education. Stroeken authored the ethnography *Moral Power: The Magic of Witchcraft* and the regional comparison *Medicinal Rule: A Historical Anthropology of Kingship in East and Central Africa*, both published by Berghahn. He recently published through Palgrave's open access *Simplex Society: How to Humanize*, a monograph applying the medicinal model to global processes. His use of "tensors" attempts to lift anthropology out of the postmodern matrix and its particularism. The theory he defends, among others in a debate in *Current Anthropology* in 2023, is a phenomenology embracing the reflexivity of structuralist analysis. He has (co-)supervised PhD projects in Tanzania, Uganda, Mozambique, South Africa, Angola, the DRC, Mali, and Ghana, as well as India, Sri Lanka, and Guyana. His editing work includes the volume *War Technology Anthropology*.

Joseph Tonda is a professor of sociology and anthropology and a writer. He teaches at Omar Bongo University in Libreville, after having taught at the Marien Ngouabi University in Brazzaville from 1985 to 1997. He has carried out teaching and research missions at the École de Hautes Études de Paris, École des Hautes Études en Sciences Sociales, Catholic University of Louvain, KU Leuven University, and several other universities. He is the author of several works, including *La guérison divine en Afrique centrale (Congo, Gabon)* (Karthala, 2002), *Le souverain moderne: Le corps du pouvoir en Afrique centrale, Congo, Gabon* (Karthala, 2005, translated into English by Seagul in 2021), *L'impérialisme postcolonial: Critique de la société des éblouissements* (Karthala, 2015, currently being translated for Duke University Press), and *Afrodystopie: La vie dans le reve d'autrui* (Karthala, 2021). He is currently finishing the book *Ecoanimismes: Le suicide de la nature humaine dans le continent noir*, a reflection on the colonialism of human nature.

ILLUSTRATIONS

PREFACE AND ACKNOWLEDGMENTS

The purpose of *The Post-Global City* is to open up a new field of analytical inquiry that takes seriously technological developments in urban Africa, as these are rooted in local, historical realities while also partaking in transnational, global processes. We thus aim to correct the stereotypical image of Africa as a continent either devoid of technology or filled with broken technologies or solely with technologies coming from the Global North or Asia. This volume focuses on accounts and critiques of new "rising Africa" ideologies and practices threaded in and around state megaprojects (geothermal, hydroelectric) together with networked start-ups that circumvent or contest the state and patriarchal hierarchies (artisanal oil refineries, female vendors online, techie start-ups across diasporas) and post-global South–South connections. Without ignoring technologies responding to marginalization and exploitation, often expressed in nativist, occultist, and Christian fundamentalist language (the subject of many studies), it responds to new imaginaries, affects, and individual self-confidence that assert young Africans should, and are showing that they leave colonial and postcolonial inferiority complexes behind, instead building new nonstate connections across post-global cities. We aim to rethink colonial and postcolonial approaches to knowledge production in African cities by bringing into focus how the subaltern designs, innovates, and mobilizes technologies for everyday use. The chapters also encompass large and small settlements, a university campus, as well as enclaves that display some levels of temporality, and the protagonists are not only those who live in these areas but also those who visit them and move in and out for social, economic, and other reasons. *The Post-Global City* is the first book to explicitly and persistently inquire into the dialectics between technology and the urban in Africa.

The volume showcases the emergence of Belgium (KU Leuven University) as a center of Africanist, anthropologically situated science and technology studies in association with colleagues elsewhere in Europe, the United States, and across the African continent. The contributors are a unique blend of junior and senior scholars, and they are working at African, European, and American universities. All chapters, except for the introduction, draw on original ethnographic fieldwork carried out in urban spaces in Cameroun, Democratic Republic of the Congo, Gabon, Kenya, Nigeria, Sudan, and Tanzania. They bring together voices from both Francophone and Anglophone Africa. Also here, the volume is unique.

Funding for the research for most of the chapters of this edited volume came from the Fonds voor Wetenschappelijk Onderzoek (the national fund for scientific research in Flanders), which provided financial support for two projects on technology cultures in urban Africa: Comparing Technology Cultures in Urban DR Congo (1960–Present): Kinshasa, Kikwit and Lubumbashi (Odysseus grant, 2014–2019, FWO G.A005.14N) and Technology and the Postcolonial City: Anthropological Explorations of Infrastructures. Mobilities and Urbanity in Postcolonial Kinshasa (1960–Present) (ERC Runner Up grant, 2014–2017, FWO G.0.E65.14N). Both were designed by Katrien Pype while she was a postdoctoral scholar at MIT (2011–2012). Her previous research, on popular culture and media in Kinshasa, mainly focused on representations (in television fiction, songs, dances, etc.). Around 2010, during fieldwork, Katrien was confronted with major infrastructural transformations in Kinshasa. President Kabila's governance was very much anchored in so-called public works, of which renovating and upgrading the electricity and water grids in the city accelerated (although at the time of publishing this volume, these remain very much unfinished). At the same time, social media gradually became more and more in use in Kinshasa. Technology talk was everywhere: in the public media (and especially in Kabila's propaganda), on social media platforms, but especially in the everyday conversations with Kinois, who had to adapt their daily movements to the blocked roads that had turned into construction sites, and who began dreaming of a Dubai-like Kinshasa. Many of these fantasies were nourished by billboards around town, promising comfortable urban environments made possible by well-maintained, tarmacked roads, well-functioning electricity grids, state-of-the-art hospitals, and so forth. These ethnographic observations pushed Katrien to develop a research project that would ethnographically investigate the new forms of expertise, knowledge, affects, urban experiences, and cultural forms that infrastructural changes in the DRC, and beyond, generated. The subprojects of this research agenda were oriented toward three domains: communication, health, and energy.

The core team comprised the PI, Katrien Pype; three PhD students, Barbara Carbon, Trisha Phippard (Lawrence), and Nick Rahier; and Griet Steel as postdoctoral scholar. All carried out their own field project in urban areas in the DRC, Kenya, and Sudan, respectively. Various scholars joined the team for a few weeks or longer. Contributors Joseph Tonda and Vivien Meli visited the team in 2018 and 2021 respectively. Other colleagues who came to Leuven and provided invaluable feedback on ongoing work while also sharing their own work in progress on related topics are Patrice Yengo, Elisio Macamo, Alessandro Jedlowski, Cele Paul Manianga, Olunfunke Olufunsho Adegoke, Sasha Newell, Scott Ross, Nanna Schneidermann, Lys Alcayna-Stevens, and Josiah Taru. The following members of the advisory doctoral committees have provided invaluable insights on drafts of the PhD work for Barbara Carbon, Nick Rahier, and Trisha Phippard: Lys Alcayna-Stevens, Reginald Cline-Cole, Filip De Boeck, Joost Fontein, Paul Wenzel Geissler, Clemens Greiner, Bruno Lapika, Clapperton Chakanetsa Mavhunga, Patience Musasa, Koen Stroeken, and Steven Van Wolputte. In the summer of 2021, most contributors to this book and two of the editors (Omolade and Katrien) congregated in the medieval site Alden-Biesen, eastern Belgium, to workshop an earlier version of the chapters. Peter Geschiere and Victoria Bernal discussed the drafts and provided generous and excellent feedback.

The work in this book also builds on long-standing Africanist anthropological research at KU Leuven. At the time of starting this project, it was hosted by the Institute for Anthropological Research in Africa (IARA), which morphed into the Department of Social and Cultural Anthropology in 2021. The anthropology of technology was introduced into IARA by this project and has since inspired other technology-oriented research. We would like to thank IARA and the Department of Social and Cultural Anthropology at the KU Leuven for the intellectual, collegial, and logistical assistance they have provided during this project. Annelies Geens and Ann Weemaes deserve special mention because of their special care for the various activities organized around the project—particularly logistics for participants at some of the workshops.

US-based scholars and academic infrastructures likewise provided significant scaffolds for this book. From the incipient phase of the technology cultures in urban Africa projects onward, the project could count on the wavering support and invaluable input from Clapperton Chakanetsa Mavhunga. Katrien is thankful for the many years of sparring over research ideas, exchanging literature tips, and commenting on drafts. Mike Fischer, coeditor, was the host of Katrien's postdoctoral fellowship at MIT, and has shown a keen interest in technology cultures in Africa ever since they first got in touch in 2009. Mike's excitement about this collection, and especially his feedback on the book's organization and the analyses, have rightfully turned him into a coeditor. Victoria Bernal held a nine-month visiting professor position at IARA (2018–2019), during which time she observed and commented on the progress made. Jeroen Cuvelier, Thomas Hendriks, and Peter Lambertz gave feedback on some earlier drafts.

We are very grateful to the Department of Afroamerican and African Studies and the African Studies Center at the University of Michigan for providing funding for Omolade's research in Nigeria. Our gratitude also goes to the series editors—Kelly Askew, Laura Fair, and Pamila Gupta, as well as the acquiring editor, Marcella Landri, for their support of this volume. Thanks to the anonymous reviewers for providing insightful comments, and to the copyeditor for their expert care on this manuscript.

Finally, we especially acknowledge the many interactions with colleagues and interlocutors in the DRC, Cameroun, Gabon, Kenya, Nigeria, Tanzania, and Sudan, without which the ethnographers would not have been able to collect the empirical data. This book is as much theirs as it is ours. And we hope that the open access version of this book will enable them to find joy and satisfaction, but above all pride.

Post-Global City Formations

Technology and Africa's Urban Futures

OMOLADE ADUNBI, KATRIEN PYPE,
AND MICHAEL M. J. FISCHER

At the celebration of its golden jubilee anniversary in 2013, the African Union, established in 1963 as the Organization of African Unity, rolled out "Agenda 2063: The Africa We Want," enumerating what it calls "*An integrated, prosperous and peaceful Africa, driven by its own citizens, representing a dynamic force in the international arena.*"[1] Agenda 2063 suggests we think about the future of Africa as belonging to and shaped by Africans. The reshaping of the future of Africa, the agenda suggests, would include investment in science, technology, and innovation. The science and technology component of Agenda 2063 did not come as surprise considering that many technology icons such as Mark Zuckerberg, Bill Gates, and others have paid several visits to cities such as Nairobi, Accra, and Lagos, boosting the image of Africa as a rising technology giant. These visits have added to speculations about Nairobi, Kigali, and Lagos becoming the new Silicon Valley in Africa. In this volume, we contextualize technology in ways that center Africans in the making of technologies that create interaction between cities and suburbs, creeks and city centers. While not discountenancing the idea that Agenda 2063 is crucial in how Africa positions itself as a site for science, technology, and innovation, we suggest that Africa has always been a site for innovation through everyday practices by its citizens. We pay particular attention to everyday practices that are connecting cities as centers of innovation and technological development in ways that suggest the emergence of what we call post-global city formations. By the "post-global city," we mean the new reconfigurations of growth in technological innovations in but certainly also beyond the global city through vibrant start-up communities, and the emergence of networks of tech entrepreneurs, apprentice engineers, and other experts, that make connections between cities that may be inserted in the global economy but have little prominence, for example, from San Francisco to Lagos, New York to Nairobi, Brussels to Kinshasa, Singapore to Kigali, and Nairobi to both Lagos and Kigali (see Fischer 2023a, 2023b, 2023c, and 2025, Fischer and Sadruddin forthcoming 2025). "Post-global" thus is a relational term and contrasts, as we show below, with the "global city" (Sassen 1991). The post-global city often grows within and without the porosities of the city. Cities connect individuals and groups who design and co-design technologies that navigate the contours of rural and urban centers. Cities serve as the hub of incubation of ideas that manifest as technologies. Post-global cities do this along flows of influence, expertise, capital, and affect differently than global cities. To demonstrate the emergence of the post-global city, this volume showcases nine examples of everyday practices in the making of technologies. We start with the most difficult to evaluate, capturing the ingenuity of practitioners, and proceed to the everyday of astute, inventiveness, and pragmatics of learning to live in these spaces.

First, we take on perspectives on the new internationalizing start-up, digital, and engineering economies that, as Katrien Pype describes in her essay on Kinshasa's emerging tech scene (chapter 1), can lead to a post-global city—which we have taken as the volume title and focus of inquiry. These new economies have also been hailed in slogans such as "Africa rising," meant to highlight new technical means that the young and educated may use to democratize bureaucracies, level the playing field of wealth creation, and reshape the political state. The second set of perspectives are the mediated (and media) worlds of smoke and mirrors (in finance, music, and religion) that seem to dominate the psyches of everyone from politicians to Pentecostal preachers (Tonda in chapter 2). The first set of perspectives can be measured with the tools of business plans (successful, flawed, failed, or awry); the second is measured in fancy cars, gowns, gated mansions and communities, and other status-creating commodities, always outrunning themselves, creating new distinctions, and often reinforcing the state of violence and the violence of the state. They are often driven psychodynamically, incorporating and undoing the economic logics of the post-global.

As Tonda illustrates, there is an argument being developed, largely by some African theorists, that after the necessary intellectual efforts at deconstruction of colonialism, postcolonialism, neoliberal globalization, and the decolonial, there comes into view (like a rubbing of an inscription on a grave or memorial) something we call the post-global that is productive, dangerous, and potentially a new imaginary that recycles and intensifies legacy spirits, ghosts, and prophets into new heterotopic (to use Michel Foucault's term) urban social formations.

Pype, in describing the post-global city, is less focused on the colonializing "discipline and punish" panopticon of camps (or immobilizing mechanisms producing poverty) or on the folklorizing and stereotyping by the media culture than on the centrifugal or outward forces creating networks across geographies, operating around, under, or beyond the state and the international "order." These newer forces are globalizing and sometimes redistributive, as with the artisanal oil refineries described by Adunbi (this volume, and his earlier work 2015, 2022), the internet apps for housewives engaged in transnational trade from their homes (Griet Steel, this volume), the now famous M-Pesa mobile money (Koen Stroeken and Mohamed Ghasia, this volume), the local physician demand for modern X-ray machines in Kikwit, a midsize city in the Democratic Republic of the Congo (Trisha Phippard, this volume), and perhaps the redesigning of moto-taxis (motorcycle taxis) imported from China to suit local practices (Vivien M. Meli, this volume). These are all bottom-up initiatives with expanding reach. Many are South–South initiatives rather than oriented to former European centers of the political economy.

Pype's term "post-global city" focuses attention on "new geographies and imaginations of other spaces, 'elsewheres,' as they are related to tech innovation," which in Kinshasa "emerge through the links between [for instance] Congolese designers, their studies abroad, the spaces of assembling the devices, and the new destinations of desire for Kinshasa's (aspiring) tech entrepreneurs . . . embedded in post-neoliberal networks of 'global cities'" (Pype, this volume). The "forms of mobility and migration" in these tech imaginations, she writes, "differ from trajectories steered by neoliberal capitalism" and are accompanied by a "particular configuration of political affects that speaks about the endurance of colonial violence into the twenty-first century, and the imagination of new, more dignified postcolonial futures." Among her examples from Kinshasa are Congolese-made watches (but also smartphones and computers), with advice on marketing from Kigali and elsewhere, in an effort to democratize the means of production in a new economy.

The notion of a post-global city builds upon the "global city," which is a formation of the neoliberalism of the 1970s–1990s with it an imagination of easing financial flows across continents among major metropoles (e.g., *The Global City* [Sassen 1991]). Global cities only have secondary concern for upgrading the "hinterlands," which it was claimed would also be stimulated by investment and growth from the metropoles. The global city builds upon the earlier "colonial city," often divided into old city and new (city and cantonment in India; medina and modern town in Morocco [Rabinow 1995]). It helps reorient our gaze away from these and uncovers a new, often South–South, formation, and a co-shaping of the post-global city with "new dialects" (or dialectical relations among) "political affects, patriotism, pride, but also shame and cultural alienation" (Pype, this volume).

The post-global city, in contrast to the global city, breaks away from the neoliberalism of directing aid and loans down through governments and then insisting on strict accounting procedures and often shadow cabinets of "consultants" to oversee the flows of money, thereby hobbling local governmental capacity-building, and often further and further indebting recipient national economies. When local redistribution of funds keeps the wheels turning, the internationals see only corruption and threaten more outside disciplining, such as in the most drastic "structural adjustments" of the 1990s, leaving countries' educational and medical systems devastated, lacking funds and equipment in order to save the "credit" and "reputation" of the country on capital and lending markets (Duffield 2001, 2007, 2019). The post-global city is an answer to these dilemmas "from below." The post-global city will have its own dilemmas, but, for the moment, the idea of it provides a framework for trying to locate "other" centers of growth, generativity, and creativity. Some innovations, like M-Pesa, launched in Kenya as a mobile money transfer platform by cell phones in 2007, are able to expand across borders: M-Pesa now operates in eight countries, providing a real-time financial platform that serves those who are often ignored by regular financial institutions (see Fischer 2023 for the IT and financial structures beyond just M-Pesa). The post-global city is etched onto something "other" than colonial/global flows of ideas, capital, knowledge, and desires. What these "others" are is the subject of ethnographic investigation. For example, recognizing Congolese and other African traders in Chinese cities (Guangzhou in particular) can provide us with new maps of how supply chains work, how they grow, how they move up the value chain, and how these movements are embedded in affective circuits that have largely been uncharted so far. Though not charted, these formations can find space in the discourse of the "Africa rising" mantra.

"Africa rising" is the catchphrase in Africa of this post-global city formation, centered on engineers, scientists, physicians, and entrepreneurs: some of them trained in universities abroad but returning home, others are local "engineers of the practice" (mechanics, machine repairers) or local designers, ranging from innovations in women's wear to oil refineries, others are systems analysts who can mobilize information systems to upgrade and monitor and get school lunches into the school system or those who do similar things for public hospitals, rebuilding what has been destroyed by war or state neglect, or designing technologies for everyday use. *Limitless Africa*,[2] a podcast hosted by True Africa and produced by a Togolese American, Claude Grunitzky, is one of a number of programs in the diaspora trying to publicize developments of rising Africa. It is a weekly podcast that focuses on subjects ranging from entertainment and art to politics and the environment, presenting an uplifting idea of Africa as a rising giant in many areas of human endeavor. The narrative of the podcasts, while acknowledging many of the challenges of Africa, also seems to align with the African Union's Agenda 2063 without necessarily making it explicit in its interviews. The podcast showcases ideas from leading entrepreneurs, potential changemakers, tech enthusiasts, and young technocrats who constantly advocate for Africa and Africans in the global space of all human endeavors. But there are also local engineers navigating the contours of technology in ways that connect the rural with the urban in many of the spaces ethnographically captured in this volume.

STUDYING TECHNOLOGIES IN URBAN AFRICA: EMPIRICAL AND ANALYTICAL LINES

The Africa-Rising Narrative

The continent of Africa closed the twentieth century with many analysts projecting that the twenty-first century would be Africa's. Despite the many conflicts that engulfed the continent toward the end of the previous century, scholars began to speculate about the future of the continent. In some political science and economics literatures, African states continued to be represented as "failed states" or as grappling with various levels of conflict, sometimes economic and at other times political (see, e.g., Herbst 1990; Clapham 1996; Van de Walle 2001). Some of this literature went on to describe Africa as a continent facing a permanent economic crisis (Van de Walle 2001). Yet anthropologists and historians of Africa situated the impasse on the continent within a global economic and political predicament by suggesting that we look closely at Africa *within* these global phenomena rather than singling out Africa as a continent of "crisis" (Ferguson 2006; Roitman 2013; Adunbi 2015; Murray 2017). And so, in the first decade of the twenty-first century, *The Economist*, having previously predicted gloom and doom for the continent, suddenly made headlines with an issue powerfully titled "Africa Rising" (December 2011).

The Economist wrote, "After decades of slow growth, Africa has a real chance to follow in the footsteps of Asia," suggesting that Africa could take a cue from countries such as China, South Korea, Indonesia, Malaysia, India, and Thailand that enjoyed rapid economic growth during the first decade of the twenty-first century. These years were defined not just by how global economies were performing but also by the emergence of new technological forms. Nowhere is this new technological era more defined than in the continent of Africa, where novel cultures of technology and its uses have emerged. This seems to put an end to the long-lasting stereotype that suggests "Africa does not have technology" and the notion that in Africa, people only use cheap, but also less performative and less durable, technologies. Such discourses ignore the centrality of technology to the long history of Africa, a long history that includes the insertion of technology into the various sectors of life, ranging from administration to education and the health sector.[3] It is this ignored history that, for example, gave rise to the dictum "poor technologies for poor places" that dominated in the domain of health care, as Geissler (2011, 14) reminded us in the same year as *The Economist* issue "Africa Rising" appeared. Geissler added, "African colleagues [doctors, nurses, scientists] are not content with this [dictum]" (14). For them, the lack of resources and capacity was more a matter of "no longer" or "not yet" (14). They were expressing a sense of anticipation similar to that which *The Economist* voiced. In similar vein, half a decade later, Clapperton Mavhunga, a historian of technology cultures in Africa, writing in his introduction to a book on technology, science, and innovation in Africa and following in the footsteps of earlier accounts such as the work of the late Calestous Juma (Juma 1989, 2011, 2023; Juma and Obwang 1989; Juma et al. 1995), observed, "There seems to be a feeling that Africa's time has come" (Mavhunga 2017a, 1).

The narrative that Africa's time has come, a mantra equally emphasized at the golden jubilee anniversary of the African Union where Agenda 2063 was crafted, has been cemented by the widespread embrace of "new technologies" on the continent in the twenty-first century. This perception is anchored in the dominance of mobile telephony as an answer to the prohibitive and elitist nature of telephony prior to the advent of the Global System for Mobile communications. The mobile phone revolution swept through the contours of technology embraced in many African countries beginning in the late twentieth century and culminating in a form of dominance in the early twenty-first century.[4] The advent of social media further cemented the important role that technology use began to play in Africa's twenty-first century with the emergence of platforms such as Instagram, Facebook, Twitter, and so on. At the same time, the story of Africa rising is not limited to how telephony shaped a new economy but also encompasses how social life became transformed from the rural to the urban centers of many African landscapes. The talk of smart cities and of rapid techno-industrialization recentered the urban as a site for the incubation of ideas in ways that create rural-urban interaction. It also inspired a new vocabulary: For example, "incubators," and "start-ups," "tech hubs" and "mentors" have become key tropes when talking about the development of a business idea, economic formations, and patrons.

We suggest that the Africa-rising trope needs to be questioned, for a variety of reasons. Not everybody benefits from this new trend of Africa rising, and those who benefit do not do so in the same way. Yet these older, but also newer, forms of exclusion remain very often under the radar. Furthermore, the dialectics between transformation in technology use and social life in African cities is not straightforward. This volume posits that in order to properly understand the ways in which new forms of technology are shaping urban life in Africa, we need to pay attention to the particularities of the transformation. After all, in certain instances this change may lead to new forms of colonization, or "bedazzlement," as Tonda (this volume) calls it. An "engaged ethnographic research" (seeing opportunities and blockages through local eyes), we argue, is best suited to explore the relationships between technology and city life in Africa.

The Africa-rising narrative and the concomitant Afrofuturistic imagination professed in novels, films, mass media, and social media discourses prioritize, as mentioned, technology as the bedrock of Africa's new moment. A good example of media production of Africa's new moment is epitomized by a CNN International weekly program called *Innovate: Africa*. In an episode watched by one of the editors of this volume on April 30, 2022, in Brussels, the CNN host narrated how new ideas and innovations were changing the African landscape, creating new materializations of technological culture in many parts of the continent. With the tagline "These ideas and technological innovations from Africa could change our world in the future," the host rolled out some of the innovations from the continent, amplifying its relevance for a global audience by arguing that they could not only change the future of the African continent itself but also dramatically transform the world as we know it. That episode centered around m-health (mobile health services) and showcased entrepreneurs in Lagos, Accra, and Cape Town who installed systems through which to fight against counterfeit pharmaceutical drugs; digital platforms for medical consultations; an app allowing patients to get regular updates about their health records; and a text-to-speech app to help visually impaired students read in the classroom. Watching this program brought to mind the ways in which the idea of "innovation" has gained currency in the last few years (Nowotny 2006; Adunbi 2022).

The idiom "innovation" has gained much traction globally, and it seems to combine well with the rubric of "creativity," which for so long has been a privileged entry into the study of African forms of adaptation, inventiveness, and resourcefulness in contexts of precarity, dispossession, periphery, lack of high-quality materials, and an abundance of low-skill workers. In the discourses around innovation and creativity in Africa, we see some dangers as well as opportunities. The main danger is that the rubric of innovation is often situated within economies considered to be informal. It ignores the important role that skilled entrepreneurs play in making technology. When technologies are designed by those who operate outside of the purview of the state and their corporate allies, such efforts are dismissed as belonging to an informal sector. As Adunbi (2022, 33) has argued, we need to move away from categorizing economies as formal or informal when discussing Africa, because those considered to be "informal" make important contributions to economic growth.[5] In this volume, we apply the same logic to the development of technologies in Africa. Thus, we do not want to abolish the concept of innovation, but, as our chapters show, it is important that scholars represent Africans who develop and use technologies not as merely "tinkering" with the technology to suit their own purposes but as innovatively and creatively experimenting, testing, trying out, and "developing" technologies that fit social and economic ambitions, and urban and rural cultural practices. Attention to that kind of innovative work entails a radical rupture from the stereotypical representation of Africa as a space defined by tradition, the old, the used, the broken down beyond repair.

While lack of well-functioning technologies seems to define much of the literature on Africa, the fact that many global technologies draw on raw materials (minerals) mined in Africa makes the representation of the continent in the study of technology more contentious. Coltan and cobalt mines in the DRC; oil extraction in Nigeria, Gabon, Angola, Chad, and Cameroon; and uranium mines in Niger are all representations of how Africa shapes uses of technology outside of the continent.

Yet often ignored globally is that many of the mining societies that literally unearth the cobalt, oil, uranium, copper, aluminum, and so on can only carry out their work because of an array of older and newer technologies, some of them imported but many others invented locally. Most scholarship on mining societies tends to focus on the political economy of extractive practices as well as its social imbrications in ways that render the skills, craft, and creativity of miners invisible. In literature where the contributions of miners are discussed, they are referred to as "artisans," a term that diminishes the importance of their craft and the ingenuity they bring to making possible the technologies we use (Wilson et al. 2015; Pierre 2020; Adunbi 2022). We therefore apply the logic of caution to move away from seeing the craft of miners as "artisanal mining," not only because of its racial connotation, as Pierre (2020) argues, but also because of the miners' important contributions to making technologies possible. This volume takes these cautionary notes seriously, hence our focus on the relationship between the development (design, production, adaptation, modification) of technologies and the city in Africa. By looking at how technologies incubate in African cities, we call attention to the important ways in which African entrepreneurs take seriously their innovative approach to the use and development of technologies, from the development of smartwatches in Kinshasa's suburbs to the crafting and design of machines for refining oil in the suburbs of Port Harcourt and Yenagoa in Nigeria. The use of WhatsApp for the marketing of clothing materials in Khartoum is not just about posting these materials on social media platforms but also about the utility of the post itself and the strategies developed by Sudanese women in circumventing practices that impede their trade. Using WhatsApp as a trading platform, furthermore, creates new forms of urbanism in Africa. Several chapters in this book address how the insertion of technologies shapes urban interactions and city life.

Pype (2022a) has argued that practices of learning and information sharing within Kinshasa's emerging ecosystems cannot be understood without acknowledging the analogy with precolonial forms of "composition," of assembling people with various skills, capacities, and resources. Adunbi (this volume) makes a similar argument for welders and refinery designers in the Niger Delta in the urban center of Port Harcourt as well as in the rural creeks where the designs are tested out. Such forms of collaboration and invention, "traditions of invention" (Guyer 1996), risk being rendered invisible if we merely transfer Western logics and rubrics of technology cultures to the study of technology on the African continent. Our contributors avoid definitions and understandings of technology that locate their design and use in the Global North, for example, in Birmingham regarding coins and arms; or in Silicon Valley regarding digital technologies. This volume is a call for, and illustration of, taking seriously the study of cultures of technology in African cities from within. This is why we argue that writing about technologies from within provides a window onto everyday practices of Africans as makers of technologies rather than as consumers, as they are often portrayed in much popular discourse as well as in academic literatures. We therefore shift attention to how technologies get crafted, recrafted and repurposed in ways that make them interact with urban spaces in Africa.

AFRICAN TECHNOLOGICAL URBANISMS

It is high time that scholars begin to write about African urban life from the perspective of technology. While there are numerous works about infrastructure and citizenship in Africa (Larkin 2008; Degani 2023) and about non-Western urbanisms (Murray 2017; Amin and Lancione 2022), there is no scholarship addressing the performativity of technology in urban Africa. A growing body of literature draws attention to the digitalization of African societies (Keja 2022; Bernal et al. 2023); this volume, however, expands the gaze beyond digital technologies to include transport technologies, technologies for energy production, and medical technologies. We understand digital infrastructures as one among various kinds of technologies that cocreate urban configurations, flows, and experiences. After all, multiple layers of technological cultures and their imaginaries have contributed in variegated ways to urban life in many African regions. As we argue in this volume, the way to make sense of these multiplicities of technological interactions with urbanscapes is through an ethnographic mapping of the relationships between the locales and the urban, between citizens and communities, and of the how of technology design, development, production, and deployment, thereby helping to make sense of the various material and social transformations on the continent.

Best known in the Africanist literature are the mining towns (Bryceson and MacKinnon 2012) that emerged around minerals such as diamond, iron ore, coal, gold, and manganese in the colonial period. Water dams, wood logging, and oil extraction generate their own forms of urban life, especially in the forms of concessions and enclaves. Some of these urban forms were and still are company towns, where all residential units and facilities are owned by a company; others may have been hybrid from the onset; and some have generated improvised forms of cohabitation, sociality, and economy over the course of their existence. A few of these communities, like Johannesburg (Harrison and Zack 2012), turned into megacities over time. Others only had a short lifespan and dwindled out when the resources diminished, either fully disintegrating or evolving in other forms of urban livelihood (Kamete 2012; Mususa 2012). Still other communities never grew into a major urban hub but remained "enclaves," such as the semiurban community that has developed in and around the Inga water dams in the western DRC since the 1970s (Carbon, this volume). In such a context, the "urban form" is not defined by mass traffic or huge markets but rather by the appearance of commodities, practices, and imaginaries associated with getting ahead in urban life and the ensuing frustrations and compromises (e.g., good salaries but living away from family and cities; dealing with "small town" social pressures in or outside churches and segregated spaces). Hendriks (2022, 104), writing about a timber concession in northern Congo, describes how a forest camp generated an "urban ambiance" because of generators, loud music entertaining the camp workers in the evenings, pop-up bars with beers cooled in refrigerators, people showing smartphones, and participation in the activities of Pentecostal churches. The experience of "the urban" in this locale thus is very much defined by the presence and use of various technologies: mechanics, electronics, and, increasingly, digital devices.

Taking the urban scale as the point from which to ethnographically explore emergent cultures of technology in Africa allows a focus distinct from how states interact with and shape practices within their territories. While we acknowledge the significance of state practices for how technologies function and come into being, our interest is in the ways in which technology cultures shape everyday urban life and livelihood practices. After all, "citizenship," a concept that is based on urban life itself, is constantly assessed, reevaluated, and reimagined in African urban spaces (see Stroeken and Ghasia, this volume). These new articulations of contemporary citizenship in African cities cannot be understood without taking into account the amalgam of various kinds of knowledge scaffolding citizens' urban livelihoods. Many of the examples in this volume draw attention to the performativity of technologies and materials in shaping urban life in Africa. While many of these materials and objects appear in urban ideologies, we think it is important to look also at the urban practices that they generate. With "urban practices" we refer to a set of discursive, embodied, and institutional behaviors, interactions, decisions, and trajectories that city dwellers express, and engage in, in order to navigate the urban space, to engage with urban kin, power, and value.

A poignant example of attending to the discourses and practices that the technology cultures in urban Africa spawn is the recent social scholarship on the effects on the environment of mining towns and resource enclaves, and on how city dwellers experience these effects and make sense thereof. Many voices in Africa denounce the environmental degradation that has been caused by technology use and innovation. Carbon (this volume), for example, describes how the building of the Inga water dam in western Congo involved deforestation. Her interlocutors remember how trees "that would have been cut, would grow back overnight, thereby indicating that the ancestors were not happy with such drastic alterations to their landscape." In Nigeria's Niger Delta communities, the artisanal oil refineries and other oil-extractive practices pollute and degrade both rural and urban centers (Adunbi 2022). But alongside the Africa-rising narrative, protest against environmental damage caused by technologies installed in colonial times appears. Along new multinational technologies, and along local technologies that seek to keep oil in the local economies, we also observe various practices that bring attention to the plight of communities. Even if the imagination of "greener" urban futures spurs technological innovation, urban residents may apprehend the latest extractive novelties with a critical eye. In Nakuru, as Rahier (this volume) shows us, efforts by the Kenyan state, in collaboration with German and other international investors and scientists, to turn steam from the Menengai volcano into geothermal energy are met with suspicion and distrust and give rise to various theories of exploitation supported by occult science. Concomitant practices of protest, exclusion, purification, and repair emerge as well. At the same time, we see new ways in which technologies are imagined, designed, and mobilized for everyday use in many of the African communities our contributors ethnographically mapped.

EXPERTS, MAKERS, AND USERS

In this volume, our desire is to give visibility to otherwise invisible yet important African urban residents who, on a daily basis, produce new technological knowledge that is (re)shaping material environments. These actors mobilize specific know-how, skills, and capacities in dialogue with their material and social environments. The technologies they produce go beyond the notion that Africans are cloning or tinkering with technologies that are Western-made. As we demonstrate in this volume, many communities across Africa are producing technologies from scratch, and in the process they redefine their relationship to the environment, landscapes, and city life. African cities would not function without various experts who repair cars, unlock and repair mobile phones and other smart gadgets, or weld buckets, portals, fences, and artisanal refinery pipes (Adunbi, this volume). We want to draw attention to engineers who repair cars, motorbikes, mobile phones, refrigerators, and other gadgets—electronic or mechanical—in their workshops in Port Harcourt, Lagos, Kinshasa, and other urban centers, and those who design, experiment with, and invent technologies and put them to use, ranging from healing anointments to machines and computer hardware and software, and from cooking utensils, water purification systems, and green pesticides to social media platforms. The protagonists of our chapters are engineers, inventors, creators, literally "makers." They collaborate with vendors, delivery boys, taxi drivers, and nurses and cater to users, buyers, patients, and ordinary citizens.

Exciting questions emerge: Do different urban environments "think" differently depending on the available technologies? What kind of cityness leads to which technology forms? Do urban spaces facilitate recognition and deployment of ideas and material in innovative but conceptually different ways? Are gender, religion, race, ethnicity, morality, and political subjectivities engaged in different ways in the city, with different categories or mazeways of concept formation? Several of these latter questions have been addressed in historical writings and in ethnographic writing that does not always deal explicitly with the dialectics between urban life and technology cultures in Africa. Hart's (2024) reconstruction of the policy efforts in urban planning in colonial Accra, and the kinds of resistance that these brought about, informs us that "Accra citizens sought to embrace technological advancement and economic opportunity while protecting their own social, cultural, and economic autonomy." She argues that these negotiations still resonate today (Hart 2024). The study of the deployment of fertility machines imported from abroad by medical practitioners in northern Congo among the Mongo ethnic groups during the colonial era, also illustrates how cultural ideas impacted technology usage. As Hunt (2016) documents, the intent of the machines was to help married couples, but the end users turned out to be mostly *femmes libres* (unmarried women) rather than married women. During ethnographic research on Dutch ultrasound machines in Tanzania, when observing and interviewing pregnant women, doctors, and administrators Mueller-Rockstroh (2011) was pushed to ask questions about and bring to awareness the "intended and unintended [effects], beneficial to some and harmful to others" (Mueller-Rockstroh 2011, 17), of such imported technologies: Technologies are not asocial or merely technical. We build on these and similar scholarly writings but want to apprehend how the urban context co-organizes technology cultures in Africa.

This volume is attentive to situations where it is not only Africans inventing, using, repairing, or at work, but also regional or transnational migrants, including expats present for short periods as in the Inga dam (Carbon, this volume) or in the Menengai crater in Nakuru, where geothermal energy should be captured (Rahier, this volume). In Kinshasa's tech ecosystem (Pype, this volume), migrants return after having spent some years in South Africa, France, Germany, or the United States and try to find a foot in the local tech ecosystem (Pype 2022a). These returnees dwell in Kinshasa's fancy city center, where dollars, fancy hotels, conference rooms, business cards, and investors provide ample opportunities. Other (aspiring) tech entrepreneurs, with hardly any experience in the Global North, often have less easy access to the formal ecosystem. They set up their own forms of collaboration, expertise, and opportunity seeking in the economic ecosystem, hoping to gain access to resources in the more affluent formal ecosystem one day.

The technologies themselves are often the source of various affects of anxiety (Larkin 2008, 9) and of suspicion and distrust (Heald 2011; Masquelier 2012; Pype 2022b), while in other instances they generate trust and hope. As Pype (this volume) writes, pride and dignity are added to the affective map when we listen carefully to discourses about technology and urban life in Africa. But the same goes for boredom. During students' visits from Kinshasa to the Inga site, the engineers on the Inga dam are reminded about the prestige of their status as engineers. At the same time, they feel stuck in the enclave and long for a more exciting life in the capital city (Carbon, this volume). While their know-how and professional investment in the repair and maintenance of the Inga dam are key to a basic functioning electricity grid in Kinshasa, they feel abandoned and isolated and desire to leave the enclave. Not only in the Inga camps, but most residents in enclaves, concessions, and even on campuses prefer life in the big city, where, as they imagine, opportunities are many, food cheaper, and solidarity networks larger (see Stroeken and Ghasia, this volume). The infrastructure of such networks draw on various technologies, and it fosters urban experiences that become the backbone of everyday practices of city dwellers. In this way urban form, technologies, and infrastructures are entangled, continuously co-shaping one another.

URBAN FLOWS

Technologies are indeed the infrastructure of urban webs. The chapters in this volume are set in workshops where moto-taxis are assembled and repaired, in the healing spaces of so-called tradi-modern healers, in the residential camps for engineers, in the bushes where artisanal oil refineries are set up, even in living rooms where women operate digital entreprocess, and even the doctor's office where deals are brokered between a prospective mother and a surrogate mother who encountered each other in the virtual world before arranging to meet in a doctor's office. Such spaces are buzzing with movement, experimentation, and anticipation. The tools and materials around which all activity is centered are as diverse as motorized vehicles and smartphones.

In the study of urban livelihoods, much attention is paid to the flow of people toward and from the city. Another strand of literature defines cities by their physical infrastructure (Murray 2019), while other forms of infrastructure that make cities an assemblage or disassemblage do not get the attention they require. However, as the case studies in our book showcase, the infrastructure of a city encompasses more than just the physical; it includes human, material and symbolic infrastructures and various kinds of knowledges that are produced in cities amid structures of hope, intention, and possibility. Therefore, chapters in this volume bring to the fore flows of nonhuman entities, such as words, and rituals; objects like money and devices; and materialities like water, oil, sand and sandbags for cement, and motors. This perspective on urban life helps to shape a proper understanding of a city as an assemblage of different forms of technologies, some of which can also aid in its disassemblage.

The "street," a long-standing space of analysis in Africanist literature

(Beck et al. 2017; Hart 2016; Sheldon 2018), becomes important to our analysis. After all, objects travel along streets and roads. The chapters by Adunbi, Meli, Phippard, and Rahier in this volume indicate that the material and immaterial objects flowing through Africa's streets are actants in their own right—they have agency, and are connected to ideas of city life. Khartoum's moto-taxi drivers transport luxury products such as perfume and lingerie, desired assets of urban girls and women (Steel, this volume), from the living rooms and warehouses of well-connected upper-middle-class married women to their customers; Ugandan taxi drivers transport sim cards (Vokes 2018), a necessary commodity for urban livelihood (Archambault 2017; Pype 2021), while their Kinois counterparts are sometimes sent to deliver money and thus end a debt. From anthropological research in South Africa, we know that informal moneylending is typical for urban townships and small-town settings (James 2014, S27). Some of the urban flows structure movement along the familiar lines and boundaries of kinship and of socioeconomic class, while other flows, for example floodings, digital data traffic, and donor blood, may overrun these boundaries partially or totally. Through urban transport, delivery boys like the ones described by Steel (this volume), transporting children's clothes, cosmetics, and lingerie through Khartoum's streets, connect women with clients beyond cosmopolitan networks while preserving the social reputation of the female sellers and their clientele. Similar forms of urban connectivity are established through taxi drivers who bring pizzas to Cairo's gated communities and thus literally connect menial workers with wealthier families.

Technologies thus generate webs *within* the city boundaries; they connect cities with other spaces such as rural settings as well (see Steel, Adunbi, Phippard, and Meli, all this volume). While often these connections are embedded in urban planning, ethnographers can point to the ways in which citizens extend the urban space in ways beyond the planned, and sometimes beyond the city's boundaries. In many African cities, moto-taxi drivers extend the viability of roads (see Meli, this volume). They can move easier through unpaved urban spaces and thus connect areas in the city that are usually only accessible to pedestrians but, thanks to the motor and the skills of its driver, now also to passengers. The newly paved roads then produce situated networks that are historical and that cannot be understood without taking into account the agency and affordances of technologies.

Very different webs come into being through the artisanal oil refineries in Nigeria's Niger Delta—often categorized by the state as illegal—where urban residents set up oil infrastructures using materials from national and international oil companies. Sometimes these materials have been discarded; at other times innovators improvise with locally acquired materials.

Such ethnographic observations allow us to reconsider urban flows in African cities. Flows are not only historical, they are also co-shaped by technologies. Acknowledging the role of technology in these urban flows provides an intimate insight into the various connections that the urban fabric in Africa is made of. Along with the fact that technologies need to be maintained, repaired, and updated, we are reminded that cities are constantly in the making. In this book, we situate "the urban," as in "the urban experience," the "urban fabric," and "the urban assemblage," in relationship to technologies and in relationship to other places, cities and villages, while mediated by technologies. Our contributors acknowledge that these relationships are fragile, historical, and constantly reassessed and negotiated.

HOT SPOTS

One of the defining parts of the webs that technologies generate is what we call "hot spots," which connect people, communities, objects, aspirations, and imaginations in the various technology cultures in Africa. For example, Boro park in the city of Port Harcourt, where there are cybercafes in which people compose job letters, get online, and print essays, serves as a web that connects the rural with the urban in a variety of ways through the reshaping and mapping of imaginaries into products that are mobilized for use. These hot spots can be considered spaces of overlap and thus are spaces through which to consider the parameters of urban inclusion, exclusion, and congregation (Pype 2016b). Probably the best-known hot spots of African cities are the places where taxi drivers congregate, waiting for clients, whose personal trajectories in the city require assistance from motorized transport systems. Passengers of moto-taxi drivers who have suffered unfortunate accidents find themselves congregating in the compounds of traditional practitioners in Kikwit, where they rely on medical technologies to heal their fractures. Other forms of hot spots exist as well, for example around various communication technologies (Pype 2016b) like public radio and TV sets (see Pype 2010), citizen-broadband houses (Pype 2016b), and video stores (Schulz 2006). Hot spots around print media are the so-called *parlementaires debout*, groups of people reading newspaper articles hung on a cord or spread out on the pavement (Banégas et al. 2012). Their social and political potential is very well known by African urban authorities, who sometimes forbid these congregations and in certain instances, especially during political instability, use violence to disperse these groups.

Hot spots in urban Africa are sites of innovation and help produce technological knowledge. University campuses provide an excellent example: Buzzing with technological expertise and experimentation, students and professors constitute an important, though often ignored, space of technological innovation and technology transfer (see Stroeken and Ghasia, this volume). Hospitals, producing congregations of various kinds, have for a long time been the site of technological innovation. Microscopes, needles, vaccines, and other materials invented to monitor and modify health and fertility are the objects of technological invention, adaptation, and innovation, and their presence is often the reason why people travel to hospitals. Other hot spots of care in African cities are the houses of "tradi-modern" practitioners. As Phippard's research in the Congolese city of Kikwit (this volume) reminds us, victims of road accidents may suffer for a long time before arriving in a care facility center in the city. It is in the urban space that microscopes, blood centrifuges, X-rays, tradi-modern practitioners, new creams, crutches, and walking sticks are available. Medical equipment therefore constitutes some of the most significant technology of the city.

Hot spots can be situated in city centers, bars, mechanic workshops, welders' corners, and on pavements, very often marooned in suburban spaces, but they can also be curated in a rural setting and in the more private spaces of individuals, such as bedrooms (Gilbert 2018) and living rooms (Steel, this volume). Some hot spots may be hidden, for example when treatment for afflictions with a stigma is offered, or where practices couched in mystery are performed, or again in bedrooms and living rooms. Hot spots thus allow us to rethink urban connections and nodes by looking into the people, objects, affects, and spaces that combine. They bring people and things together, even if togetherness is fraught with friction and competition. It is from these hot spots that we can learn much about how urban life is organized and how various human and nonhuman actors coproduce city life.

URBAN RHYTHMS

Analyzing technology cultures in African cities opens the lens for a particular set of times and spaces around which these cultures are built. Speed is a quality associated with urban life in general and in Africa as well. In the world of technologies, creative dexterity defines the pace within which practitioners move, engage and produce because, just as the city is the place of fast money, so is the form of technology that is produced in the city. Fast money, a defining characteristic of fast oil capitalism in several countries, is an example of how technologies shape cities. Some protagonists of the various chapters in this book skillfully take advantage of other flows that constitute urban life. In Kinshasa, for example, moto-taxi drivers (so-called *wewas*) benefit from their facility to move swiftly and quickly in traffic jams where cars are blocked, and on sandy roads where cars either cannot enter or only very slowly can maneuver.

Indeed, there is no flow without its opposite, the fixed, the sedimented, the stuck. In major cities, traffic brings traffic jams. Traffic is one of the most familiar markers of urban flows. While stuck traffic can be considered a symptom of the mismanagement of urban space and of an excess of capitalist desires, we think about traffic jams as producing a particular form of urban life. In certain areas in African cities, traffic jams become so socially and economically powerful that city dwellers adapt their rhythms, their daily activities, and their movements (Melly 2017). For example, pedestrians, moto-taxi drivers, and car drivers purchase food and commodities on the sideways, exchange gossip and information deemed newsworthy, and assess political and economic futures while attending to radio shows broadcasting public and more intimate life stories. Traffic jams thus give rise to specific economic and social practices, and generate urban publics, which can become politically very powerful.

The ambulant vendors trying to find customers in the traffic jams are only one among various categories of experts who capitalize on the need to halt urban flows, or to fix things that can get broken through them. In Kikwit, fracture healers literally need to set bones that have been broken while driving on a moto-taxi. Other makers and inventors deliberately take immobility as a value for their designs and forms of business. Upper-middle-class women in Khartoum (Steel 2017 and this volume) who desire to become Facebook traders from their living rooms but want to preserve their reputation, literally render themselves immobile and stay at home. They safeguard their honor based on other flows: those of mobile data and of commodities and of money that circulate around them rather than with them. Their opposites, the ambulant vendors, a familiar sight in many African cities, embody an urban figure associated with precarity and movement-because-of-lack.

Finally, technologies in African cities create urban flows that assemble and disassemble through ritual forms in various complex webs. Rituals have their own rhythms while also imposing a particular rhythm on the life of those participating in the ceremonies. What we call ritualization of technology life suggests we pay attention to technology cultures and the ways in which technologies such as formol, cameras, sound blasters, digital photography, and smartphones have gradually been inserted in healing rituals, prayer practices, ceremonies of enthronement and succession, and marriages and funerals in the lives of African urban residents.[6] The field of religious media has been one of the most surprising analytical spaces in which the dialectics between urban society and technology have been explored. Starting with Evans-Pritchard's classic distinction between witchcraft and magic, it has led to theories about mediation in urban settings. Meyer's pioneering work on Pentecostal media in Accra has in particular drawn attention to the agency ascribed by Pentecostals to the camera, the screen, and film props (Meyer 2006, 2015). In this context, their agency is ultimately traced back to a spiritual world creating a rhythmic effect that ties together hot spots, webs, and other forms of connectivity that facilitate multiplicities of different assemblages and (diss)assemblages. An emphasis on flows of technologies, in and outside of ritual moments in African cities, allows us to consider urban life as constantly in a state of flux such that it keeps incessantly responding to human and nonhuman agencies.

ORGANIZATION OF THIS BOOK

This volume brings together voices from across many spaces in Africa. It focuses on accounts and critiques of new Africa-rising ideologies and practices threaded in and around state megaprojects (geothermal, hydroelectric) together with networked start-ups that circumvent or contest the state and patriarchal hierarchies (artisanal oil refineries, female vendors online, techie start-ups across diasporas) and post-global South–South connections. Without ignoring technologies responding to marginalization and exploitation, often expressed in nativist, occultist, and Christian fundamentalist language (the subject of many studies), it responds to new imaginaries, affects, and individual self-confidence that assert young Africans should, and are showing that they can, leave colonial and postcolonial political and economic complications behind, through building new nonstate connections across post-global cities (Pype, this volume). The volume showcases the emergence of new ways of thinking about technologies by paying attention to different ways of comprehending the relationship between urban and also rural spaces.

Chapter 1: Invention/Design, Transnational Assemblage, and Desires of Elsewhere

Pype, as already indicated, takes us to Kinshasa and the invention of a "Congolese" smartwatch, and connections of start-ups to places outside Congo (America, Brazil, South Africa; but also China, South Korea, and Rwanda). These are the new spaces of desire for Kinshasa's tech entrepreneurs. Pype defines their Kinshasa as a "post-global city," a city that occupies a spot in a network of post-neoliberal economies, where Kinois hope to find dignity and promise rather than racism, alienation, and shame. The latter, by contrast, are the affects they associate with the global city. In this sense, the "post-global" is undecidably phantasmagoric and real, since Guangzhou and other Chinese cities are also global cities (where black skin is not always treated well) as well as possibly post-global, with communities of Africans who have managed the supply chains and mercantile linkages to forge new transnational lives. The design and assemblage surrounding the watch is but one of a series of interconnecting devices, including a computer, a smartphone, and a portable solar charger. The drive for technology solutions to living in the contemporary world with élan, and not just getting by with bricolage, is vigorous and insistent, drawing on local and diaspora knowledges.

Chapter 2: Imaginaries and Electric Media

As noted already, Tonda takes us to Libreville and Brazzaville, where television screens broadcast seductive images coming from state propaganda and from abroad, the former colonizing empires, and the United States. It reminds of Victor Tausk's early 1919 paper on "influencing machines," the radio in those days, although Tonda does not follow Tausk's argument into schizophrenia; in passing, Tonda refers to Jean Rouch's film *Le maitre fou*, marginalized practitioners of the Hauka all-night dance and trance rituals who mimic the bureaucratic and military order, but are Songhay migrants from Niger, resettled in the peripheries of Accra and Kumasi. Even more "regulatory" is the De Gaulle dance, which evolved from the Ekoda from Equatorial Guinea, using marching formations with military-administrative hierarchies to control the crowds of dancers (Tonda 2021, 122–32). More free form are trance dancing and human tower acrobatics of the Gnawa ritual performers in Casablanca, who migrated there in the 1930s from Marrakech

(Portelli 2023), living a floating life, supplying entertainment for the workers, and working on the subconscious of the dancers and participants as they fall into trance. Today's Congolese rumba broke from earlier dance forms that mimic the disciplining of the body and instead provide body-to-body excitement. Tonda paints a painful image of the impact of screen images on central African citizens: These images generate desires and aspirations of a capitalist or authoritarian world, and, at the same time, they evoke an "Afrodystopia, the place of unhappiness, both real and unreal." Mass media are depicted as technologies of capitalism, materializing a neocolonial occupation of minds and bodies. Tonda thus describes how technologies facilitate the flow of dream scenarios, without the viewers being able to enter or alter the script themselves. Here we penetrate one of the most difficult realms of urban life: the imaginary and how electronic technologies impact the urban imaginary.

Chapter 3: Hydroelectricity and Third-Generation Engineering Enclave

Barbara Carbon writes from the camp around the water dam in Inga, western Congo. She first delineates the urban form of the camp, which she calls an "enclave." It was built to house the workers who built the hydroelectric dam in the 1970s, while temporarily housing expats and engineers sent from the national electricity company in Kinshasa. Centering the figure of the engineer, a protagonist in technology cultures, though an understudied professional category, Carbon analyzes how the workers sent from Kinshasa juggle the boredom and stress involved in living in an isolated work environment, and the prestige their identity as engineers brings. She thus problematizes the symbolic connotations often attributed to highly skilled professionals and provides a much-needed detailed exploration of the social positioning of engineers in Africa.

Considering post-global cities, we need to think of not only megacities (Kinshasa) or deindustrialized ones but also relatively new urban growth with new mixtures of ethnicities, classes, skills, vocations, and aspirations. If we think of the post-global city as "as a space of desire, ideas, mobility, and affects that emerges in the contemporary tech economy . . . and that [while] intimately tied to the 'colonial city' . . . also orients its gaze away from it . . . we need to take seriously the social performativity of technology and study its interactions with political affects, patriotism, pride but also shame and cultural alienation" (Pype, this volume).

Amid the assemblage of living quarters, lifestyles, masculinities, and moral aspirations, two contrasting masculinities emerge, that of the "rascal," hustler (*gaillard*), and trickster, who prided himself on working the system, dressing flamboyantly, and living life large; and that of the earnest (often Pentecostal) young engineers who (like Max Weber's Protestants) dedicate themselves to monogamy and gaining wealth and status through hard work and eschewing corruption. The latter bemoan that by refusing to participate in common corruption schemes such as submitting inflated receipts for supplies (and splitting the difference between shopkeeper, superiors, and themselves) they are accused of plotting against team leaders. Although well paid, with good accommodations (free electricity and water) until they marry, they are made to feel liminal both as mature men and in their jobs (neither comrades with the workers nor with the expatriate and Congolese supervisors). Unlike the rascals, they are constrained in social activities and concerned about their reputation, often finding a role preaching in churches, two of which are dedicated to different Pentecostal founders.

The personal psychological stresses of the more marginal rascals and the more work-ethical engineers are embedded also in the larger social scale of the resource enclave and "modern town" of fourteen thousand involved in the construction of the large Inga hydroelectric dams in the 1960s and 1980s to supply electricity to Kinshasa and other towns in the Central Province of the DRC. Both resource enclave and mega-infrastructure project, Inga is cut out from the forest along the Congo River, made more livable by pouring DDT into the river to kill the eggs of black flies that cause river blindness. Several generations of workers now live in this urban assemblage, the older ones squirreling away what they can of stolen materials and planting trees in the house plots in the hopes that, when they are forced to move, they will get more compensation. Some of the earlier generations of workers have been allowed to stay as hunters and agriculturalists to help feed the population.

So while the engineers look forward to a time when they will have created a skilled labor force that can run the dams profitably without foreign supervision or World Bank funding, other older-generation employees are biding their time until Inga becomes less of a construction site, when, however, their homes will be cleared away. Conflicts between lifestyles, opportunities, and moral configurations enliven the canvas, while on the horizon lurks an influx of Chinese engineers and workers who are to build a third dam, which will further change the mix of people and global connections and generate new South–South geographies and affects, as indicated by Pype (this volume).

Chapter 4: Geothermal Energy and Mountain Spirits

Rahier brings us to Nakuru, a midsize city in Kenya, once (before Nairobi) the economic heart of Kenya, where the Geothermal Development Company, a government-owned company, has committed to transforming the national energy sector by turning the steam emanating from a dormant volcano into geothermal energy. The project is embedded within an ambitious program for greener urban futures. It is an important part of the Kenya 2030 Vision, bringing electricity to all Kenyans and shifting from hydropower to geothermal energy. But drilling in the volcano proves to be a risky endeavor, working in an underground filled with unknowns, and combining, as Rahier's Kenyan interlocutors tell him, a combination of science and luck. The Kenyan, US-trained expert who is in charge of the drilling operations tells Rahier that no existing technology can accurately visualize the complex underground structures, and so there are many unknowns causing premature inferences. Even experts from Iceland (which pioneered the technology) and Germany (with its machine expertise) have no better underground vision. Informatics, too, only helps so far: Complex structures and temperatures can be translated into data but do not fully map, or allow drillers to grasp, the entire volcanic structure. The social concomitants of technology also require negotiations of mysteries. Not only does Rahier's ethnography show that "negotiating trust in geothermal exploration in Menengai is a highly volatile undertaking that depends on the endless possibilities and endless interpretations of the technology," but the "deep science" here involves bringing together various forms of secrecy, both the secrecy of scientists hiding their knowledge and work from the Nakurene population, and the secrecy or mystery of the supernatural, which guides some of the scientist-engineers but which especially informs those who dwell in and around the volcano and who fear becoming dispossessed or chased away. Local blacksmiths make deals with the supernatural or occult to answer the unanswerable, reminiscent of anthropological accounts of mining in Bolivia (Nash 1979; Taussig 1980). This chapter thus situates high-tech performance technologies within Kenyan epistemologies and within urban lifeworlds. Rahier makes excellent use of a concept from Pype, that of the technology contract, a contract between the technologists, technicians, and the local population, and among the various participants in the project. The geothermal project is one of two large-scale engineering projects (Hughes 1993, 1998) in this volume and involves expertise from Iceland and Germany, while otherwise employing Kenyan engineers, labor, and political support. Rahier's contribution and the previous chapter, by Barbara

Carbon, together constitute a third anchor of perspective for the volume, a perspective Michael Fischer has called the "anthropology of the meantime," the all-important temporalities, negotiations, and implementations that allow projects to proceed (or not), that put pragmatic criteria of evaluation to the imaginings of promoters (who, as Rahier notes, sometimes project a Rhineland industrial region growing around this geothermal energy transformation). In addition, following Tonda and Pype, and in tandem with Carbon, Rahier contrasts the subjectivities in play between those who are able to exploit volatility and "live large" (whether CEOs or local hustlers) and those who are bound to a Protestant work ethic and morality.

Chapter 5: Clinical Experience and City Technology

Phippard's ethnography of X-ray technology in the Congolese city of Kikwit opens up an analysis of what she calls "technology of the city"; that is, certain technologies are only found in cities and thus attract people to the city because of their sheer presence. This is the case for X-rays, which are difficult to produce in rural areas characterized by a shortage of electricity and basic equipment. Yet, Phippard adds another layer to this notion of technology of the city, as she observes that many Kikwitois make use of the X-ray after having had an accident with a moto-taxi, the preferred mode of transport in Kikwit as in many other African cities. The network of moto-taxis, X-rays, doctors, and city dwellers produces a care-scape centered around the technologies and expertise (or lack thereof) required to handle them. Yet the meanings attributed to the objects, experts, and their work are often ambivalent and sometimes contradictory, thus showing that the relationship between the urban and technology is always unstable and often the terrain of competition and contestation. The ethnography is enlivened and richly developed through the biographies of, and negotiations between, a famed bonesetter with years of practical experience and accumulated anatomical knowledge and a local hospital physician who tries to get a newer X-ray machine with better resolution that, alas, cannot be used for other technological reasons. It is the collaboration between the bonesetter and the physician that provides the center of this account, and the pragmatic success of the bonesetter brings people also from the city.

Chapter 6: Bend-Skin Dancing and the Moto-Taxi

Meli takes us to the town of Mbouda in Cameroon (population 111,000), where the metaphor of bend-skin (from the dance) is used to described the intricacies of moto-taxi navigation around traffic and over the often unpaved roads and suburban paths into the countryside, narrowly avoiding accidents, carrying goods (from farm to urban market) and people, venturing through spaces not on the map of any urban planner. Drivers sometimes double as repairers, sellers, garage responsibles, assemblers of new bikes, master cannibalizers of old bikes to repair broken ones, teachers, and so on, accumulating vast repertoires of knowledge and mastery. Meli describes the bend-skin drivers as urban connectors. They literally make roads and shape city flows. They connect people in the city (those visiting one another) and establish the material connections between the rural and the urban. "Bend-skin" is the name moto-taxis are known by widely in Cameroon. The service is beginning to go digital with the entry of Bee Moto, a hailing and delivery app offered in Cameroon and the DRC. The founder, Patrick Timani, has a German university degree (Pforzheim) and a microfinance certification (Frankfurt School of Finance and Management); he returned to Cameroon in 2015, founded Bee Moto in 2017, and created delivery partnerships with the equipment manufacturer for the Cameroon national football team and with an insurance company. In 2022, the company was among the sixty awardees of the Google for Startups Black Founders Fund. *Bendskins* is now also a 2021 Cameroonian film, directed by Narcisse Wandji, a somewhat dark melodrama but putting the adventurous, precariat, drivers, and their livelihoods and needs on camera.

Chapter 7: Cunning and Technological Citizenship

Stroeken and Ghasia propose the concept of "co-citizenship," based on reflections about how urban cunning (*ujanja*) operates in the city as a space of war of technicities colliding, a place where "every sound, smell, or view . . . exude[s] technicity." Not only in capital cities such as Nairobi and Dar es Salaam, but also places like Morogoro, urbanites know that "those without technicity live their lives in jeopardy." Where the state is absent, withdrawn, or distrusted, citizens need to operate beyond or alongside the state. Car drivers need to maneuver their vehicles on any free spot of the street; students and professors communicate over social media platforms because the intranet software and infrastructures are unreliable. Citizenship is asserted through technological cunning. There is resonance with Bill Readings's (1997) early account of the neoliberal ruin of the university by excessive concern with metrics and productivity, and the offloading of access to the internet from public university funding in the Global South; but also, more interestingly, there is a fit with the themes of Carbon and Rahier on the contrasting subjectivities embedded in work ethics for success and survival: cunning/trickery/rascal masculinities versus a sharing ethos allowing networks of friends to succeed, with return on gifting later in life.

Chapter 8: Diaspora, Discretion, Disguise, and the Digital in Female Entrepreneurship

Steel provides another example of urban tactics used by Africans, in this case, women in Khartoum who become online entrepreneurs. In order to successfully manage their businesses in food and kitchen equipment, clothes and bed linen, they may include male relatives in the business and set up fake accounts to mask their gender. Another tactic is to switch smoothly between offline and online vending strategies. Steel's ethnography is an exemplary case study in the ways in which "hidden" technologies, such as WhatsApp and Facebook usage in the women's living room, can set in motion urban infrastructures (of taxis, of money exchange, of delivery boys). That same private space facilitates flows of commodities from Dubai, London, and New York to Khartoum. Diaspora, discretion, disguise, and the digital are the axes around which these urban female entrepreneurs organize their economic activities.

Chapter 9: Repossessing Local Resources with Vocational Apprenticeship and Experimental Design

In the final chapter, Adunbi situates skills gained through long apprenticeship, applied to experimental designs, to retake oil that the multinational oil companies have been taking from the Niger Delta, leaving behind a wash of toxicities, environmental degradation, and anger. Adunbi takes us to the two oil cities of Port Harcourt and Yenagoa, long on the forefront of environmental justice movements, and repression of both activism and political resistance (Ken Saro Wiwa and the Ogonis, Isaac Adaka Boro and the 12 Day revolution, the insurgents of the early twenty-first century, etc.). Hanging out on street corners with the welders, iron casters, masons, and designers, Adunbi explores their informal workshops where they devise new technical techniques for retaking what they think should be theirs. Rather than to dismiss them as a lesser form of technological development, to call these "artisanal" refineries is correct and should be a badge of honor (successful craftsmanship). Without such local mechanical knowledge among machinists, metalworkers, masons, and builders, many forms of industrial enterprise would never have gotten started. This war over infrastructure, between David and Goliath, is the material means of establishing possession and claims to rights over resource extraction. To what extent the spread of small oil refineries can shift the political calculus and bring in additional income remains to be seen. How long will it take the modern sovereign, using its military might, to "crush" the new oil infrastructure that challenges its control? Or will it acquiesce in a more limited hegemony? Meanwhile, how do local imaginaries play out in a landscape of trouble and three forms of violence (corporeal, structural, and fetish-imaginary)?

NOTES

1. For more on this, see, for example, "Agenda 2063: The Africa We Want." https://au.int/en/agenda2063/overview (accessed October 14, 2024).

2. For more on this, see, for example, https://trueafrica.co/category/news/environment/ (accessed November 1, 2024).

3. A notable exception is Hart's historical ethnography of urban planning in colonial Accra (2024).

4. Alongside the technological innovations, new social and economic practices emerged. For example, flashing, or pinging, a system of text messaging developed by Research in Motion, makers of Blueberry smartphones, became an effective and cheap communication strategy for most mobile telephone users, who saw an advantage in using the services to engage with everyday life in Africa (Donner 2007; Pype 2016a). Pinging enabled a system that lets users circumvent the often prohibitive cost of texting instituted by mobile telephone operators, especially for those texting outside of the borders of the nation-state.

5. We see much value in Hart's approach to "informalization" as a historical process that "marginalized and criminalized long-standing African economic and spatialized practice" (2024).

6. Some of these technologies have begun to earn a pivotal role in political rituals such as national broadcasts by presidents of countries in Africa, religious leaders, and others. There are examples of political speeches simultaneously broadcast on radio and television stations, Twitter (now X), Facebook Live, Instagram Live, and other social media platforms (Adunbi 2017). Today, national independence anniversaries and religious ceremonies such as harvests have become sites where technologies interact with urban spaces through the use of these platforms for connecting with local, national, and global audiences.

CHAPTER 1

The Post-Global City

South–South Geographies and Political Affects in Kinshasa's Emerging Tech Scene

KATRIEN PYPE

Since the mid-2010s, Kinshasa has become an epicenter of digital tech creativity in the Democratic Republic of the Congo. Participants in the growing geek[1] community (*éco-système*) are gaining tech skills through attending formal and informal training in artificial intelligence, software design, and assemblage of devices. Incubators, start-ups, and accelerators are new forms of economic institutions in this ecosystem that, very often with international capital, guide these geeks and turn them into aspirational young Kinois (from Kinshasa), entrepreneurs eager to set up a tech business.[2] Many of these geeks (and their "mentors") are enchanted by the Africa-rising narrative, a scenario that defines a brighter African future through new investments and new forms of training and education, and which is mainly professed by national governments of African states, but also media such as CNN and *The Economist*, and are sponsored by governmental and private institutions and organizations of the Global North. Many of these geeks are or want to become tech entrepreneurs (Pype 2022a). Their world provides a different narrative about digital futures and the DRC than the conventional one in which the DRC is identified as a provider of coltan, a mineral on which our global digital society is built, but where tech knowledge and tech infrastructures, apart from the mining technologies, seem absent. In this global narrative, the DRC is described as a country looted of its major resources, yet hardly any attention is given to the knowledge, tech expertise, and aspirations that hum in the DRC's urban lifeworlds.[3] It is also a world "in the meantime" (Fischer 2018), a space of unfulfilled desire, very much encapsulated in the here and now, merging colonial frustrations and post-colonial anticipations.

Let me start with a vignette from fieldwork about the background of a Congolese smartwatch, the Nuvens watch:

On a late afternoon in August 2019, Prince Mpembele arrived more than two hours later than we had agreed upon. I was waiting on the upper floor of the bar Planète J Socimat, located Kinshasa's fancy city center. The bar boasted loud rumba music, while a giant white screen broadcast music video clips from the popular international station Trace TV. Fashionably late, Prince arrived in a posh BMW, showcasing white earbuds, and carrying two large smartphones in his left hand, evoking a swag style. He complained about the fact that he had been chasing the sole smartwatch at his disposal. A potential customer was using the only test piece Prince had. We had scheduled a meeting in which Prince would give me some background information about the Nuvens smartwatch, which he marketed in town. As I learned during my conversation with him, the "Congolese" degree of this smartwatch resided mainly in the fact that Ken Kelvin Mbaz, Prince's brother, and thus Congolese by birth, but living and working in Brazil, had designed it. The conceptualization and assemblage of the smartwatch took place in Brazil and South Korea. Nevertheless, the watch was marketed on Kinois television[4] and in our conversation as a "Congolese invention" (*eza congolais*, "this is Congolese"). At times, Prince talked about an "African device" (*une machine africaine*).

Similar transnational networks emerged when I attended networking events among Kinshasa's (aspiring) tech engineers. Rwanda, South Korea, and China were often mentioned as countries where their peers had more opportunities than France or the United States. It was argued that innovation and initiative were far more encouraged and appreciated in Asian and African societies than in the Global North. Looking carefully into the geographies of tech innovation in Kinshasa, one observes a predominantly South–South-oriented network of ideas, capital, and products. These new geographies provide a novel perspective on Kinshasa's international positionality, on Kinois' experience of globalization, and on the role of technology therein. In this community, Kinshasa suddenly appears as what I propose to call a "post-global city."

The main goal of this chapter is to take seriously these new geographies and imaginations of other spaces, "elsewheres," as they are related to tech innovation in Kinshasa. It is exactly in Kinois' narratives about tech that a specific set of cities (Kigali and Guangzhou) in the Global South have become particularly meaningful. I qualify the networks connecting these other spaces and Kinshasa, and which emerge through the links between Congolese designers, their studies abroad, the spaces of assembling the devices, and the new destinations of desire for Kinshasa's (aspiring) tech entrepreneurs, as "post-global" because these are embedded in post-neoliberal networks of "global cities."[5] The forms of mobility and migration in these tech imaginations differ from trajectories steered by neoliberal capitalism. If cities such as New York, Tokyo, and London became global cities (Sassen 1991) during the 1970s, when the international political economy was redesigned by neoliberal principles, thirty years later, Chinese, Indian, and Brazilian economies have turned Shanghai, Dubai,[6] Rio de Janeiro, but also Kigali into attractive spaces for economic and social pursuits. This has strong political and social consequences for daily life in Kinshasa, and especially for the ways in which Kinshasa's geeks imagine their present and future. Intercontinental migration has been redirected: Where initially former European colonies and, later on, North America were the desired destinations of outward migration, a gradual shift toward the East and the South is observable (Ding and Pang 2018; Braun 2019; Owen 2015).[7] Not only travelers with commercial interests but also aspiring tech entrepreneurs are attracted by these new destinations. Since the 2010s, an increasing number of Kinois have been traveling to Guangzhou, Dubai, Cairo, and Ankara. Some may only be staying for a few weeks, long enough to do some purchases and fill a container with commodities to send back to Kinshasa, where these can be sold in institutionalized markets, but also on pavements, in school, at work, in church, via social media, and by ambulant vendors. Others stay longer, study, set up a home, and postpone their return to Kinshasa.

Within tech narratives that I collected in Kinshasa, the attraction of these other destinations is often accompanied by a particular configuration of political affects that speaks about the endurance of colonial violence into the twenty-first century, and the imagination of new, more dignified postcolonial futures. In these stories, (aspiring) tech entrepreneurs quite vocally situate tech expertise within a transnational network of power, opportunities, and dignity. But it will become clear that this post-global network is not devoid from critique, fear, and risk either.

The main goal of this chapter, then, is to put forward this concept of the post-global city as a space of desire, ideas, mobility, and affects that emerges in the contemporary tech economy in Kinshasa. The post-global city builds upon the global city, which in itself is intimately tied to the "colonial city" but also orients its gaze away from it. I argue that the dialectics between political affect, citizenship, and technology co-shape the post-global city. If we want to understand contemporary forms of mobility, desired futures, and tech expertise in the Global South, then we need to take seriously the social performativity of technology and study its interactions with political affects, patriotism, and pride but also shame and cultural alienation.

With this material, I want to contribute to the study of the dialectics between the cities and technologies in sub-Saharan Africa by foregrounding how cities are embedded in specific networks because of particular technologies and affects accompanying technological production, circulation, and consumption. Technologies are connectors, linking urban spaces with one another, positioning cities within translocal networks, and tying inventors, investors, brokers, sellers, instructors, repairmen, and users. These networks, or tech-scapes à la Appadurai (1996), comprise bodies, objects, ideas, capital, and affects, and they shape and are shaped by city dwellers' imaginations of personal and collective futures (the good life), and by comparisons with the local and the elsewhere. In these networks and imaginaries, the urban and national scale at times intersect or overlap.[8]

This chapter is divided into five sections. In the first section, I briefly introduce Kinshasa's tech community. Then, I discuss "Congo shame," a sensation of cultural alienation that one can hear being talked about in Kinshasa, which has origins in the colonial period and shapes much discourse about "Kinshasa in the world." The third part puts at center stage the "Africa rising" narrative and analyzes pride and efforts to promote things "made in the DRC." I then explore how Kinois *ingénieurs* imagine China and Rwanda as new centers of innovation. In the final section of this chapter, I summarize the particularities of the post-global city.

The material for this chapter was collected during field research in Kinshasa on technology and the city that started in 2014 and ended in 2021. I visited Kinshasa regularly, following inventions and attending events in which innovations were showcased and debated. I carried out formal and informal interviews with tech innovators, sponsors, and potential users. Digital media (such as WhatsApp group lists and Facebook pages) have become very quickly significant spaces of communication and data collection in Kinshasa's tech community. In 2020, due to the Covid-19 pandemic, I resorted to online interactions only with my interlocutors and continued following their digital platforms of networking, training, and exchange. Most names have been anonymized for ethical purposes. I did not change the names of inventors and public figures (such as political leaders). This chapter is one in a series of publications on innovation and tech creativity (among others Pype 2016, 2017, 2018, 2021, 2022a, 2022b).

KINSHASA'S TECH COMMUNITY

Kinshasa boasts a growing entrepreneurial tech community of which the center of gravity is Gombe, the upscale municipality that houses presidential buildings, offices of ministries, embassies, NGOs, the UN and other international institutions, international companies, luxurious hotels, Western-style restaurants, expensive gyms and nightclubs, large villas, and apartment buildings with more than twenty floors. This space is the economic and political heart of the city and the country and of the local formal ecosystem (Pype 2022a). Here shops sell brand-new computers, laptops, tablets, smartphones, and accessories of established brands, often providing a small warrantee and customer service. In other municipalities, one can easily purchase used tablets and tech products, or new tablets and computers from Chinese brands sold in warehouses, in small shops, or on the pavement. Gombe is also the space of choice for events by international networks such as CongoBusiness-Network and CongoBusinessAngels, often coordinated by Congolese entrepreneurs from the diaspora, whose ambition is to connect their international business with members of the highest political circles in the DRC.

Until the late 2010s, initiatives of the local tech scene, such as hackathons, fairs of Congolese mobile phone applications, and formal meetups among technologists, were restricted to Gombe; in the last few years, formal and informal events have gradually been organized in adjacent municipalities such as Lingwala and Ngaliema.

Foreign embassies, with especially the US embassy as a forerunner, NGOs, and international telephone companies have teamed up with local tech lovers to boost tech creativity. For example, for several years, the French telephone company has been organizing annually the Salon of the Congolese Mobile Phone application, a full-day event in the gardens next to the parking lot at the so-called "GB premises," and free to attend. In the 2018 edition, which I visited, more than ten local inventors pitched their demo for a mixed audience of local journalists, Orange employees, and peers. I counted about forty people in the tent. Most of the presenters were young men in their twenties and early thirties; an odd presenter was a Congolese man in his late fifties residing in London. Outside of the party tent, small booths had been set up where local and international companies could explain their wares and services to anyone who wanted to learn more; flyers were distributed; Black urban music played loudly through the soundboxes. Other events, usually without such side activities, are organized by Kinois geeks with very limited funds and take place in meeting rooms of local hotels. All these events provide a stage for return migrants, who can share their stories of success and failure and their thoughts on a Congolese cyberfuture.

Several of the narratives presented during such events are disconnected from the material infrastructures available in the city. For example in August 2018, a returnee from South Africa, with a degree in digital marketing from a South African university, explained during a neatly prepared PowerPoint presentation how QR codes could be integrated in Kinshasa's urban transportation system. A retired director of the National Bank of Congo, who had been invited as a special guest, asked the presenter how realistic his project was. He was the oldest man in the room, occupied by a group of twenty tech lovers, predominantly male. He found it necessary to remind the presenter that only a small portion of Kinshasa's population was using a smartphone. The reasonable question did not temper the enthusiasm among the gathered technologists; the presenter and participants in the audience turned toward the former director and laughingly told him, almost unequivocally, that "one had to start somewhere, and that such smart systems were already operational in South Africa and Kenya."

Such events attracted between twenty and fifty participants. These numbers may seem minimal for a city of about eighteen million inhabitants.[9] Yet most of these events are reported on local television (e.g., in the weekly show *Hi-Tech Afrique TV* on B-One TV; and in news reports of the public TV broadcaster RTNC1) and on social media platforms (e.g., WhatsApp groups such as Hi-Tech Afrique TV; Réseau des AFROPRENEURS; Web Entrepreneuriat Rdc; and Centre INFO NTIC BONSOMI), and thus construe a large urban public. In addition, aside of these events of formal networking and showcasing inventions and projects, a major activity is training: teaching people to code, to design software, and to set up a business project. In numerous poorer areas of Kinshasa, volunteers teach primary and secondary school children for free the basics in coding. These activities happen on an irregular basis, though there is a growing awareness among Kinshasa's children and youth that understanding algorithms and coding can lead to better futures. Since 2015, several fablabs (e.g., LumumbaLab and Lisungi Fablab) have timidly come into being, very often initiated by people from the diaspora and with logistical support from international agencies. In Gombe, incubators (e.g., Digital Kinshasa) are set up with international capital (French, American, South African) in order to stimulate an economy of start-ups.[10]

Intimately entangled with Congolese who have traveled abroad either to study or for economic or familial reasons, many products are invented abroad, demos and prototypes travel to Kinshasa, and ideas and requests for funding and for customers are imported via family networks and mass media. Indeed, several of the products presented in Kinshasa and online as "Congolese" are invented and produced within the Congolese diaspora, such as the Nuvens smartwatch and the Okapi laptop and tablet, and thus travel via this parallel, second track of Kinshasa's tech world. Such observations seem to confirm the idea that technology cannot be created and invented *in* Africa—a stereotype against which many of my interlocutors—especially those who have never been abroad—nevertheless agitate.

"Local" technologists experience ambivalent feelings regarding this dominant role of the Congolese diaspora in the local ecosystem. On the one hand, they acknowledge that the creators are as much Congolese as they are (even if some may have given up Congolese citizenship) and thus experience a sense of fraternity and belonging aside from appraisal and admiration; yet, on the other hand, frustrations are voiced about unfair advantages: Returnees gain more opportunities in Kinshasa, for example they have easier access to the higher decision boards in international offices and enter without much difficulty into government networks. These irritations are embedded within overall fraught relationships between the diaspora and people at home, who feel they are often belittled by those abroad and put in a relationship of dependency (see Pype 2020). For those with kinship or other intimate relationships with Congolese technologists abroad, such as Prince has, these relationships are opportune, and they give them also a sense of autonomy in Kinshasa's ecosystem. It is no surprise that I never ran into Prince during networking or training activities. He was a marketeer for his brother, a successful technologist in Brazil. That relationship gave him the social capital that others, often beginning tech entrepreneurs in Kinshasa, could only dream of.

CONGO SHAME

With a selling price of USD 150, the Nuvens smartwatch was out of reach for the majority of Kinois. Although, so said Prince, the *montre intelligente* (smartwatch) was an excellent answer to the thieves who operate in busy spaces in Kinshasa.[11] At the time of our interview, only five Nuvens watches had been sold in Kinshasa: two had gone to patients (a man in his early sixties and a woman around fifty years old) whose GP had recommended the device. The three other buyers were politicians. They had purchased the device out of curiosity and in an effort to support local entrepreneurs. "Ah, Congolese too can produce such high-tech products": So Prince imitated the reaction of one of the politicians when he had handed him the device. This led to a discussion of "Congolese intelligence" (*mayele ya biso*, "our knowledge") and creativity. So, argued, Prince, "If Congolese can choose between European design and African design, they will go for the European design. People do not believe that Congolese have the capacity to create, to produce something durable."

Such statements echoed utterances I have heard ever since I began ethnographic fieldwork in Kinshasa in 2003. In one of my first visits, I learned about the difficulties of a Kinois shoemaker who tried to rival "the Italian shoe producers," he said. Through his large network he managed to get interviewed on some TV broadcasts dedicated to the iconic Congolese subculture of fashionistas, to find local buyers. Yet his clientele did not go beyond a handful of Kinois able to appreciate and purchase real leather instead of cheaper artificial materials. A similar stance was expressed by Thérèse Kirongozi, the charismatic leader of an engineering team that created traffic robots with a human shape and which attracted international attention. During one of our trips to the workshop where the robots are assembled, she had an appointment with a British female freelance journalist. The journalist hardly spoke a word of French but prepared a feature story about the invention for British television channels. Thérèse Kirongozi asked me to translate for the journalist when necessary. She jokingly told the journalist that I was like many foreigners, "curious to see Congolese who can actually think and do science."

Thérèse's joke was not innocent. It rehearsed a common trope among Kinshasa's innovators and tech engineers: a regret that they are not considered "real engineers." It is certainly a trope one often hears in Kinshasa, where the word *ki-ingénieur* is often used when talking about local inventions that do not last or do not live up to their expectations. The prefix *ki-* is used in slang to associate the stereotypes of "Kinois identity" (a fraud, a bluffer, a trickster) with particular professions (e.g., *ki-ingénieur*, *ki-politicien*, *ki-pasteur*).

Such a derogatory way of speaking about local experts resonates with the depreciative stance many Kinois take on local products and when they reflect on Kinshasa's outward gaze, what Bayart would call "extraversion" (2000). For Bayart, extraversion is an essential, acclaimed characteristic of African societies. Yet when Kinois tech entrepreneurs reflect on the higher value (monetary and symbolic) Kinois attribute to "things foreign," this extraversion becomes a problem. Such language is not unique to the discourse of technologists but is also evoked in a variety of ways in Kinois society. Kinois never tire of repeating that "Congolese are *complexé*." Or, "We are suffering *un complexe*," "an inferiority complex" (*complexe d'infériorité*). A *complexé* denotes a person feeling a sense of inferiority, which I prefer to read as a symptom of cultural alienation.

The *complexé* is a cosmopolitan positionality. It is defined by an awareness of contrast and is accompanied by a set of moral and affective judgments. This can be due to a difference in education. One can often hear people emphasizing their proficiency in French (a colonial language) in an exaggerated manner, for example, by articulating too much so that the sounds become hypercorrected, by using difficult vocabulary, or by copying a posh accent. In such occasions, people are sometimes accused of suffering from a *complexe d'infériorité* that pushes them "to speak better French than the French." The label *complexé* is also used to critique people who only speak French with their children and who slap them when they hear them exchanging some words in Lingala. A *complexe d'infériorité* is sometimes inserted in a description of gendered sociality when assessing the difficult social positioning men occupy when living with elder or economically more powerful wives. In such a relationship, these men cannot uphold the masculine ideal of being the main provider. The label is also used to indicate women's general reluctance to enter the political field, as it is argued that women think they do not have a valid voice there. Furthermore, Kinois also evoke the *complexe d'infériorité* when reflecting on religion. Members of animist churches critique Christian and Muslim practitioners who turn to global religions rather than indigenous religious communities, by calling them *des complexés*.

The *complexe d'infériorité* is not only evoked as an explanation for linguistic or social behavior but often also used to critique the "Congolese way of life," when compared with practices, manners and habits elsewhere. Such comparisons mainly pertain to dress and consumer objects. For example, a person can be accused of being *un complexé* when that person critiques women for wearing jeans and T-shirts and advocates the "more African" *pagne*; or for only wearing wigs; or for applying skin lighters excessively. A similar *complexe* about Congolese design was also observable within the clothing and textile industry in the early years of my fieldwork in Kinshasa (2003–2010). It is only when VLISCO began a glossy billboard campaign of

"African" design around 2010 that the local fashion industry found a new breath.[12] Furthermore, such a *complexe* is apparent in Kinois' appreciations of technological devices and spare parts for cars, radio sets, and household utensils. The already-mentioned traffic robots are sometimes ridiculed, especially by young Kinois who aspire a Western, cosmopolitan lifestyle. They depreciate the traffic robots for being too far removed from the prototypical image of a traffic light. In such perspective, a hierarchy exists in the ways in which certain devices are valued, based on their assumed origin. Many Kinois prefer devices with a European, American, or Japanese origin and undervalue, even disdain, anything produced locally.

The cultural alienation also seeps into the political and economic spheres. For example, a *complexe* can be experienced regarding the state's faulty infrastructure. Telling in this regard is the announcement that "Congolese would not feel any *complexe* anymore" when in 2016, the ministry of postal services, telecommunications and new technologies of information and communication proudly communicated that postal codes had been created for every single province, city, village, and neighborhood:

> For example, Maniema has Code 63, Kinshasa has Code 10, etc. . . . This will allow each Congolese to be able to benefit from a precise localization for the receipt of parcels and mail. For online shopping, now no more *complexes*! You can easily fill in the details of your place of residence and receive your packages purchased on the internet. E-commerce will develop even more in the DRC.[13] (My italics)

(Aspiring) tech entrepreneurs such as Prince and Thérèse claim that the *complexe* obstructs innovation and impedes a healthy urban, even national, economy. In August 2020, Jordan, a thirty-something software developer and consultant for the Congolese state, posted a *voice* (voice message) of more than four minutes on one of the WhatsApp groups gathering Congolese tech lovers. He contributed to a discussion in which "Congolese" were lamented for "lacking vision." With a strong, self-assured voice and a particular French accent one hears among young upwardly Kinois men, he claimed that

> in Africa, the problem is not that people are lacking vision. No, what Zuck [Mark Zuckerberg] has done, many people have done in Africa as well. It is nothing. You just need to use servers. The problem is the *complexe*. If one of us produces something, he will not get the support of his family nor friends.

They will prefer what the Europeans have made. Maestro Jims has made X-cash; it is the same as PayPal. But if we do not use X-Cash, then X-Cash will never get the same magnitude as PayPal. So, do not repeat anymore that here in Africa, we are not smart enough, or that we are lacking a vision. We are *complexé*, we do not support one another.

Many on the WhatsApp group agreed with Jordan's assessment of Kinois sociality: Because of the *complexe*, people do not believe that Congolese can produce valuable commodities, machines, software, and so on. Some WhatsApp subscribers even argued that the *complexe* pushes certain people to use *kindoki* (sorcery and witchcraft) on inventors in order to make sure that they would *not* succeed.[14]

History and Cultural Alienation

The experience of cultural (and economic) alienation in African societies has been the subject of numerous scholarly and activist publications (see also Tonda, this volume). Frantz Fanon, one of the most important intellectual voices in the anticolonial struggle, rigidly denounced the cultural alienation that colonialism installed. He had observed that an inferiority complex had arisen among colonized peoples. His analysis was inspired by colonial cultural policies that promoted European languages as "more civil," and thus "buried" not only local languages but also local cultures (Fanon 1961, 14, translated by KP).[15] The figure of the *complexé* is related to Fanon's "black skins, white masks," colonized people who mimic the colonial culture so well that they become alienated from their own cultural roots. Other words, such as *bounty* in anglophone Africa, and *mundele ndombe* (a Black white person) in Kinshasa, have been used to express this radical cultural conversion to European cultures. Nowadays, *mundele ndombe* is an ambivalent denominator in Kinshasa. Depending on the context, it can be a token of achievement and success or an insult. Calling someone a *complexé* in Kinshasa, however, is unambiguously an expression of disagreement and discomfort.

Relating the dependency relationship of colonialism to the economic level, the Beninese philosopher Paulin Hountondji observed in an insightful, though rather neglected, commentary that colonialism was characterized not only by a theoretical vacuum (as scientific teachings and discoveries in Africa depended on what happened in the colonizers' labs and universities), but also by an industrial vacuum: "In the overall process of the production of knowledge, colonies functioned as immense data banks, as storehouses of bare facts and information that were exported to the ruling country, just as they used to serve as storehouses of raw materials that were exported to the same ruling country" (1990, 8). This industrial vacuum had (and still has) strong political and economic consequences, as it defined African countries as receiving countries of "traveling technologies," designed and produced in the West.[16]

Kinshasa's technological extraversion may very well have been imposed during colonial times, but it remains very much a social and economic reality and experience of the twenty-first century, confirmed and sustained by various social and political projects that do not always come from outside but sometimes even from inside, as is the case of the culture of *kindoki* and the elite culture in the city.

Made in the DRC

(Digital) technology seems to allow for a new narrative. Along with an Africa-rising trope apparent all over the globe, Kinois engineers and makers display a strong sense of pride and conviction about their technical capacities and capabilities (see also Carbon, this volume), to the extent that many of their engineering efforts and experiments are captured in narratives about patriotic contributions to the national economy and to building an international reputation of the "brand DRC." Billy, a tech engineer in his early thirties setting up cryptocurrency in the DRC, organizes online trainings in coding, website design, and cryptocurrency on digital platforms such as WhatsApp for free. He considers the investment of his time and mobile data to be a patriotic act. As he earns enough with the management of intranets and web design for private companies, he wants to contribute to the growth of a skilled tech community in Kinshasa and elsewhere in the DRC.

The Africa-rising era seems to provide momentum to fill the industrial vacuum Hountondji wrote about so many years ago. In Kinshasa, various international initiatives have sprung up in the Africa-rising atmosphere. Since 2012, hackathons and events such as "Kinshasa Innovation Days" have been organized. Coworking spaces to be used by aspiring tech entrepreneurs such as Digital Kinshasa and Ingenious City and fablabs such as LumumbaLab and others have popped up. These are financially and logistically supported by public and private capital, mainly coming from international embassies, NGOs, and foundations. These institutions and organizations turn toward the digital ("Digital for development") and aim to produce new, "disruptive" futures.[17] Such initiatives are socially meaningful as they nourish the dream of a new form of development, revalue the role of engineers in Kinois society, inspire individual prospects, and unleash conversations about national, patriotic contributions.

One could argue that, more than the music world, the classic space of a promotion of Congo pride, the tech world is nowadays the sphere of choice in Kinois society where Kinois (politicians included) actively invest in "Congo pride." An early manifestation of this is the slogan "Made in RDC" (and online "#madeinrdc"),[18] which has gained political significance and is used by institutional actors, the press, tech innovators, and laypeople, and which is eagerly attributed to tech innovations.

The slogan "Made in RDC" was invented as part of a political project of the Kabila state (2002–2019), intended to awaken the local economy and to boost local inventions. A Fond pour la promotion the l'industrie ("fund for the promotion of the industry") was set up. Its announcement happened via electronic and digital media, and billboards were placed on the major axes around town where international investors pass through when traveling from the airport to the city center. Another initiative of the Kabila state was the establishment of a "salon," a fair, set up in the Pullman hotel, one of Kinshasa's upmarket hotels, where state agencies and big and small enterprises could showcase their products and services. The salon exposed *des biens et services produits en RDC* (goods and services produced in the DRC), which included goods and services in the agro-alimentary industry, cosmetics, plastics, technology, *artisanat*, carpentry, fashion, and so on. This initiative aimed at "valorizing local content and normalize local offers," so the official tagline of the salon's marketing material announced.[19] Examples are food (coffee, jam based on strawberries grown in the DRC, herbs and tea drinks), clothes and interior decor textiles (like pillows), locally bottled water, the construction of a cruise ship (*Emmanuel 4*) and of an electric car (Benzoula). Services, car -and truck-renting companies, but also incubators, new policy programs, and cultural events (e.g., "slam made in RDC") have quickly seized the label "Made in RDC."

Congolese inventors in the diaspora are defining their designs as "Made in RDC" as well.[20] Sephora Lukoki Kapinga, a web journalist for Slkaanews. org, in an article one can find under the rubric "Made in RDC," showcases watches designed by Michelange Katende, a South Africa–based Congolese entrepreneur. Her description is evocative of the association between emigrants, tech invention, Congolese patriotism, and a firm belief in the possibilities of Congo/Africa rising:

It is essential to invest in Congo, by extension in Africa, and to bring our expertise to the nation. Our generation is aware of the issues at hand and of its role in trying to change the course of history. If our generation does nothing concrete, it will pay the consequences. We can already see this with the domination of foreigners on the African continent. So we must do our part. Each journey is an inspiration. SLK News is committed to encouraging new businesses and defending the interests of the people above all else. Beyond a watch company, Michelange Katende represents a generation zealous to bring a new perception of Africa. A generation that believes that sooner or later the sun will eventually rise for the cradle of humanity.[21]

The label "Made in RDC" does not speak about the location of invention and creation but positions the object/initiative within Congolese post-global society. For example, Katende's watches are made in South Africa, but the smartwatch with which I opened this chapter, and other tech innovations made by Congolese or by makers who identify as Congolese but live abroad, are all labeled as "Made in RDC." Two dimensions seem to justify this epithet: First, the invention is made by people who *identify* as Congolese despite the region in which they live or work. Second, the invention is described as contributing to the Congolese economy and the national and international appeal of "things Congolese." All in all, the political intentions behind the usage of a mark such as "Made in RDC" draw attention to the role of Congolese "raw material": not only minerals, but also ideas and efforts that can materialize in objects. The usage of this label speaks to inventors' ambitions to contribute to national (Congolese) prosperity, even if the innovation has been made in South Africa, Brazil, or the United States.

A Slogan to Critique

As happens with much political language, the slogan "Made in RDC" has been inserted in political critique, especially when Kinois denounce the state's lack of transparency and its culture of corruption and fraud.[22] In Kinshasa's tech world, the slogan is also often used to expose the gap between the promises and plans made by the state and their implementation. This criticism has been most manifest in the collective indignation around the state's decision[23] to invest in Industry Five, an American company, which has been granted the right to produce and assemble tech devices on Congolese territory. The deal meant concretely that 1.4 million smartphones and tablets would be produced in the DRC, and, so the Congolese minister of industry, Julien Paluku, repeated during various press moments, "It will entail one thousand jobs." Nevertheless, the private-public partnership, established during the summer of 2020, has received harsh criticism by Kinshasa's *ingénieurs* for two reasons. First, in October 2019, the same minister had promised Dieudonné Kayembe Kabukala (the inventor of Congo's first tablet, the *motema* tablet) that the assembly of his invention could be done in Kinshasa. This announcement had nourished dreams about installing local factories in Kinshasa, where every single component of a tablet (and other devices) would be fabricated. Now the Congolese government had shown that local politicians were not interested in launching local entrepreneurs, nor in turning them into *millionnaires*, as President Tshisekedi had promised when he introduced the National Program for the Digital in September 2019. Second, the new deal between the Congolese state and Industry Five would mean a boost in the economy of *eastern* Congo, where "it will take the young away from the rebel groups in the region," rather than in the capital city.[24]

With the agreement between the Congolese state and Industry Five, the label "Made in RDC" (which in press reports appeared as "Made in Congo") suddenly got stripped of its "Africa rising" potential. Rather, many of the protesters argued that American investors and know-how would use Congolese raw materials, now interpreted as the bodies of Congolese factory workers, to assemble high-tech devices. In this and similar debates, Kinshasa's *ingénieurs* are eager to make connections between the *scandale géologique*, referring to the extraction of coltan minerals, without which the digital economy cannot function, and the continued role of the Congolese state in making this happen. The "real raw mineral" is their talent, so Kinshasa's (aspiring) tech entrepreneurs like to proclaim. The contract with Industry Five counters the Congo pride Kinshasa's *ingénieurs* have begun to believe in; furthermore, it once again positions the state as an opponent of the citizenry.

Amid the protest, the Congolese state was reminded about its responsibility to its citizens and was accused of being hypocritical toward Dieudonné Kayembe Kabukala. For years, this recent graduate of the Université de Kinshasa has been traveling abroad to represent Congolese creativity at various diplomatic and economic events. In 2012, for example, his tablet was nominated *lauréat* (honorable mention) at the Android Challenge Africa competition; Kayembe Kabukala represented the DRC twice at the Abu Dhabi World Fair and once at the Francophonie (2017) in the category "innovation and youth." The ministry of industry has even awarded him six patents.

Kayembe Kabukala has been working since 2008 on this tablet and likes to label his invention as "African" for various reasons. First, it operates in the four national Congolese languages (Kikongo, Lingala, CiLuba, Swahili), in contrast to devices from the Global North and from China.[25] Second, the hardware contains a mini-solar panel, through which the tablet can be charged—thus responding to the instability of electricity mains in the DRC. Third, while the tablet runs on Android, the goal is to set up a "Congolese" operating system, Okapi OS. In 2015, when I met Kayembe Kabukala for the first time, he tried to motivate peers to design apps that speak to Congolese users and could be integrated into his tablet. Late in 2019 Kayembe Kabukala traveled to China to visit factories that could produce parts for his device; in December 2020 he toured francophone West African countries, such as Ivory Coast and Benin, looking for partnerships with local political leaders and tech communities.

Relevant for our discussion is that the Congolese state and Kinshasa's tech entrepreneurs have different perspectives on Kinshasa's positioning within international networks. The deal with Industry Five is mainly an economic initiative, accompanied by development-related language (diverting potential child soldiers into factory work). By privileging American investors and creators, and Congolese as people putting US-designed parts together in factories, the Congolese state confirmed Kinshasa as a global city, functioning within established structures of capital, labor, and design that perpetuate neoliberal dependencies. Yet Kinshasa's technologists and entrepreneurs imagine their city as a space of tech creativity, a city where "African" devices are not only assembled but first and foremost designed, a post-global city. This obviously can happen only when inventors who identify as Congolese (despite where they are located) are prioritized. This difference between the global city and the post-global city also means a different interpretation of the "Made in RDC" slogan. The Congolese state seems to accept a minimal definition, that is, assembled in Congo, while Kinshasa's entrepreneurs are more ambitious and first and foremost want to invent their own devices, disregarding of the location of assembly.

POST-GLOBAL GEOGRAPHIES

In mid-August 2017, together with Maman Tina, an apprentice in web design (Pype 2021), I passed quickly by the LumumbaLab (LLab) as I had heard that Filip Kabeya, the initiator of the LLab, was back in town. LLab, a pioneer among Kinshasa's fablabs, was changing locations almost every year as it was difficult to find funding to pay rent, electricity, and other bills. In mid-2017 it was situated in a two-room flat in Beaumarché, the beating heart of Kinshasa's popular nightlife. The bedroom of the flat was reserved for Filip, in his mid-thirties at the time. He was often traveling abroad for consultancy work and sometimes visited Kinshasa for a few nights only. He then used this flat to sleep and meet people. For the time being, the LLab could use the space. The rent was low because of its location, on the third floor of an apartment building right behind the notorious nightclub Cheetah 2, which only closes in the early morning hours, making it difficult for people in the immediate vicinity to maintain a healthy sleeping rhythm. The living room was small (about 1.5 by 3 meters) but neatly arranged. There was a sofa, a small table that could double as a desk, and some shelves with books to be consulted by curious visitors. *Coding for Dummies* was there and some other manuals for software development and programming, next to books about African political history and novels. Maman Tina was most excited about the drone that had been given a nice place on top of a series of books. Filip's brother and a friend, who were using the free Wi-Fi on their smartphones when we entered and who were supposed to answer questions from curious visitors, told us that Filip had purchased the drone a few months earlier, but they had not yet dared to use it. As Kinshasa's airspace is a military zone, they first would need to ask permission from the police, they reckoned. We apparently had just missed Filip, who was off to the airport to fetch a Rwandan female tech entrepreneur whom he had met during one of his recent trips to Kigali. A few days later, she would give a session on how to "repair laptops and other devices yourself, so that people would not have to spend money on repair and maintenance anymore."

This visit of a Rwandan technologist to Kinshasa is noteworthy because the DRC and Rwanda are formally in a state of war. Yet it is not remarkable given the exchange of expertise and knowledge that happens within tech circles in sub-Saharan Africa and given Kigali's reputation as a forerunner in digitalization on the continent.

Kinshasa's *ingénieurs* often position themselves within a global and post-global network of tech design and knowledge. In my conversations, technologists expressed a tension between, what I see as, the global and post-global scales of movement, affect, and capital. The latter seems more open and accessible to many young Kinois *ingénieurs*, while the former is characterized by inequality, dependency, and exploitation. By contrast, relationships with countries, institutions, and people in post-global networks are defined in terms of opportunities and accessibility.

In what follows I explore the significance of China and Rwanda in the discourses and lifeworlds of Kinshasa's (aspiring) tech entrepreneurs. Elaborating on their imagination of these two countries helps us to understand how Kinois tech entrepreneurs signify these countries as new, post-global spaces of desire. The default interpretation of post-global Kinshasa's tech scene is that they consider themselves and fellow citizens as "raw material" (see above). They do not consider their country to be rich in minerals only (*un scandale géologique*) and explicitly mention that Congolese possess intelligence (*mayele*), just like citizens of any other nation. However, so the *global* narrative goes, the economy and political uncertainties hamper these smart Congolese who have scientific merits and try to achieve tech successes, in contrast to peers elsewhere. In, what I call a *post-global* imagination, however, non-Western developing countries are presented as models to follow. Here the main points of reference are not so much Europe or the United States, which serve as point of reference in the global (colonial and earlier postcolonial) space. Rather, the economies of China, South Korea, and Rwanda and their leadership figure prominently as examples to follow in post-global Kinshasa. Thérèse Kirongozi, the leader of the traffic robot team mentioned earlier, stated explicitly when presenting the phone during a press conference (2020): "We have to follow the example of countries which have advanced, like China, like [South] Korea. They did not do magic. They worked while putting their intelligence for their country, and I believe their efforts are palpable. If we follow this model, I believe we will move forward."[26] Significantly, she did not reference the United States, where the designer of Okapi, Jean Bele, resides. In other conversations among tech entrepreneurs, Rwanda is added to the list and is applauded as one of the only African countries that takes the lead in terms of innovation.

Made in China

China is very much present in the lifeworlds of young Kinois, especially through the various cheap commodities that have flooded Kinois markets (Makungu 2012) and which Congolese migrants bring back home from trips to China (Braun 2019). In all of Kinshasa's neighborhoods, Chinese traders have set up shops where one can buy almost everything, from ties and tires to air conditioners, all for very cheap prices. These Chinese traders and storekeepers speak Lingala, often move around in public transport, and thus embody linguistic and physical proximity.[27] Furthermore, many Kinois know various individuals—family members, friends, neighbors, or peers—who travel to China for business or study (Braun 2015, 2019). These people return with a variety of stories on daily life in China, especially on food culture in Chinese cities. In 2018 and 2019, Kinois radio broadcast several times a day a commercial for the "China Card," a prepaid Visa card created by Rawbank (an Indian bank group operating in the DRC) in order to facilitate business in China. With the China Card, merchants and immigrants do not need to call Kinshasa to have money transferred via Western Union; rather, so the advertisement went, "Kinois (and Congolese) can travel with much money on the card to China, without having to bother people who have stayed behind."

The flow of travelers and commodities between China and Kinshasa has social consequences. So argued Flavie, a mother of three, and for years one of my main interlocutors in Kinshasa: "The Chinese have changed everything. Now, we buy Chinese; others go to Lufu [a town at the border between the DRC and Angola] or even to Turkey. There is hardly any difference anymore. We are not impressed by the *djikas* [Congolese emigrants living in Europe or the United States] anymore" (Pype 2020).[28] She had just confirmed that European commodities are still valued more than commodities from China. However, while until recently their role as providers of quality goods ensured a particular dependency between the *djikas* and those who had stayed behind, the easy access to cheaper Chinese commodities has changed that and diminished the authority of *djikas* in family affairs. "You do not need to be afraid of not getting any perfume anymore if you're not complying with the *djikas*' impositions. We can get good enough perfume from Lufu or China," Flavie stated.

Not many people can afford the more expensive devices of European origin and thus have in their living rooms cheap Chinese brands such as Sonyc or Nokla, mimics of better-known Japanese (Sony), and European brands (Nokia). Yet the general assumption remains that European technologies are more durable than those produced in China. To that effect, a whole range of jokes about the short lifespan of "Chinese products" circulate in Kinshasa. One of them tells how Kinois girls never have to worry getting pregnant by a Chinese man, as a Chinese pregnancy would never get to nine months.

Unsurprisingly, then, a key trope in discourse about Chinese goods and business strategy among Kinshasa's tech entrepreneurs is *kosa bachinois*, literally "the lies of the Chinese." The lying is the skillful copying of brands, goods, and commodities and acting as if they are the real thing. A telling example is the much-discussed Chinese e-platform Kikuu. "You order trousers, but you get a skirt, even one too small for a Chinese," wrote a seemingly well-informed man on a WhatsApp group of Kinshasa's geeks during a discussion of China's success stories.[29]

Within Kinshasa's tech community, what seems to be most appreciated about "the Chinese" is pride in their own culture and tradition. Hugor, a student studying marketing who has never traveled to China, told me, "There they teach their own languages in primary school. Here we use French and maybe Lingala. But no CiLuba, or KiKongo." I met Hugor during a bar meeting organized by Congolese youth who travel from time to time to China and attempt to inspire others to undertake business start-ups. I regularly heard and read references to Confucius when attending geek meetings.[30]

Most informative is the following statement I read in a WhatsApp discussion about China's success stories, and in which a comparison is made between Chinese and Congolese business culture:

Our ways of doing things is acting as if they are amazon,

1   too expensive
2   complicated way of paying
3   delivery time as if it has to come by plane
4   adding the natural Congolese fraud

so [it is] very complicated[31] to have faith in our local solutions.[32]

The statement brings American business culture into the equation and offers a critique of global culture. It does so by arguing that the Congolese act as if they were Amazon, referring to the US-based online retailer. This is a culture that, so the subtext goes, needs to be abandoned.

Kinshasa's tech entrepreneurs assess Chinese business culture as more efficient and cheaper than Congolese and American business culture. They also are convinced that a shift in the international order is happening. This shift, so they perceive, means an increasing dominance by China. Similar assumptions came up most prominently during one of my visits to the fablab LLab in 2018, which by then had moved to another part in town, Boulevard Laurent D. Kabila, one of the main roads from the townships to the city center. That evening, two return migrants were having some beers with workers at the LLab. The party of four was seated at one of the picnic tables the LLab coordinators had installed in front of the twelve-square-meter space they rented. In order to add some revenue, the fablab now doubled as a bar. Friends of geeks sometimes just spent time outside, drinking and debating, while others were coding, programming, or just surfing online in the air-conditioned indoor space. Jeras, the most vocal of the two migrants, had just returned after a stay of three years in Ukraine. He had won a fellowship from the Ukrainian embassy (calls for which are regularly broadcast on Kinois TV stations) through which he could study for an MA degree in agriculture. I arrived during a heated conversation about the unfolding political events (will President Kabila organize new elections?). But as soon as I was introduced as a friend-anthropologist, Jeras asked me what it meant that "the Chinese write 'Made in China' in English and not in Chinese?" Others responded before I could. It was quickly established that this choice of English was part of a clever strategy to expand Chinese culture through objects. Jeras, seemingly satisfied with the consensus, added that such a label "even renders the Americans afraid." The conversation turned toward speculations about a new world order in which the US economy would be dependent on African and Asian labor and capital.

Rwanda

Even more than China, Rwanda has become the space of reference for Kinois (aspiring) tech entrepreneurs. Yet when they talk about Rwanda, they narrow it down to Kigali, the capital city. This importance of Rwanda in their lifeworld may be surprising given the DRC's long-standing conflict with its small neighbor. One observes an almost generalized anti-Rwanda sentiment in Kinois society. Just like many international observers have been confirming for years, many Kinois are convinced that the Rwandan president, Paul Kagame, sustains armed conflict in the eastern part of the DRC, loots the region for its minerals, and aims to integrate the mineral-rich Kivu provinces into Rwandan territory. For more than a decade, Kinois public figures—politicians and others—have been accusing President Kagame of trying to "balkanize" the DRC. Traumatic memories of the arrival of rebel leader Laurent D. Kabila and his troops in Kinshasa in 1996 also sustain anti-Rwandan sentiment and discourse. One often hears stories of how mass mobs threw burning tires (*des colliers d'or*, "golden bracelets") around individuals with a tall and slim frame, corresponding with the stereotypes of Nilotic morphology. Such brutal murders were inspired by a fear that Rwandan usurpers had joined the Kabila forces. Several innocent victims died, leading to ambivalent feelings about Laurent Kabila's "liberation" that remain meaningful in present-day Kinshasa.

The image of Rwanda in a Kinois tech imagination is strikingly different. Here Rwanda appears as the promised land for tech entrepreneurs.[33] Stories of people who have traveled to Kigali have inspired Kinshasa's (aspiring) tech entrepreneurs to visit Kigali, to participate in tech events there, to get to know Kigali's booming start-up sector, and to launch their own successful tech career.[34] One of the innovations in Kigali mentioned often during fieldwork among Kinois geeks is the fact that in Kigali moto-taxi fares are paid electronically.[35] Such imagination is close to the public image the Rwandan state promotes via international media campaigns, supporting its ambitions to become a tech paradise for the African continent.

The image of Kigali as a space of possibility disrupts the taken-for-granted idea that Congolese geeks want to go to Silicon Valley; it is at the same time a critique of the Congolese state. Kinshasa's geeks like to emphasize the *difference* between Rwanda's ecosystem and that of the DRC. Rwanda is described as a place where tech innovators can make money more easily, where internet structures are more reliable, where citizens are "more disciplined," and where the government facilitates entrepreneurship. This contrasts with the way in which they represent Congolese society, where, as many Kinois technologists argue, *Le plan numérique ne marche pas* ("the digital plan does not work")[36] and "Congolese enjoy bars, beer, and women too much."[37] When comparing the costs of mobile data, they observe that Congolese fares are higher than in neighboring countries. Kinois geeks argue that *ce pays n'a pas de chance* ("this country does not have any luck") and blame the Congolese state for being too greedy with its taxes on companies, which in turn transfer these costs to Congolese users.

The applause for Rwanda's ecosystem within Kinshasa's geek community is not total. Nuance is observable in stories about tech surveillance.[38] A young man wrote in a WhatsApp group among Congolese tech developers about his recent trip to Kigali: "In Rwanda, there are various surveillance schemes in the city. Rwanda is strong in spying. These days, they use a small fly that lives with you, can rest in a small corner in your house, registers all your conversations and videos, and even sends it to a central institution" (July 2020). This and similar stories are powerful in a city where the former president, Kabila, has invested in surveillance cameras around town, but nobody believes that they are operational (Pype 2022b).

Ambiguous feelings about Rwanda add a new, almost secretly admired connotation to the country's name. Not all of Kinshasa's tech entrepreneurs are comfortable enough to overtly declare themselves *Rwandophiles* (neologism for "people who love for Rwanda"). An example is Jeannot, a thirty-something software developer who started a software business both in Kinshasa and in Kigali. He travels frequently between the two capital cities.[39] Even though he enjoys sharing his experiences in informal networking events, Jeannot has become careful not to boast too much about his Rwandan business. As he told me during our first encounter in 2018, there was envy regarding the savoir faire he was accumulating in Kigali. But the political tensions between the two nations also nourished anti-Rwanda sentiment in Kinshasa's ecosystem. At best, so he confided, others simply teased him and jokingly called him a *refoulé du Rwanda* (someone forced to return to his home country). Especially among the junior geeks, he felt the need to defend himself for developing a network in Rwanda.

An example of the reluctance to join the pro-Rwanda discourse is the following fragment of a discussion on a WhatsApp geek group about presumed Rwandan origins of Patrice Lumumba, one of the DRC's leaders during the independence struggle in the late 1950s. Julien wrote, "They should leave us alone; we're looking for a reparation of the social, stability in electricity, high-speed internet for an affordable fare, that's it."[40] At the time he posted this message, Julien was in his early twenties and had only begun to frequent the geek community a few months earlier. He felt uncomfortable with what he called the "Rwandophily" that he encountered there and felt it important to redirect the gaze to local realities and what needed to be corrected locally.

TYING THINGS TOGETHER: THE POST-GLOBAL CITY DEFINED

In this final part of this chapter, I try to bring together the various thematic strands of affect, initiative, movement, and technologies into a further conceptualization of the post-global city. My analysis offers a narrative about the digital and the DRC completely different from what is globally familiar. Usually, global media report on coltan mining in the DRC for global consumption. The only Congolese in such narratives are the coltan miners (very often children) and corrupt Congolese leaders. Such a story situates the DRC within a *global* imagination. My analysis describes the emergence of what I call a *post-global* narrative.

I began by describing *complexés*, people who devalue and depreciate goods and sounds (accents and language included) that have a distinct local, "Congolese" flavor, even to the extent that they value a faulty French more than Lingala, the dominant language in Kinshasa. While these linguistic and material markers of *des complexés* ("people with a *complexe*") may express an aspiration for a globally oriented, middle-class lifestyle, these same people devalue local food, languages, traditions, and lifestyles.[41] Various Kinois critique such behavior. By formulating extraversion in terms of a *complexe*, Kinois assess the problematic positionality vis-à-vis local culture and the local industry.

Based on expressions offered by tech entrepreneurs such as Prince Mpembele, Thérèse Kirongozi, Julien, and Jeannot, but also on experiences with other Kinois such as Flavie and Jeraz, who are not *ingénieurs*, I have been able to bring together narratives about agency, dignity, technology, and society. Their stories bring in different positionalities in the globalized world. As I showed, key in the tech entrepreneurs' stories is the embeddedness of Kinshasa (and at times the DRC) within translocal and transnational networks. I observed a strong orientation to "newer" spaces of reference, such as China, Rwanda, and South Korea. I qualify this network as "post-global" and label the urban space from which these narratives are told and lived a "post-global city." This concept provides a new lens on urban imaginaries and the various trajectories and flows they (can) facilitate between cities, countries, and regions, and along which money, people, goods, ideas, and affects travel. These follow routes other than the "global" routes. Post-global Kinshasa, as it appears in the lives and discourses of Kinshasa's (aspiring) tech entrepreneurs, is a space of desire, a realm of alternative economies, of futures beyond neoliberal capital. "Post-global Kinshasa" emerges when observing closely the trajectories of Congolese entrepreneurs and their inventions, and when listening attentively to their stories about desired futures. Global cities such as New York, Los Angeles, Paris, and Tokyo hardly figure in these narratives. Rather, cities in Brazil, China, and Rwanda have become more attractive. Post-global Kinois also circulate within the African continent. The geographies of the current tech imagination indicate how among young Kinois tech engineers alternative regions in the world become meaningful, even shaping new desires of mobility, destination, and prestige. Kinshasa as post-global city therefore is at once a reality and an unfulfilled dream mainly imagined by (aspiring) tech entrepreneurs, not by the state. The Congolese state remains very much operational within global structures of power and capital, themselves etched with colonial relationships.

Crucial in the ethnographic material is the insistence on affects such as shame and inferiority—which can be defined as the affects of the global city in the Global South; pride and aspiration seem to be the steering affects of the post-global city. Post-global cities thus can be considered palimpsests: They build further on colonial and global cities. This "building upon" entails a conscious rejection and marginalization of "global cities." This refusal to enter into "the global city" may be enforced (e.g., because of the lack of visa or of funds to travel to these countries), yet it is often also accompanied by strong affects, of indignation, contestation, repulsion, attraction, and desire. The hyphen of the "post-global city" is thus significant, as it contains a critique on the global city. The post-global city cannot be experienced without the exclusionary mechanisms of the global city. But the post-global universe is not friction-free either. From the discussion about the imagination of Rwanda and China, it appears that, even though these countries may be more attractive for post-global Kinois, they are very aware of the potential political and social risks of life in these countries. Post-global Kinois are very well informed about racism, violation of human rights, and exploitation in global and post-global worlds.

In deliberations about the potential downside of the spaces of desire, post-global Kinois manifest a strong sense of self-confidence and do not narrate the relationship between their own society and new centers of desire in terms of dependence. Post-global networks seem more balanced; there is less "colonization" or dominance going on at first sight, and they seem to allow more space for exploration and experimentation for the post-global citizen. The material shows how Kinshasa's tech entrepreneurs, as post-global citizens, imagine new futures not only based on economic attractiveness but first and foremost on possibilities to realize their own potential and to experience pride about their own designs and products.

The emphasis on aspiration among Kinshasa's geeks entails a major departure from the contemporary Africanist library, which focuses on global cities, and where Africa's youth are "waiting." Rather, young men such as Prince, his brother, and Dieudonné Kayembe Kabukula and women such as Thérèse Kirongozi reflect on the social and economic possibilities of digital technology and its interventions in their urban lifeworlds. They actively pursue change, both for themselves and for the larger urban, and even national, collective. That change is not yet realized; it is a condition of "in the meantime" (Fischer 2018). These aspiring, post-global tech entrepreneurs—post-global citizens—mobilize their knowledge and their relations in order to, quite literally, design their own futures. Even though many of them may be "stuck" in youth (as they do not easily find the funds to marry), they are not waiting idly. Their "in the meantime" condition is very much characterized by aspiration, hope, anticipation, and prefiguration (Pype 2022a, see also Phippard, this volume, and Rahier, this volume).

If for some the post-global city is already a reality, for most Kinois it is not a given yet, considering the fact that the *complexe* continues to steer for many their evaluation of things Congolese. The post-global city is very much under construction. The entrepreneurs struggle with global effects—of shame, racism, and cultural alienation. All in all, the post-global city is a socioeconomic project that is growing and is supported by "Africa rising" and similar narratives. It is a conscious effort of institutions such as start-ups and incubators, and of individual actors to reclaim recognition of "African" knowledge, dignity, and products. The Africa-rising narrative and the accompanying imagination of African tech futures propose, even promise, a radical break with the technological extraversion since the colonial era, which has been assessed as hampering the local economy and diminishing self-value. A post-colonial (rather than "postcolonial") and post-global affect of self-confidence is cultivated. It affirms economic opportunities for local knowledges and inventions.[42] In such symbolic constructions, African citizens (Kinois included) appear as intelligent, dignified, and deserving.

NOTES

1. I use the word "geek" here as it is a label that some of my interlocutors, in particular technologists with some experience abroad, use to describe themselves. A geek is someone with a significant interest in things technological, in particular digital and electronic. Most of my interlocutors also harbor ambitions to become wealthy thanks to their tech skills and networks within the tech community. This is a world of anticipation, aspiration, and education.

2. To my knowledge, no statistical info about start-ups and incubators in Kinshasa is yet available. International actors try to map Kinshasa's/Congo's ecosystem (e.g., Zuidberg 2018; the Briter Bridges website).

3. See Adunbi (this volume) for a similar argument about the study of technology in Nigeria.

4. Prince appeared on some talk shows on local television, in which he could introduce the smartwatch to the viewing public. In such instances his mobile phone number was mentioned, thus allowing interested viewers to get immediately in touch with him.

5. The networks Steel (this volume) describes in which Khartoum women's digital businesses are embedded are similarly global and post-global.

6. Dubai is oftentimes regarded as a "global city." For an increasing number of Congolese, trips to Dubai are part of their desired commercial and leisure activities for several reasons; one of them is that it is easier to obtain visas for Dubai rather than, for example, France or Belgium. This experience sets Dubai apart from the former metropoles. From a Kinois perspective, Dubai is very much a post-global city.

7. It is telling that a review about Congolese immigration and emigration published in 2009 (Ngoie and Lelu 2010) does not mention the Arab Emirates nor Brazil as destinations. China is identified as not an attractive space for Congolese emigration. Of course, statistics and official data do not tell the whole story, nor can they capture the significance of these spaces in the Kinois imagination of economic achievement. Yet that absence suggests a recent change of migration trajectories.

8. The Kinois imagination of "the Congolese nation" differs from, for example, the ways in which people in Lubumbashi or Goma or any other Congolese city (or rural area for that matter) relate to the idea of the Congolese nation due to its specific positionality as the capital city, as the heart of national politics, and as the largest city of the country.

9. At the time of revising this chapter (in the fall of 2024), Kinshasa is home to some eighteen million inhabitants. Kinshasa is one of the fastest growing cities on the African continent.

10. An investment group published statistical results of its market analysis for optical fiber connectivity in Kinshasa. It noted that almost 30 percent of companies have business access to the internet and 90 percent of Kinshasa's households have some access to the internet, mainly mobile (CDC Investment Works 2020).

11. Like many Kinois, I have been victim to several thefts of phones during moments of inattentiveness in public transport, in markets, and on busy roundabouts.

12. The fashion scene may be a precursor of a reappraisal of things local. Meyer (2015) describes how in Accra fashion has brought in more "African" materials and designs, which also appeared in local filmmaking.

13. Facebook post on the page of the ministry (SCPT, La Société Congolaise des Postes et des Télécommunications), October 17, 2016.

14. We can ask how far the undoubtedly well-intended international aid schemes that more and more focus on so-called capacity building (rather than aid) confirm the *complexe* and thus produce more harm. After all, such programs suggest that there is a lack of adequate capacity in the country where they intervene, and ignore the kinds of expertise that àre available.

15. See Mbembe 2010 for an insightful elaboration on how African societies are experimenting with new forms of producing dignified futures. Mbembe considers the artistic world one of these spaces. An update of his book would probably include the tech scene as another one.

16. See Mavhungu 2017 for a harsh critique of such enduring narratives.

17. This was exactly the tagline of the #Ishango Innovation Awards announced in 2020. The initiative came from Kinshasa Innovation Forum, a collaboration between the Congolese Foundation KA and the German Hanns Seidel Stiftung. Their goal is to encourage young Congolese to become entrepreneurs.

18. The slogan "#madeinrdc" was launched in 2014. It has a special twist; the first part is formulated in English and riffs on the familiar global labeling of a product's national origin. The second part is the acronym of the French name of the country, République Démocratique du Congo. On social media posts, Kinois sometimes also write "Made in 243," referencing the international area code of the DRC, when claiming a person's success or an invention, though very often as well mocking or ridiculing a particular practice or social phenomenon.

19. Salon des biens et services produits en RDC (agro-alimentaire, cosmétique, plastique, technologie, artisanat, menuiserie/ébénisterie, couture, etc), Initiative de valorisation des contenus locaux, Action de normalisation des offres locales.

20. https://slkaanews.com/2020/05/10/michelange-katende-premiere-compagnie-de-montre-congolaise/ (accessed February 11, 2021). Closely linked to the intended boost of the local industry is the effort to convince Congolese to "consume Congolese." To that effect, the slogan *Consommons congolais* ("Let's consume [things] Congolese") has been created. This slogan (which has quickly evolved into a hashtag) speaks to the *complexe* described above. There is an assumption that things Congolese are of a lesser quality than foreign products and thus need to promoted specifically.

21. Translated by KP: "Parce qu'il est primordial d'investir au Congo, par extension en Afrique et d'apporter notre expertise à la nation. Notre génération est consciente des enjeux présents et de son rôle pour tenter de changer le cours de l'histoire. Si notre génération ne fait rien de concret, elle en paiera les conséquences. On le voit déjà avec la domination d'étrangers sur le continent africain. Nous devons donc faire notre part. Chaque parcours est une inspiration SLK News s'engage à encourager les nouvelles entreprises et défendre les intérêts du peuple avant tout. Au-delà d'une compagnie de montre, Michelange Katende représente une génération zélée d'apporter une nouvelle perception de l'Afrique. Une génération qui croit que tôt ou tard le soleil finira par se lever pour le berceau de l'humanité." https://slkaanews.com/2020/05/10/michelange-katende-premiere-compagnie-de-montre-congolaise/ (accessed February 11, 2021).

22. For example, a meme depicting Trump's efforts to rig the 2019 elections was accompanied by a text stating, "made in rdc: vérité des urnes aux états-unis de Donald trump."

23. Contracts were signed in July 2020. Industry Five was supposed to begin construction of factories on Congolese territory in September 2021. As of August 2023, nothing had started.

24. July 31, 2020, on the website of the ministry of industry, https://www.minindustrie.gouv.cd/galerie/actualites/119-vers-la-relance-des-industries-detruites-par-les-forces-negatives-dans-le-nord-kivu-et-l-ituri.html (accessed February 11, 2021).

25. ZTE feature phones (a Chinese brand) sold in Kinshasa in 2009 already had the option to set their parameters in Lingala.

26. "Nous devons prendre les exemples des pays qui ont avancé, comme la Chine, comme la Corée. Ils n'ont pas fait de la magie, ils ont travaillé tout en mettant leur intelligence pour leur pays, et je crois leurs efforts sont palpables, et si nous suivons ce modèle, là, je crois on va aller de l'avant" (WhatsApp communication).

27. The presence of Chinese sellers in Kinshasa's districts beyond the city center contrasts with that of groups of Chinese construction workers who live in workers' camps and build Kinshasa's roads and skyscrapers. These laborers barely speak Lingala, do not build a social life outside of their community, and are only visible on construction sites (roads, apartments, public buildings, etc.). The Congolese politicians and local media describe these Chinese laborers as "our guests" (Pype 2010), thus framing their presence as an invited presence, not intrusive or colonizing.

28. The word *djika* derives from the slang word *belgicain* (the middle of the word has been extracted) and thus references a person who has traveled along global trajectories. A Congolese who has traveled to Europe, Canada, or the United States is therefore called a *djika*; this appellation is not used for someone who has traveled to Dubai, China, or South Africa.

29. Kinshasa's tech entrepreneurs are not blind for the limits of freedom in China either. For example, when Jack Maa disappeared in late 2020, the news circulated widely on the WhatsApp groups of Kinshasa's geeks.

30. For a media example: Shola Deen, one of the founders of Kinstartup Academy, KinInnov, and Ishango Days, is quoted in an online news magazine: "This is why we created the Kinstartup Academy. Through this television program, we make young people want to set up their businesses by broadcasting the program on national TV . . . a fair fight that takes up the famous phrase of Confucius: 'If you want to grow up a year, plant a rice plantation. If you want to grow ten years, plant a tree. If you want to chart your course over a hundred years, educate the youth'" (translated from the French by KP). https://cio-mag.com/rdc-kininnov-au-coeur-du-reacteur/ (accessed February 11, 2021).

31. "*Compliqué* is not the same as *complexé. Compliqué* means cumbersome, difficult because of various bureaucratic and social obstacles.

32. Translated from the French/Lingala by KP: "ya biso basalaka makambu lokola baza amazon, 1 trop cher; 2 moyen de payement compliqué; 3 délai de livraison neti kaka ezuaki avion; 4 ajouter l'escroquerie naturelle de congolais;donc très compliqué pour se fier à nos solutions locales" (WhatsApp text, 2020).

33. To my surprise, there are hardly any debates about Kigali Innovation City among Kinshasa's geeks. Furthermore, in Kinshasa, one hardly hears about Nairobi as the site for tech innovation. Most probably this is due to the fact that Kenya is anglophone while Rwanda has a history of being francophone. In 1996, English became a national language in Rwanda. Since 2008, English has been language of instruction in the country thus still adding a linguistic challenge to Kinois who not always master English.

34. It is maybe too soon to state this firmly, but one can ask whether Rwanda has replaced Angola as a destination country for young Kinois. The diamond business has lost much appeal among young Kinois. In the case of the tech entrepreneurs, they dream of accumulating tech expertise and skills, not of digging up an exceptional diamond. Yet Rwanda remains a difficult space to access, due to the language difference (not many Kinois are fluent in English or Kinyarwanda), and not everybody has the required networks to get invited to Rwanda. The latter remain opaque, most probably due to the tense political relationship between the DRC and Rwanda.

35. Hardly any of the Kinois technologists with whom I interacted were aware that the same (Canadian) tech innovators that had set up this system in Kigali were trying out the system in Kinshasa as well in 2019. The tryout happened in the elite area of Gombe and Ngaliema. By 2021, the initiative had proven to be unsustainable in Kinshasa, and the project was aborted.

36. Referring to the National Plan for the Digital that President Tshisekedi inaugurated in September 2019. His ambition was to turn the DRC into Africa's digital center by 2025.

37. During an online conversation (August 2020) with one of Kinshasa's leading tech entrepreneurs, I was told, "In DR Congo 22GB costs 20USD, while in Brazzaville, Rwanda and Burundi 30GB costs 10USD with the same company of Airtel."

38. One subscriber to the aforementioned WhatsApp group mentioned that "worse than leaving your wife at home while you're away is going to Rwanda, where the state is surveilling." The joke signals two different social spaces of surveillance. While within Kinois courting and matrimonial culture men are supposed to surveil the wanderings of their wife, traveling means the husband is losing that possibility (although various other technologies are set in place). The joke suggests that such a trip transforms the young Kinois man from the agent of surveillance to the object of surveillance—enacted by the Kigali state.

39. Usually people transit via Nairobi when traveling between Kinshasa and Kigali.

40. "Qu'ils nous laissent tranquille, biso tozo luka social ebonga, courant stable, internet haut débit au moindre coût epicetout" ("epcetout," typo for "et puis c'est tout").

41. Related to that: The local elite send their children to schools in Europe and the United States; they also prefer medical treatment abroad.

42. The Congo pride of the Africa-rising moment differs significantly from the *retour à l'authenticité* ("back to authenticity") program installed by Mobutu during the 1970s, which also proclaimed pride and and during which time the president also reinforced diplomatic ties with China and North Korea. Some of the main differences are (a) the relationship toward ancestrality (rather absent in the Africa-rising narrative); and (b) the main propagandists/protagonists (then mainly cultural entrepreneurs such as musicians and dance groups, now tech entrepreneurs). Both projects entail an explicit postcolonial move, a moving away from colonial stereotypes, structures, and affects. A deeper comparison between the two projects is beyond the scope of this chapter.

CHAPTER 2

Technologies of Dream Life and the Life of Dreams in Afrodystopia

JOSEPH TONDA

TRANSLATED BY KATRIEN PYPE

This contribution proposes to show how modern technologies are instituted as thaumaturgical (magical and wondrous) powers of production of the dream life and the life of dreams in Afrodystopia, the African dystopia (Tonda 2021). It is based on my work in urban sociology and anthropology, where the technologies of the capitalist world stimulate the creativity of social imaginaries. They destructure and restructure, in a continuous dynamic, the relations between "elders" and "social cadets," men and women, dominant and dominated, within what I propose to call "the unconscious of capitalism" or the "specular mega-machine of interpellation."

THE SPECULAR TECHNOLOGICAL MEGA-MACHINE OF INTERPELLATION, AND THE UNCONSCIOUS OF CAPITALISM

Among the technological devices that transform and enrich the social imaginary of cities (and villages) on the "dark continent" and elsewhere, as well as the relations between groups mentioned above, is the specular device of the mirror. Indeed, as Sabine Mechior-Bonnet writes, "To grasp the magical, miraculous nature of the first face-to-face encounter with the mirror, we must turn to the imaginary narrative of myth or folklore: Narcissus is the first hero of this troubling encounter with oneself. It is for this reason that the mirror is the 'matrix of the symbolic'" (1994, 14). In this perspective, we can consider not only "mirrors, photographs, and camcorders" (1994, 12) as material analogues of the mirror but also, in a wider way, the cinema, television, and all the machines with a portable screen or not, characteristic of the "culture of the narcissism" (Lasch 1979) that impregnates all contemporary societies.

We are considering a culture that has not suppressed the magical and miraculous dimension of the first face-to-face with the mirror, but that, on the contrary, has both internalized it in the brain and objectified it in the screen machines, the producers of the screen images of capitalism. This means that contemporary societies are governed by an abstract, specular technological mega-machine that constitutes the unconscious of capitalism. In my reading of this societal phenomenon, this unconscious can be qualified as machinic by working with the Guattarian concept, where it presents itself "as something that would hang around us a little everywhere, as well in gestures, daily objects, as on TV, in the spirit of the times, and even, perhaps especially, in the major problems of the day" (Guattari 1979, 7–8).

What I call "the technological mega-machine," specular and abstract, and which I consider "the unconscious of capitalism," its unknown brain, is not, in reality, "outside" the individual unconscious, since the gestures, the daily objects, the TV, the spirit of the times, and so on, are not conceivable or thinkable "outside" of the power of the reflexive thought constitutive of the contemporary technological and scientific episteme of which they are the mirrors. They mirror the unconscious of this episteme. They are close to what Lipovestki and Serroy (2007, 10) write about the global screen: "We passed from half a century of the screen spectacle to screen communication, from the one screen to the all-screen; here is the era of the global screen. The screen in any place and at any time." My understanding of this global screen differs because it locates the global screen at the same time in the objectivity of the material structures and of the "major problems of the day," and in the subjectivity of the mental structures where it functions like an unconscious. specular mega-machine of interpellation. In this chapter indeed, this global screen functions as an immense mirror that continuously acts as an "affect of interpellation," at the same time external and internal to the individuals. This allows us to widen the Althusserian concept of interpellation following Jean-Jacques Lecercle (2019, 67): who develops it further:

> The . . . affect of interpellation is not only social (in its origin) or psychological and moral (in its result) but also bodily in its effect: One will thus speak of a perlocutionary effect, effect of the illocutionary force of interpellation that

seizes the body of the individual that it subjectifies (and one will also speak of a pervisionary effect). I suggest two theoretical places where this corporeal seizure of the interpellation by address has already been described. In the primitive scene of the Althusserian interpellation . . . , the whistle of the police agent, in the *cantonade*, interpellates me, in both senses of the term, as a subject, because it can only be me who is targeted, and it is my body that first reacts to this aggression: I stop dead in my tracks, I turn around, my heart beats wildly, etc. And, second, we can read the description given by Favret-Saada, in *Les Mots, la mort, les sorts*, of the taking of the bewitched by the vital force of the sorcerer.

In my perspective, what I will call the "immense mirror of interpellation," the "abstract specular mega-machine," the "unconscious of capitalism," or its "machinic brain" that acts as an "affect of interpellation" is situated at the same time outside and inside individuals, in the logic of the Guattarian unconscious. Thus it is constantly produced by this affect of interpellation that seizes individuals and makes them turn around, at the same time according to the paradigm of the whistle of the policeman (Althusser) and that of the witch's powers (Favret-Saada). The interpellated subjects are infantilized, which condemns them to live in the omnipotence of the thought or of the image-screens, and therefore without possibility of overcoming of the mirror stage described by Jacques Lacan. As I contend, in the society of screens, that is to say, this society where the individuals are constantly confronted with blind mirrors that are screens, people are constantly interpellated to enter into childhood and thus to live in the hallucinated world of the dazzles of the mega-machine of the unconscious of capitalism. This makes the subjects themselves a component of these screen mirrors constitutive of the mega-machine. In other words, in the society of screen machines, each subject is for the other both a screen mirror and a screen image, both becoming conscious of their social positioning in the screen images that they project reciprocally. In doing so, this "awareness," which is achieved through a confrontation with reflected specular images, is translated into representations of oneself as a valued or devalued subject, big or small, important or insignificant, desirable or undesirable, and so on, but always in a state of powerlessness and impotence in the face of the capitalist mega-mirror of interpellation.

In this framework, all technologies created by human brains are caught in the specular mega-machine that figures the unconscious of capitalism and are, by design, infantilizing. They are so because they are not only devices of interpellation but also and simultaneously, by their power of interpellation, devices that subjugate by creating power within "social relations." Indeed, experts, that is to say those who know and who master the mechanisms of functioning of these technologies, possess a power created by the knowledge and the mastery of these technologies, and they exercise it on those who do not know and do not master anything. They trade a power and a knowledge (a power-knowledge) in the field of the social relations; they have to update this power-knowledge permanently by never-ending processes of learning due to a constant stream of innovations that characterize the field of the sciences and the technologies. On the side of the subjects who are excluded from the mastery of these technologies, and who have to pay services to the experts, their infantilization is produced by "ignorance" that makes them dependent on the knowledge-powers of the specialists, and also by their constitution as subjects subjected to the technologies by the effects of dazzlement, wonder, fascination, and seduction that these technologies produce.

Because these technologies are commodities and circulate on the market, they behave as "things-subjects" calling humans, to subject them to their power, which is not the power-knowledge of the specialists but is their power as objects. This power is historical and social and is always "put on scene" in "exhibitions," as Giorgio Agamben underlines (1998b, 79):

> Just as Bosch, at the dawn of capitalism, drew from the spectacle of the first great international markets of Flanders the symbols suitable for illustrating his mystical-Adamite[1] conception of millenarianism, so Baudelaire, at the beginning of the second industrial revolution, drew from the transfiguration of merchandise in the World's Fair the emotional state and the symbolic elements of his own poetics. To an eye as attentive as his, it appeared henceforth evident that the merchandise had ceased to be an innocent object, whose practical use exhausted the enjoyment and the sense, to load itself with this worrying ambiguity to which Marx was to allude twelve years later by speaking about its "fetish character," its "metaphysical subtleties," and its "theological quibbles."

The mirror, as a commodity, is a fetish; while the fetish as a commodity is a mirror. The society of screen machines, producer of screen images (among which humans live only as screen images of the possessed objects that possess them), is a fetishist society in which the superfetish reigns. The superfetish is emancipated from the role of merchandise, since it controls, inside the immense machine mirror that constitutes the unconscious of capitalism, the creativity of the inventors of screen machines whose dazzling power conditions their sale on the market. This dazzling power has as a key concept the solar dazzle (*l'éblouissement solaire*) to which all the screen images (as commodities) aspire. It is in this sense that we must understand their "mystico-adamite" power, in the sense of Bosch; it is also a power to produce "metaphysical subtleties" and "theological quibbles," in the sense of Marx.

Thus, in a fetishist world, governed by capitalist sorcery (Pignare and Stengers 2007), the loss of power and knowledge generated by the mastery of technologies that are commodities has the effect, in the social imaginary, of extending the domain of the invisible, fantastically enriched with the most modern and sophisticated technologies, such as supersonic airplanes, televisions, guns, and so on. It does this in the world of the night, the world of witches' powers. This is a world where the "child witches" (Tonda 2008), products of the machinery of the unconscious of capitalism, are credited with being masters of these technologies. The immense abstract machinic mirror of interpellation, by this example of the child witches, manifests thus as a device of infantilization consubstantial with the omnipotence of the children's thought processes, but also that of adults in the world where capitalism seems to have become a religion (Löwy 2006). This is how the thaumaturgical power of producing the dream life and the life of dreams in Afrodystopia, the African dystopia, functions in the sub-Saharan worlds of the Congo Basin, in Brazzaville, Kinshasa, Libreville, but also elsewhere on the "Black continent." This is a chimera, a place of nowhere whose inhabitants have been devalued, dehumanized by colonial domination, by the material force of war technologies, and by the dazzling power of psychic technologies, religion, and money in the first place.

THE HEROISM OF REVOLUTIONARY BODIES AND ITS INTERNAL AND EXTERNAL ENEMIES

If we pay attention to the ways in which boundaries between older and younger generations are drawn by the technological advances on the "dark continent," we grasp more fully the thaumaturgy of the technologies of the dream life and the life of dreams in Afrodystopia. What characterizes these generations is not, for example, the revolutionary heroism embodied by Che Guevara; in other words, it is not a heroism supported by the technology of sophisticated weapons, as in the blockbuster *Black Panther*. What characterizes the heroism of the Congolese revolutionary *maquis* of the 1960s is that it is built on the fabrication of the heroic body by means of physical and mystical combat techniques matched with techniques of moral formation: the revolutionary hero is a fighting body with a morale of steel. This revolutionary body and morale form a subject whose entire life has as its horizon the struggle that must defeat imperialism and its technologies, whose power is reduced, in the imagination, to the symbolism of the "paper tiger."

In the former People's Republic of Congo, the writer Emmanuel Boundzeki Dongala (2005) imagined the defeat of imperialism by a most archaic technology: a bow and arrow carried by a "Pygmy," the legendary man of the forest ecosystem, determined to liberate Bantu communities from the imperialist enemy. The "Pygmy" warrior, with his bow and arrow, was thus put at the opposite extreme from the imperialist American and French with their bomb-carrying planes, their guns, and all the sophisticated technological arsenal that accompanied them. The revolutionary imagination drew its strength from the techniques of producing the body and mind of the combatant, in connection with the elements of nature that the images of the Vietnam War presented as part of the enemy: The revolutionary combatant was subjected, like the nature that protected him and that he constituted as the American enemy, to the devastating fire of the napalm poured by the terrible B52s.

Projected on the big screen, *Apocalypse Now* showed the life of the revolutionary fighters' dreams, as well as the life of the revolutionaries' nightmares. The technologies of imperialism had the objective of transforming the indifferent psychic, physical, and social space of the revolutionary into a nightmarish space, that is, into a dystopia. On the side of imperialism, however, these technologies served to produce and perpetuate the dream life of which the American dream was and still is the key concept. In both cases, it is a question, for imperialism, in the use of its technologies, of working on the regression of adult humanity to childhood, that is to say, to the world of the omnipotence of ideas and desires whose emblematic object in the American dream is Coca-Cola and all that it represents and that represents it, for example the dollar.

This American dream of Coca-Cola, a mirror screen of all imperialist dreams, has challenged the Congolese by seizing their bodies and transformed them into allies of the imperialist power that, in so doing, ended up exterminating the revolutionary dream carried by the Congolese hero of anticolonial resistance, Patrice Lumumba. But this dislocated dream was not only Congolese. It thrived among all the sub-Saharan *maquisards* (resistance fighters), who, in Angola, Cameroon, Mozambique, Congo-Brazzaville, and Guinea Bissau, were caught up in a dreamlike interpellation other than that of Coca-Cola and Euro-American technologies that diffused, in the specular mega-machine of imperialism, messages of the "free" and "democratic world." In the People's Republic of Congo, the anti-imperialist struggle was led by the youth organized in the Youth of the National Movement of the Revolution, especially in its armed branch of the Civil Defense. This struggle was waged above all against the "obscurantism" embodied by the "old men," who reputedly possessed the magical technologies of the "reactionaries" they were assumed to be, and which turned the revolution into an antisorcery movement. This led to a paradox: The specular mega-machine constitutive of the unconscious of imperialism and capitalism included, as a result, the "mystical force" of the "old," that is, the "social elders."

However, this constitution of the "social elders" as a counterrevolutionary power with mystical technologies allied to the imperialist power was, at the same time, their own definition of themselves as "social cadets" because the cadets had transformed into political elders armed with the "ideological weapon," as it was called. This was, in fact, the national manifestation of a global phenomenon of infantilization of the inhabitants of the territories under imperialist domination. What was and still is unknown is that the revolutionary "war of dreams" against imperialist dreams, supported by technologies of mass death, repeated, on a symbolic level this time, the historical experience of the school, where knowing how to read and write made children the parents of their parents, thus plunging the latter into the night of "ignorance" and of "powerlessness." This means that knowledge created during the night is a power-knowledge that elevates the cadets to the status of "knowers (those who know)" or "experts." This war prolonged and still prolongs the history of colonization, which, under this angle of symbolic violence, produced the colonized as ignorant children and nonsubjects. The concept of the "colonial situation," like that of the "postcolonial situation," is from this point of view a concept of domination or subjection of the social elders by educated cadets who acquire the power-knowledge of modern technologies, of which writing is a major component.

THE MEGA-BRAIN MACHINE AND NICKI MINAJ

The preceding developments show that it is not only the world of Big Brother's telecoms (Orwell 1984) that has become commonplace, to the point that surveillance screens are ordinary objects of the owners. Also, more profoundly, the rupture of the boundary between psychic life and objective or physical life has been so significant that those who, in therapeutic traditions, once made the mirror a magical technology of consultation, in competition with or replacement of water or any other reflecting surface, have appropriated the computer as a tool of diagnosis through digital vision. I have known a powerful diviner-healer who called himself "Television" (*television*) in the Democratic Republic of the Congo. The breaking of the barrier between the psychic life, invisible, in each of the humans by other humans, and the visible life, physical, that everyone can see, is significant, even if the meanings each one gives to the visible things can diverge according to cultural qualifications (in the sense that one speaks about culture of a group). Even if these ruptures do not imply a homogenization of the meanings, significant is this continuity from the interior or psychic screens to the exterior or physical screens.

In African cities, the opening up of psychic screens to material or physical screens results in a phenomenon that is not often emphasized: Interior screens, like psychic screens, are mirrors of the desires, aspirations, disappointments, illusions, and nightmares of African cities. In other words, Brazzaville and Kinshasa, called in Lingala *Mboka Mundele* the "Village of the Whites," which were originally villages of mostly single men, have given these screens the creative capacity that Castoriadis gives to the imaginary. Thus, the "screenosphere," which Gilles Lipovestki and Serroy (2007, 11) reserve to physical or material screens alone, can be widened to include psychic screens, in the sense that they function, in the relation between the two registers of the real, as the imaginary in its capacity to create images. In short, I propose to conceive the inner imaginary (the psychic screens) in its relation with the screen machines and to think the whole thus constituted as a capacity of absorption and creation of images.

This proposal implies two consequences. The first one is that the subjective screens function inside as objective screens, because of the subjectivation of the images created and diffused by the objective screens. Conversely, the objective screens function as subjective screens: They are invested with the same capacities of creation of images as the subjective screens. The screen machines, indeed, create images on the model of the images generated by the psychic machine. In other words, the psychic life, consisting in the creation or in the production of images, concepts, ideas, has a material analogon in the machines made by man. Technologies thus fill, if one can say so, the role of the brain, which makes the technological sphere function as a huge brain in which human brains operate.

The second consequence is the agency that these two brains, in their dynamics, assign to the images, notably to the images of what we call the body-sexes, that is to say, the human bodies hypersexualized by the capitalist system. I have described elsewhere how screen machines not only create body-sexes, images at the same time mental and physical of human beings reduced to objects of libidinal desire, but also confer to these an agency, that is to say, a capacity to act on the relations of domination. This agency of the dominated bodies-sexes, notably that of the female bodies-sexes, is ambivalent. It can turn them into objects by reducing them to technologies of seduction exercised by "body-commodities" selling themselves to whoever can afford them and enjoy them to the point of their destruction. But it can also allow them to be inscribed in the relations instituted by the capitalist system and its market of the image-sexual screens, as means of capture and capitalization of the desire, by producing itself on the material screens, as machines of production and intensification of the dream life. I illustrate this with two cases, the first is what was called in Libreville, *tuée-tuée* ("fatal beauty," Tonda 2006), this body-sex that was delivered to whoever could "pay" for it, provided that the "client" was able to "bet" (take risks) and thus to consume it sexually without protecting himself from the risks of contamination of the AIDS virus.

The second case works with the image of Nicki Minaj, notably in her clip "Anaconda," staging the undulatory dazzles of the body-sex of this artist that was presented as a powerful selling point of her screen image, in the market of the screen images of capitalism. The producers of the "Anaconda" clip generated a hypersexualized dream life both within the clip's narrative and beyond it. Inside the clip, we see a young man completely captivated by the undulating dazzle of Nicki Minaj's body-sex, which, by the end, proves to be hallucinatory. The young man lives a powerful daydream from which he awakes to the disappearance of the object of his desire produced by the capitalist mega-brain that had penetrated his individual brain and had made him live an illusory dream life, different from the one that the powerful lead in real dream places, those heterotopias that their financial means allow them to frequent.

Beyond the narrative depicted in the clip, but inside the capitalist mega-brain that the system of screens and image-screens materializes, it is the whole population whose desires are captured by the libidinal undulations of Nicki Minaj's body-sex. By this mechanism, this population is captivated by the desire of the capitalist mega-brain, of which the image of the star's technological body-sex is precisely an image-screen. This image-screen of the dehumanizing system sells and incites the consumption of sexual images of the Black woman, in a logic of domination inseparably colonial and capitalist. It is what I have called elsewhere postcolonial imperialism (Tonda 2005). It is in the logic of this imperialism that the body-sex at risk of the killed-killed is born, whose name repeats the suffix of the prostitute who, from this point of view, is killed twice, to live in the world under the sway of the immense technological brain of capitalism, which captures and capitalizes, to its profit, the desires of the human beings reduced to body-sexes. This immense brain is constituted both inside and outside the individual brains that it colonizes and that it incites to dream, by being their unconscious, the capitalist unconscious.

Such is life in Afrodystopia, the place of unhappiness, both real and unreal, since it is also called the "dark continent," a chimera, a place of nowhere, populated by screen images, like the slain Gabonese, screen image of Nicki Minaj, creation of the industry of the capitalism of dazzling, different from the society of the spectacle theorized by Guy Debord. In Debord's society of the spectacle, the real has moved away in the representation, while in the society of the dazzling, the representation is incarnated by the thaumaturgical power of the technological devices in the individual brains, invested by the capitalist macro-brain. What I call the dream life is then the life that produces the activity of this unconscious and that is the life of the real paradises represented by the image-screens. By real or terrestrial paradises, I think of places such as clubs for the rich, their palaces, and other types of heterotopias like the African Disney villages, fairy-like places in urban enclaves. It is as well about these futuristic creations where the precarious populations are excluded, as in the Cité du Fleuve project in Kinshasa, or in Libreville, where a poster of the unfinished futuristic city was shown to all passers-by. What these utopian or futuristic cities mean is that they are first of all products of advanced engineering, capable of generating habitable spaces from liquid spaces: the river in Kinshasa and the sea in Libreville. They also signify the materialization of the white man's village that confines Black people to disinherited spaces, where the psychic machines work to live "elsewhere" while at home. In Libreville, the working-class neighborhoods, called *mapanes,* are marked by the multiplicity of satellite dishes that allow the excluded to live their European soccer passion. Such is *Mboka Mundele,* the village of the whites, in which the Black people born in the villages have a psychic experience of single white women: the wives of Christ, the sisters and mothers of the missions. The treatment of these women, through the creativity of the psychic screenosphere, will produce the inverted image, the demonic negative of the mirror, the secular revelation of these sisters and mothers of the church that will be the "free women," called in Lingala the *ndumba*.

THE MEGA-MACHINE AND THE INTERPELLATION OF PRESIDENTIAL BRAINS

The mega-machine that interpellates through the dazzling body-sexes of, for example, the superstar Nicki Minaj and of Gabonese images of "fatal beauties" (*tuées-tuées*) (Tonda 2006), both mirror figures of capitalism, is also present as an unconscious device for the production of the dream life in the brains of the leaders of the "Black continent." Because their desire is to live in limitlessness, the principle of capitalism, they have to sell to the "people" the illusion of the dream life through their speeches according to the same model implemented by the Pentecostals, agents of the religious economy of miracles (Pype 2012). Historically, the dream life in the two Congos (Republic of Congo and the DRC) was conceived of as the life of the *ambianceurs* and *viveurs*, meaning the life of partygoers (*fêtards*), which gave rise to local expressions such as *baviva* (party lovers), *bisengo ya la joie* (the pleasure of joy) (Gondola 1999), and *fêti na fêti* (unending party). The interpellation of the population by a presidential brain, during a meeting of a presidential election campaign in Congo, participates in this logic of production of the dream life. For example, the candidate Denis Sassou Nguesso, who wanted another term in power, concluded his speech during this campaign, by this expression: *Kaka fêti na fêti ehhh!*, which can be translated "Let us be in permanent celebration ehhh!"

The president thus *interpellated* the Congolese citizens who were following him live, or who were going to follow him on the screens of smartphones or television to continue to live phantasmatic or imaginary rewards distributed by the "political authority," to take up the language of a Dutch novelist and doctor of the seventeenth century, Mandeville (Dufour 2011).

According to Mandeville, there are three "classes" understood as "groups" that exist in a society. The class of "villains" is that of people who refuse to disobey their animal instincts, because they are not fooled by the imaginary retributions of the political authority. The other class is that of the "neurotics." They are the "honest people," known by this name in the eighteenth century. They believe in the law and want to respect it. The last class is that of the "perverts," "constituted by the worst of men" (Dufour 2011, 71). Following the logic of Mandeville and Dufour, the Congolese president would belong to the class of perverts and scoundrels occupying the "political instance" by distributing phantasmatic rewards to the class of neurotics, the class of honest people, to whom the representatives of the composite class of scoundrels and perverts sell the imaginary, that is to say, what we call here the "dream life."

This transaction (*vente*, "sale") is done through the technology of the screens and is characteristic of the society of the dazzling in which African men and women are captured, captivated by the dream of the Other, dream of the machines to produce the dream life, materializations of the unconscious (Guattarian) of capitalism. Indeed, these captivated audiences and those who were interpellated to live in the *ambiance fêti na fêti* (never-ending party) are certainly captivated by the president campaigning for his own succession. Though, it is easy to see that the campaigning president inscribes his interpellation in the logic of that of the captivating and capturing of the global screen, such as I have redefined it, and of which fictional narratives such as *Fahrenheit 451* (Bradbury 1955) and *1984* (Orwell 1950) are paradigmatic examples. The dream life is thus the fantasized life of those who can enjoy themselves. This reminds us of all the clichés of the colonial ideology of the "good Negro," of the "primitive . . . soft, sociable and laughing," that is to say, this "big child, naive and fully disposed to receive Civilization" (Hug 2003, 147). In other words, it is about the life of the subject who would never go beyond the "mirror stage." We would thus have reached today, in the society of the spectacle such as *Fahrenheit 451* describes it, a society of bedazzlement that does not have for its model African societies, but the technological societies where the culture of narcissism reigns, according to which "archaic myths and superstitions reappeared in the very heart of the most modern, scientifically enlightened, and progressive nations in the world" (Lasch 1979, 245). The dream life produced and diffused by the sophisticated screen technologies is, from this point of view, the life of "contemporary thought forms of the most primitive societies" that dreams allow us to explore in our sleep, because according to the sociologist Roger Bastide, the "dream is an exploration of these darknesses accumulated in us for millennia, a trace in contemporary forms of thought of the most primitive societies" (Bastide 2003, 28).

Another example of a presidential brain caught in the abstract megamachine of interpellation by dazzling practices is the Gabonese president, Omar Bongo Ondimba, model of the *Parisian-sapeurs*, or *sapelogues* (fashionistas). For the latter, before they were called *sapelogues*, their reference district was the Bacongo district of Brazzaville. For the Parisian-Sapelogues of this neighborhood, the Gabonese head of state embodied the life to which their bodies aspired through luxury clothing disguises. But this dream life, which must be understood as the "white life" embodied by the Gabonese head of state, is also exemplary in that it was simultaneously a life of unhappiness, that is, a dystopian life, in the precise sense that dystopia is the "place of unhappiness," and that Afrodystopia is the concept of this dream life inseparable from a life of unhappiness. The problem is then to know in what way this Afrodystopic life possesses this characteristic of the thaumaturgical power of white technology in African history.

In order to show this link, it is important to know that the Gabonese head of state, who brought his designer suits from Paris to the seaside palace in Libreville, accompanied by call girls, was at the origin of a scandal known as the "Smalto affair,"[2] named after the fashion designer Francesco Smalto, who was accused of "aggravated pimping" for having delivered his choice suits accompanied by "brand-name escorts." The scandal was mainly explained by the fact that "the rumor in vogue in the call girl milieu is that the Gabonese president is HIV-positive . . . and that he refused condoms when these call girls, with whom he had sexual relations, talked to him about it."

These gravelly details are significant here because they allow us to establish the close link between the dream life, the *bisengo ya la joie* (life of "permanent celebration") embodied by an African head of state, model of the *Parisian-sapeurs* and therefore a figure of realized utopia; and on the other hand, the life of misfortune, dystopia, the "place of misfortune," symbolized by AIDS, which in Gabon and Congo is referred to as the "disease of fire" or the "disease of lightning," so called because of the burns it produces on the skin of the sick. The significant point on which the dream life of the *Parisian-sapeur* joins technology as a thaumaturgical power is the following: In the Gabonese, but also in the Congolese, social imagination, the symptomatology of this fire or lightning disease has given rise to what is called in Gabon the "night gun."

In Gabon, the "night gun" references a disease that in Congo is called *mwanza*, which means "lightning" (Tonda 2005). It is common knowledge that power struggles in the political, social, and economic fields are carried out in Gabon with this mystical technology of "night guns," just as in Congo, notably during the civil war of 1997, when Mwanza fired at the enemy camp. These "mystical" wars thus consisted of a symbolic appropriation, that is to say, a magical appropriation of the archaic technology of fire, of which lightning, tamed, is paradigmatic. Through firearms, the "white power" has become anchored in the social imagination of the continent. The technology of fire mastered by whites was then instituted by and in the imaginary as a magical power, and the whites occupied the structural place of spirits, notably the "revenants. The possession of firearms was a fundamental element in the slave trade and in colonization. It is in this sense that social, political, and economic power is inseparable from the mastery or acquisition of technologies of protection and aggression that are called "fetishes." It is also, in this sense, that money, like the state, is a superfetish of domination associated with the most sophisticated weapons, among which are the "mystical" weapons. The state of Wakanda, in the film *Black Panther*, illustrates, from this point of view, the technological paradigm of the most sophisticated weapons, both material and mystical.

Thus, Bongo was the head of state embodying the utopia of the dream life only because at the same time he embodied the dystopia as the life of the power of Death, of which the triad AIDS-gun-night is the materialization. Historically, Bongo's forty-two years in power took place in the shadow of the French military technological power. The military Camp de Gaulle was located adjacent to Bongo's vast private estate in Libreville. The dream life, which Bongo embodied in the eyes of the Congolese community of Parisians, was thus simultaneously a life of dreams, that is, the life that people live in the dreams of others, and which, in Central Africa, is a life that produces misfortune. The "white power" materialized by the Camp de Gaulle in Libreville materializes the life that the white colonial power continues to live in Gabon as the psychic life of the colony. After all, in the colonial situation, defined by Balandier (1951) as an unequal situation in which a racial minority dominates the equally racial majority, is a situation characterized by the technological domination of the minority. The white power is from this point of view a technological power of which firearms are the materialization. But this white technological power was so deeply rooted in the psychic life of the populations that it was translated into symbolic techniques and technologies that were and are certainly of part of the imaginary realm but whose physical or biological manifestations are socially and culturally attested. The white power, technologically evidenced, became moreover associated with the power of Money and Death, whose dreams are nowadays places of life for the living and the dead (Tonda 2021).

THE MYSTIFICATION OF THE MACHINE UNCONSCIOUS
OF CAPITALISM

The psychic life of the colony marked by the power of arms makes Bongo the one who lived in the manners of the colonists, that is, in the dreams of the colonized. To live in the dreams of the colonized is to feed on these dreams, in other words, to transform the colonized and the neocolonized into living images of the dream of the colonizers and the imperialists. Therefore, the *viveurs*, the *ambianceurs*, the partisans of the life of *fêti na fêti*, instituted themselves as *jouisseurs* in the dreams of others, and thus those who feed on their own lives. This phantasmagoria of the everyday life is of course what Marx calls the "mystification of the nonimaginary," which he explained as the fact that "a social relation presents itself in the form of an object existing outside of individuals and that the determined relations in which these enter into the process of production of their social life present themselves as specific properties of an object" (in Jappe 2003, 45–46). The object of the "mystification of the nonimaginary" that manifests itself in the "reversal of reality" is money, according to Marx' logic, but, as I argue, it must be inscribed in the logic of the mystification produced by the abstract mega-machine that the technologies of capitalism materialize.

NOTES

1. Adamites were early Christian groups in northern Africa in the second, third, and fourth centuries. During medieval times, several cults in western Europe were inspired by the Adamites.

2. "Smalto jugé pour 'proxénétisme aggravé': Le couturier italien envoyait des call-girls au Gabon pour vendre ses creations," *Libération*, liberation.fr (accessed June 13, 2022).

CHAPTER 3

Inga as Enclave

The (Dis)comfort of Being Serious Men

BARBARA CARBON

The *cité* of Inga is the agglomeration of camps built near the Inga I and II hydroelectric dams that were constructed between 1968 and 1982 in the Kongo Central Province of the Democratic Republic of the Congo. Inga provides electricity to urban centers such as Tshela, Boma, Matadi, and Kinshasa but also generates energy for the mining industry in Katanga (Willame 1986; Showers 2011; Misser 2013). It is situated in a remote, rural location 57 kilometers from the city of Matadi. Inga I and II have a combined capacity to produce 1,775 megawatts of electricity. The Congo River flows at an average speed of 4,200 cubic meters per second near the Inga dams, where there is a 112-meter difference in elevation over a distance of about 15 kilometers.

During my thirteen months of ethnographic fieldwork, conducted between May 2015 and December 2016, the dams did not operate to their full capacity due to inception faults, limited maintenance, and an accident in 2015 that damaged one of Inga II's eight turbines, the G24. The rehabilitation of the G24 was completed at the end of 2016, which coincided with the end phases of my fieldwork, during which I predominantly engaged in participant observation inside and on top of the Inga II dam with the workers involved in its rehabilitation. I also spent lengthy amounts of time with these workers and other Inga inhabitants in their homes and in public spaces such as churches, bars, the local hospital, and water collection points on the Inga site.

In this chapter, I approach Inga as a relatively new and growing urban center that brings together people from different ethnicities and classes who have different skills, vocations, and aspirations. I provide an assemblage of living quarters, lifestyles, moral aspirations, and masculinities to illustrate how techno-expertise forms Inga's social world. My central argument in this chapter is that it is the requirement of technological expertise, more permanent forms of labor, and the presence of *ayant-droits*[1] and their families together that produce Inga's social geography. Over the years, the Inga enclave has accommodated a mix of highly skilled and unskilled labor for the operation and, initially, the construction of the dams. Many of the workers in Inga stay there for a substantial amount of time. Some families have lived there for several generations, making its social life differ substantially from other camps where the majority of inhabitants are temporary laborers.

To develop this argument, I look at Inga from the perspective and living conditions of young university-trained engineers whose cultural styles and lives differ from but coexist with the more "rascal-like," physically tough kind of masculinity present in some other sub-Saharan extractive contexts and resource enclaves (Ferguson 1999). Quite often, men in such settings have been described in terms of their spending behaviors, often on sex, drugs, and alcohol as a result of quick and often temporary access to money (Cuvelier 2011, 2017; De Boeck 1998; Hendriks 2013; Jønsson and Bryceson 2009; Bryceson et al. 2014). The engineers challenge this notion by aiming to be respectable men and making good impressions and personal connections with older engineer families and local inhabitants in order to further their career.

In order to provide a phenomenological account of the engineers and their life in Inga, I first contextualize them in Inga's social and professional context. Despite their initial excitement to have obtained a post within the SNEL,[2] the engineers often described their lives in terms of stress and entrapment once relocated to Inga. They also experienced a certain animosity among the *Ingatiens* (people born and bred in Inga), who consider them *mingizila* or *arrivistes/venants* (newcomers).[3] The material comfort experienced by the young men failed to compensate for the levels of distress accompanying life in a high-tech, artificial working context. I explore these initial difficulties of the young engineers as they strove to become respectable men and assume their position as figures of success within the Inga society, a careful balancing act resembling that of a liminal phase they must go through in order to take their rightful place in Inga society.

In the next section of the chapter I elaborate on the engineers as figures of success and how they interact and influence other young men on-site. This then leads into exploring how their position of comfort and privilege impacts the experience of inequality on-site for themselves and those struggling to win a regular income. I elaborate on how *Ingatiens* operate on-site, anticipate the future project of Grand Inga, and relate to the engineers. I then consider the position of lesser-skilled staff, women, and expatriates in Inga's social geography and describe where people are located according to the site's camp system. I conclude by contextualizing Inga within the literature on resource enclaves by comparing it to cities, villages, and the post-global city (Pype, this volume). Studies on extractive industries have accentuated the resulting social change in terms of migration, the urbanization of rural areas, and changing gender relations (Epstein 1981; Lahiri-Dutt 2012). This chapter adds to this body of work by exploring Inga's particular living arrangements and how they contribute to the discomfort experienced by the young engineers.

The extraction of resources requires specific technologies and a labor force that knows how to work with them. This, in addition to the isolated nature of the spaces where natural resources are usually extracted, leads to the formation of particular urban forms often referred to as resource enclaves (Adunbi 2020a, 39). Inga as a resource enclave enables the engineers to be hyperconnected and partake in transnational networks as well as experience a deep sense of separation from their friends and families. I conclude this chapter by connecting the stresses experienced by the workers to those caused by the dams on Inga's environment and local communities. I argue that artificial living conditions in a high-tech context often augments inequalities and that these in turn lead to feelings of distress and friction between the different groups of people trying to live together. Simultaneously, they also enable emancipatory practices to overcome existing social and spatial divisions and the resulting psychological discomfort.

ENTRER DANS LE SYSTÈME, OR THE PRESSURES OF SUCCESS

One evening in March 2016, I found Germain and Benjamin in deep conversation on Germain's front porch. Germain is a young electronic engineer employed at the conversion post where low-voltage energy is transformed into high-voltage energy. Benjamin is a mechanical engineer who was hired to supervise the rehabilitation work on the G24 conducted by the SNEL. Although both men had only arrived in Inga about six months ago, they had already expressed a desire to leave. Benjamin seemed sad, talking in a low voice, saying he had been feeling so low he didn't even ring his girlfriend. Apparently he had been told that he could no longer supervise the work conducted on the G24. He said he had been accused of plotting against one of the directors with the aim of replacing him. He had also been accused of passing on information about their work on the G24 to the directors in Kinshasa, thereby bypassing his Inga superiors. Benjamin had been praised, however, for his quality of work and commitment by an expatriate mechanic, Philippe, there to help the SNEL team with the rehabilitation of the G24. Benjamin and Germain said they had been invited to "enter the system," meaning they had felt pressurized by certain superiors and colleagues to enter schemes that would help enrich them.

Both men said that they didn't want to enter this game as they believed that such practices were at the source of the difficulties experienced within the country. Their religious persuasion also prevented them from feeling that such actions were morally justifiable. Germain, Benjamin, and some other young engineers who had been appointed in Inga to conduct specific engineering tasks in line with their expertise felt responsible to change the existing culture of corruption within the company. Eager to marry[4] their girl-friends in Kinshasa, they hoped that by staying loyal to the direction in Kinshasa they would more easily progress within the company and earn more money. Although they all got married before the end of 2016 and had a child by the end of 2017, their choice to denounce rather than enter the "system" did not make their promotion a smooth process. Nor did it make them feel more at home in Inga, where Benjamin and Germain were both accused by colleagues of plotting against their leaders. The initial months in Inga, and even their work there, can be understood as a process of becoming adults, the young engineers making great effort to earn their place within the SNEL hierarchy through exceptional skill, intelligence, and hard work under stressful circumstances.

Benjamin had to find a way to get his team members on board to conduct the rehabilitation work on the G24. On many occasions, I observed Benjamin working almost by himself while the other team members were conversing in their staff room, resting in one of the dam's rooms and corridors, or busy with work that did not involve Benjamin. The more experienced but less-schooled senior employees didn't like being supervised by younger engineers, and their younger colleagues felt frustrated that they had to do hard physical work while earning less than their newly arrived superiors. No longer the youthful students free to act as they wished but not quite the married men with bigger professional responsibilities and children, the engineers experienced the first months on-site as a trial period that can be analyzed in terms of a liminal phase (Turner 1969). Once the wives of the engineers arrived on-site, part of their journey in becoming respectable men had been accomplished, but the challenges in work continued until they received their first promotion, for which Benjamin was still waiting in 2021. The SNEL workers who had grown up on-site didn't have to work this hard to be accepted. The fact that they refused to partake in the local schemes but instead reported them to their superiors in Kinshasa meant that the engineers couldn't fully be integrated into the immediate social world of Inga. If one looks at it as a part of an initiation ritual, this could be interpreted as their never quite reaching the stage of reintegration (Turner 1969).

Their "outsider" position made their life on-site less comfortable and augmented their feelings of isolation. This was partly overcome by sticking together but also through church life, through which they sought other local and transnational connections. Benjamin greatly admired the Amish communities in the United States and fantasized about a future life with horse and carriage, away from modern technologies. As a follower of the American prophet William Branham, Benjamin believed that modern technologies were enticing people to do "unnatural" things and succumb to sin. He believed that by not respecting the natural world, humans were disrespectful of God's creation. Living in Inga, where there are two Branhamist churches with about one hundred followers each, was a bliss to him because of his desire to live in a rural place with few earthly "distractions." Simultaneously, he felt an inner conflict because of his employment at the dam, where he had to engage with modern technologies every day.

Benjamin had access to the latest technologies through the work he was conducting with expatriates. This enabled him to be in touch with the wider world. Training offered to the local staff often enabled the engineers to travel abroad and benefit from the transnational networks and resource flows in which the dam was embedded. New technologies were introduced to Inga through travel by foreign experts to Inga or travel by Inga's engineers abroad in order to learn how to operate these new technologies. Later Benjamin had opportunities to take his expertise to other dams within the DRC and train others. Even though considerate effort was made to train the Congolese staff on the new incoming technologies, there was always a period during which the foreign nationals held power over the Congolese by the mere fact that they had mastered these technologies before the Congolese did and had the choice over whether to share the knowledge and in which way this would happen. On several occasions I observed this power imbalance lead to situations of abuse and humiliation. The money provided by the World Bank for the rehabilitation of Inga I and II was predominantly utilized to buy goods from outside the African continent, and the highest-paying jobs were predominantly filled by white foreign nationals.

The artificiality of the living conditions in Inga, where life revolves around work, made Benjamin feel isolated, stressed, and even depressed. Living in Inga meant that he could not seek the company of family and friends, other women even, as this would immediately be known by other people on-site. The other engineers also struggled from the artificial living conditions, which entailed that people from different countries, regions, and religious persuasions lived together in a limited amount of space. In cities, there is a similar diversity in population but more privacy and a greater sense of anonymity, also a clear separation between work and people's private lives. In Inga, the same people often figure as colleagues, neighbors, friends, and family. When arriving on-site, individuals say *Nakóti libúlú* (I enter the hole, pit, depression) and when they leave Inga, they say *Nabimi prison* (I am leaving the prison). Another engineer expressed a feeling of being lost, as if he were "in the middle of a forest where there is nothing to do except work."

INGA'S FIGURES OF SUCCESS

The engineers attempted to be accepted on-site in part by the deployment of their engineer status. By being recognized and respected as engineers and being addressed as such, the young men achieved a greater sense of self-worth despite the sometimes hostile environment they felt at work. Finding their place amid the cultural styles of the local workers and that of the expatriates whose lives they on the one hand envied for their wealth and expertise and on the other hand rejected because of their visible hedonistic and patronizing tendencies,[5] they achieved their own version of how in their eyes respectable men should act and look. Cultural styles refer to "practices that signify differences between social categories" (Ferguson 1999, 95). These performative practices are internalized and acquired over time, capable of change according to time and context. They are both structurally determined and a result of personal cultivation (Ibidem 1999). But some things are more difficult to acquire over time or, once acquired, difficult to hide. As much as it was impossible for some local young men to dress and speak like the engineers, even though they aspired to do so because of the status attached to the profession, it was also impossible for the engineers to undo their engineer style or hide their class and educational backgrounds in an attempt to fit in with the working-class employees they worked with. As *mingizila* or *arrivistes*, they regularly became the butt of jokes, particularly related to their inability to speak the local language or understand the linguistic codes used inside the dams.

The mechanics working for Benjamin were tougher looking than he and his engineer colleagues, smoking inside the workspace, overalls unzipped to expose their sleeveless shirts and upper arms, *chiffons* (cloths made from old T-shirts) wrapped around their head. During wedding parties or at church services, they made a big effort to look stylish and wear clothes fitting their position at the dam and personal wealth. The style of the engineers was more serious and less expressive, comparable to that of present-day techno-geeks in line with the more globalized business style of managers and entrepreneurs (Connell and Wood 2005 in Elliott 2020, 29). The engineers could be considered more recent figures of success, in line with the Pentecostal ethos of monogamy and obtaining wealth through hard work and studiousness rather than corruption (Pype 2012). The SNEL engineers, like those in IT and computer engineering, as figures of success, are admired in Congolese society because of their intelligence and creativity (Pype, this volume). Whereas many Congolese men invest in public display of masculinity through clothing, working out, and exhibiting wealth (De Boeck and Plissart 2004; Pype 2012; Gondola 2013), the engineers could afford to be dressed more humbly and unostentatiously. Relying on their skill and inventiveness, they resembled the style of the *staffeurs* (Pype 2007), dressed in a smart but not particularly expensive manner.

The engineers as "figures of success" differ strongly from those that emerged during the late twentieth century in sub-Saharan African societies. The latter were often of dubious morality and admired for their ability to trick people and benefit from dodgy business deals. Others were admired for their ability to conduct miracles or even just possess great physical strength and fervor in combat (Banégas and Warnier 2001; Havard 2001; Malaquais 2001; Marshall-Fratani 2001; Meyer 2001; Pype 2007). The engineers seemed much more motivated by what Weber (1930) described as a Protestant ethic of hard work in his account of the accumulation of wealth in the textile mills of North America. In several branches of Protestantism, work came to be considered a calling, and spending time and money on luxuries a sin. This enabled Protestant believers to accumulate wealth, which in turn boosted the further development of the capitalist system (Weber

1930). Germain and his colleagues mainly invested in other business ventures and became more wealthy despite not overtly displaying this wealth on-site. Elsewhere, however, they were building houses and guesthouses for foreign nationals who would pay them a good rent. As engineers, they also focused on delivering good work and figuring things out rather than being motivated solely by money. Whereas several of the multinationals suggested newer and more expensive technologies to replace the old ones, the engineers happily followed Philippe's suggestion to fix the old turbines with the means they had. This implied hard work but also a possible ending of the SNEL's dependency on multinational companies funded by the World Bank and particularly geared toward profit-making.

Several local youth mimicked the figures of success of a more dubious morality. Bonaventure, for example, a young musician and jack-of-all-trades, often walked around the camps in basketball clothes and a large cap on his head. Bonaventure had, like other local youth, a more "rascal" appearance, a style much more frequently described in other camp contexts (Cuvelier 2011, 2017; Hendriks 2013). Bonaventure proudly declared himself to be a real *gaillard* (tough guy, hustler) after a few conversations with me even though he came across as a sensitive, poetic, perhaps not so hardened young man. Bonaventure went to secondary school at the Institut Technique Protestante in Inga.[6] He tried to make a living by working small jobs for the SNEL and the other companies on-site (painting, decorating) or by performing at public events as a rapper. One of the songs he composed was entitled "*Sosa nge baka*" ("You must search to take"), expressing that life for him was a constant search for opportunities. When we met, he said he was an engineer, but when he realized I was a researcher, he said he had also worked as a journalist. Other female expats told me that Bonaventure had resorted to selling them bags of fruit after realizing that they wouldn't offer him a job at the dam. His versatility enabled him to survive on-site despite not being an expert in any of the trades he pursued. Near the end of my fieldwork, he had been imprisoned for impregnating an underaged girl. He already had two daughters with his former girlfriend. When Bonaventure returned from prison, he expressed great regret. To redeem himself, he had been asked to help a cousin oversee the construction of a garden with sculptures at the entrance to the Inga II dam. It was clear that he had made a considerable effort to present himself like the other engineers. He told me that it was now time for him to be more *sérieux*. His flamboyant sunglasses, however, and ostentatious attitude when leaving the site on his loud motorbike gave away his attempts to uphold his aspirational rascal identity whilst deeply longing to be respected like the engineers and SNEL directors on-site.

Admired for their ability to rehabilitate the G24 turbine by themselves, the young electric and mechanical engineers gained the respect of the wider Congolese population. The young engineers tried hard to live up to the image of respectability, thereby hoping to proceed upward within the SNEL hierarchy. They were an inspiration to Congolese students visiting from Kinshasa and influenced the cultural styles of local youth like Bonaventure, who were eager to be employed at the dam and receive the public respect given to the *ingénieurs*. SNEL employees were often addressed as "*ingénieur*," even when they had not completed formal education. Several of the employees of companies like Alstom or Frankotozi, hired in Kinshasa, were also addressed as "*ingénieur*," this referring to their skill and status as a result of working for these companies rather than owning an actual degree in engineering. It was a way to show respect to the workers on the dam. Representing skill and intelligence, the engineers were perceived to be the future of the country, giving people a sense of pride. For the engineers too, this mattered, despite their frustrations with having to rely on expatriates for guidance and new equipment.

RISING PRESSURES

The rehabilitation of the G24 meant that Benjamin and his team had to work for excessive amounts of time, doing shifts of twelve hours or more, six days a week. They worried about the consequences of making mistakes while trying to harness the enormous amounts of water rushing through the turbines at 320 cubic meters per second. Previously, three Inga II *chefs* (superiors/directors) had lost their job because of the mistake that led to the damage to the G24. The fear that this could happen to Benjamin and his colleagues stopped them from being assertive, worried that the responsibility for things gone wrong would fall on their shoulders. The pressure of the water as it hits the runner blades after being guided through the penstock and spiral casing can be used as a metaphor for the pressure experienced by the workers. But whereas the water eventually leaves the draft tube and gushes out through the tailrace back into the river, the engineers had no sufficient opportunities to release the emotions resulting from the constant pressure of work and trying to fit in. Because the engineers had to work hard on their image of being respectable and serious and had nowhere to indulge without everyone know-

Figure 3.1. Electrical engineer working on Inga II bridge, January 2016.
Photo by Barbara Carbon.

ing about it, they spent more and more time at home, away from the public eye and more and more entranced by their TVs.

The living circumstances in Camp Plateau did not offer opportunities to release the stresses experienced by the young engineers. The camp where they resided resembled most camps in Camp Plateau, which had the appearance of suburban areas, following grid-like street patterns. Some of them comprised only a few tarmacked streets. This meant that colleagues were also neighbors within these camps, and most engineers expressed a certain frustration related to this. The camps were initially created by foreign nationals (Belgians, Germans, Italians, etc.) in preparation for the construction of Inga I and II in the 1970s and 1980s. The houses where the engineers and better-paid workers reside are connected to low-voltage distribution cabins receiving electricity through the power lines coming from the Inga dam's dispatch center. The fact that their detached homes are electrified, differentiates Inga from other urbanized areas in the DRC, often characterized by a lack rather than an excess of electricity. This further encouraged the workers to stay home and seek solace in the comforts of their own houses. The spacious houses, surrounded by yards with freshly mowed grass and space to park one or two vehicles, made the newly arrived engineers feel lonely despite the efforts to furnish their homes prior to the arrival of their wives.

The local population, who did not have access to such material comfort and locked doors, compared the lifestyles of the engineers and the majority of the SNEL workforce to European culture, more enclosed and geared toward the self. The engineers were well aware that their success was accompanied by the limiting experience of being entrapped inside the Inga agglomeration and fearing the public eye. As a result, they very much looked forward to their monthly shopping trips to Matadi, where they initially also had to fetch their pay until two banks opened in Inga late 2016. When visiting Matadi, they often went to eat *ntaba* (goat meat) in one of the local bars. Less devoted Christians or Catholics who didn't feel as concerned about abstaining from alcohol would spend more time in Matadi and enjoy its nightlife. Germain, who preached at the local branch of the Pentecostal church, La Borne, and Benjamin, however, felt that they could not be seen in bars. For them, the only real break from work was when they visited their families and friends in Kinshasa and spent time with their girlfriends. Working overtime in that sense was often a benefit, meaning they could take longer breaks away. Their training abroad was also a welcome break from their daily life in Inga. In Inga they spent time away from home only when going to work, visiting close friends (usually from church), or going to church. Sometimes the engineers would walk out to visit small container pop-up shops, pharmacies, or the local mobile phone store. Occasionally they would attend a wedding celebration at the local hall or pick up some food from the local restaurant.

Behind the corner of Germain's house, in Camp Trois, was the house of the Bambala family, where I stayed during the first half of my fieldwork in Inga. Michel's promotion in 2019 enabled the family to move to Camp Shongo, where they had a bigger garden and a big allotment to grow vegetables. Michel Bambala is an electrical engineer with two children. In 2016, he was Germain's superior at the Conversion Centre. Michel met his wife Andrea in Inga while she was visiting her sister, also married to an Inga SNEL engineer. Two of the sister's nieces also reside in Michel's house, both eager to meet and marry an engineer. It was not unusual for SNEL families to be related to one another, especially as children often succeeded their fathers or uncles within the SNEL. Blood ties were even more common amid the Kongo population on-site. Originally from Kinshasa with family histories in the Kasai region, Andrea often spoke Ciluba to Germain, who also defined himself as

Figure 3.2. Inga workers waiting by the new dredger in the Inga II reservoir, September 2015. Photo by Barbara Carbon.

Muluba. They all prayed in the church where Germain was preaching. Michel spent most of his time at work. When home, he watched TV or performed household tasks like mowing the grass or fixing electric appliances like the hand dryer or air conditioner when they stopped working. Michel particularly enjoyed watching programs on big infrastructural projects and modern technologies. Now and then he would invite home respected members from church or visit his brother-in-law and the latter's family. In Kinshasa, the couple were building a big house, anticipating a professional promotion accompanying a *mutation* (transfer) to Kinshasa. This eventually happened in 2023. But at the time, life for him in Inga was peaceful, he had less to prove than the young engineers (his father also being an SNEL director in Kinshasa) and seemed happy with his comfort and family with young children.

The young engineers often visited the Bambala family. This made them feel like they had a local family while they were waiting for their partners to come and join them after marriage. The two beautiful nieces in the house provided a pleasant distraction to the young men, who hoped that being close

to the family would help them with their careers and make life on-site easier. Germain began to find it very difficult to resist the flirtations of one of
the nieces who showed great interest in him and particularly in wedding a
successful engineer. He also felt that maybe the family had begun to expect
this from him. When he eventually married his long-term girlfriend from
Kinshasa, the relationship with the family changed, and Germain began to
have difficulties in work.

The stress experienced by the engineers was in part relieved by the arrival
of their wives, but that event was accompanied by a different kind of pressure.
Despite the material comfort and the ability to watch as many soap operas
as desired on TV, the women often complained of feeling lonely once they
arrived in Inga. Their partners away all day, they often felt bored and frustrated, not always welcome in the home of the Bambala or other engineer
families. Germain's wife, Olive, explained that she was quite used to living
indoors, which was the case for her in Kinshasa too, but at least there would
be other family members there. Or maybe she could have gotten a job in Kinshasa with her degree in economics. Benjamin's wife, Rachel, a psychologist,
also felt somewhat isolated but quickly immersed herself in the online selling
of textiles from North African countries and Dubai. Rachel was physically
isolated from the wider world through her Inga residency and yet hyperconnected with the wider world through her permanent access to electricity and
the internet and by participating in transnational trading networks. She very
quickly began running a successful business from home using social media
in order to support her husband, she said, and relieve him from some of the
pressures he felt as sole earner for the family. Steel (this volume and 2017)
describes how in Khartoum also, mobile phones and social media are used
by women as an alternative to "physically moving through space" (Steel, this
volume) when they are confined to their homes because of social conven-
tion regarding their gender and class. For the engineer women in Inga, it
was certainly also their position of privilege that glued them to their homes.
Women in Camp Kinshasa, often working class, experienced a lot more physical freedom (in part due to working responsibilities) than their counterparts
at Camp Plateau. Once Rachel had children, she worked a lot at night as the
day became filled with caring and household responsibilities. For the families
without children, the men often complained that, returning home after a long
day of work, they had to engage with their lonely wives until late at night,
which resulted in feeling tired at work the next day. For the engineers with
growing children, work at the dam was at times experienced as an escape

Figure 3.3. Mechanical engineers working in the Francis turbine. Photo by Barbara Carbon.

from their busy home lives. Despite the hard work and internal rivalries, there was a strong sense of camaraderie and a solidarity between the men, who felt that, regarding their family life, they were all in the same boat.

NAVIGATING THE PRESSURES OF INEQUALITIES

On January 22, 2016, at 7:30 p.m., I left the house where I was staying in Camp Trois to visit Bonaventure, who lived with his grandmother together with several of his aunts and their small children. His grandmother, Maman Nkao, was employed at the SNEL hospital, and her late husband had been an SNEL employee. She supported the entire household with her income despite being in her late sixties. Maman Nkao was a follower of the prophet Kimbangu. She spent every Sunday at the local Kimbanguist church, which could easily hold three hundred followers. People arrive at the church at 9:00 a.m., and, on most Sundays, the service goes on till after 4:00 p.m. Bonaventure divided his time between Matadi and Inga, seeking opportunities to make a living.

He didn't attend church and spent a lot of time in Camp Kinshasa composing songs or hanging out with other young people in Camp Kin who were equally trying to make a living through fixing bikes and motorbikes or giving people rides to and from the Plateau. Maman Nkao resided in one of the bigger houses on the main road on the east side of Camp Plateau[7] between Camp Fwamalo and Camp Kokolo connecting the north and south part of the Plateau. She loved to tell me stories about the prophet Kimbangu and how much he mattered for the people in the Kongo Central region.

As I walked out of the house, Germain drove past on his way home from work. He offered me a lift since his pregnant wife wanted fish from Camp Kin. Olive had obtained her degree in economics one year earlier, had only recently moved to Inga from Kinshasa and didn't feel comfortable making her own way to there. Since they didn't know where to find fish there or whom they could trust, they asked me to accompany them as they knew I had been spending time with the women selling fish on a regular basis. He would drop me at Bonaventure's house on our return, although he didn't trust Bonaventure very much. There was a certain disdain in the engineering community for the local people, particularly those who did not attend church or who consumed drugs or alcohol. From the way Bonaventure dressed and behaved, the engineers concluded that he was not really someone they wanted to be associated with. To them he was nothing more than a *diambeur* (derivative of the Lingala word *diamba*: marijuana) or *mumeli bangi/diamba* (smoker of marijuana). To Bonaventure, the engineers were snobs from Kinshasa who really shouldn't be working in the Kongo Central region.

The fear experienced by the engineers to visit Camp Kin was related to the fact that it was predominantly inhabited by people with family ties to the local *ayant-droits*, the inhabitants of nearby villages and the Congolese workers who had helped to construct the Inga I and II dams. Those who were young builders during the construction phase are now aging men with large families. Some of these men are the descendants of those elders responsible for selling the land to government officials during the 1950s. This means that their presence was tolerated on basis of their *ayant-droits* status and claims to the land that may be evacuated for the construction of the Grand Inga project.[8] And although there are great concerns regarding the future displacement of people, several individuals said to me that they were planting fruit trees in anticipation of the displacement. The more they owned and could prove their connection to the land, they hoped, the more they would be compensated by the World Bank. Rahier (this volume) describes how in Nakuru, the image of a well-head discharging steam became iconic for Kenya's geothermal aspirations despite the fact that no wells had actually produced any electricity by 2021. In a similar way, the attention given to Inga's communities at risk of being displaced by International Rivers, Congolese NGOs, and civil society convinced these communities that the Grand Inga project would definitely go ahead. When local groups protested, it was because they feared that the project wouldn't actually benefit the majority of Congolese people. Despite the prospect of future displacement and living in small, predominantly wooden houses,[9] some detached, others semidetached, local families preferred to stay and continue to enjoy free access to housing, water, and electricity.[10] There are also many schools in Camp Plateau, offering education at a low price for everyone on-site.

The plan at the time of Inga's construction had been to destroy the temporary camps upon the work's completion and to encourage the builders to return home. Camp Six was not destroyed but given to soldiers and their families who reside on-site to help protect the dams. Camp Kinshasa was given to those laborers and their families who turned to hunting, fishing, and cultivating a variety of crops after the dams were built. The majority of Inga's estimated fourteen thousand inhabitants reside in Camp Kinshasa. Their presence today is tolerated because they help feed the population and provide domestic services to both SNEL and expat company workers. The better-educated SNEL workers and engineer families believe that the standard of living in the camp is below theirs. Some fear that the families who live in Camp Kinshasa envy them for their jobs (believing locals could be doing their work) and wealth and also dislike their presence because of their different ethnicity. In addition, they are well aware that the SNEL is considered responsible for the loss of the land that belonged to the ancestors of some local families who still claim a right to it. Several of these elder *chefs* (customary chiefs) are still pursuing compensation for the loss of land. Most engineer families are worried that the local *chefs* have ancestral powers, which according to their Christian beliefs should be understood as the practice of witchcraft. As a result, they fear that they could be spiritually targeted by the local people or even poisoned.[11]

Although the young engineers and their wives felt sorry for the inhabitants at risk of being displaced, they found peace in the notion that the communities living there have always known they have no right to be there. Portraying them as unwanted settlers, willing "to live like pigs,"[12] they distanced themselves from the people living in Camp Kinshasa and other "informal" camps on-site in a way that resembles European class distinctions, where middle-class people tend to describe those of lower classes as "unhealthy, undisciplined and degenerate" (Mosse 1985 and Stoler 1995 in Çankaya and Mepschen 2019, 628). During our visit to Camp Kinshasa, German and Olive tried to speak Kikongo to Maman Eugénie, the only woman at this hour who was available to sell them fish. Maman Eugénie[13] owns a popular bar (for both expatriates and SNEL workers who prefer to drink somewhat further from home) on a street central to the main section of Camp Kinshasa. This street with cafés, container pop-up shops, and a small market is accessible by car, whereas the other streets in Camp Kinshasa are usually too small and sandy. By trying to speak Kikongo, Germain wanted to show respect and make a good impression on the few locals who had now gathered around to observe the transaction. No longer the confident preacher and engineer who would normally drive around the site as though he owned it, his posture now suggested a certain sense of humility, resulting from the discomfort of being out of place. It was the first time in about a year that Germain had bought fish in Camp Kinshasa. Before his wife arrived, he had mainly sustained himself on *fufu*,[14] pasta, biscuits, tins of sardines, and the occasional meal he would receive in the house of a selected few that he would trust enough to accept their food,[15] usually people he knew from the church where he preached. After getting the fish, we drove back to Camp Plateau, where they picked up some bread from a family bakery in Camp du 24 Novembre. Germain and Olive then somewhat reluctantly left me with Bonaventure before returning to Camp Trois, where he and several other engineers resided.

BELONGING AND TEMPORALITY'S EFFECT ON THE EXPERIENCE OF ISOLATION

Jerome grew up in Inga and completed his bachelor's degree in mechanical engineering at the Institut Supérieur de Techniques Appliquées in Kinshasa. His father was an SNEL employee who died while Jerome was studying. As a result, Jerome could not obtain his master's degree. Early-career mechanics and electricians like him are usually given smaller houses, adjacent to one another in camps like Camp Nouveau, Camp du 24 Novembre, Camp Fwamalo, Camp du 20 May, Camp Bundi, and Camp Sikila. Rank and seniority, but also personal connections, usually determine where one will be housed. Usually workers are moved to bigger habitations once they are married or promoted. Some women, like Jerome's sister-in-law,[16] still reside in SNEL houses after their partners have died, giving them a chance to rebuild their lives before they eventually move on. Some inhabitants of Camp Plateau have moved to Camp Kinshasa after divorce, death of their partners, or losing their jobs with either the SNEL or expatriate companies, hoping for a future opportunity on-site. During my fieldwork, Jerome was living in Camp Sikila. His son lived with his ex-partner in Camp Fwamalo. Once he married and had three more children with Regine, he moved to a bigger house in Camp du 24 Novembre.

Several of Jerome's team members refused to go to the bars because of their religious persuasion, but Jerome didn't mind, providing nobody in his company indulged in dancing. He also spent time in the two bigger bars in Camp Plateau, Skoll and Maman Delo, where many of the expatriate work-ers spent their evenings, often accompanied by local women. Jerome in this way felt less frustrated about his life in Inga and was also able to move more freely from Inga to Matadi, where his mother lived, than the engineers from Kinshasa. He also had a sense of ease about him when he was in Inga. He had a better understanding of how to navigate the social context than the engi-neers who were not born there. As a child of Inga he also experienced more freedom and a certain privilege in work, particularly that offered by those of the region and who had known him his entire life. The older men in his team who were less fervently religious also met in small bars dispersed around the site after their workday. Although they regretted that Inga had lost some of its charm (there used to be a swimming pool and regular concerts during the early years after the construction of the dams), it was a peaceful place for them to reside, especially once they had learned not to mind other people's business and not to care about what others thought of them. Papa Makuza explained that it was important not to care: "*Il faut s'enfouttre,*" or in Lingala: *kokipe te* or *Tala yango pamba* (don't care, don't give it any attention). If you care too much about what people think of you in Inga, it was said, you will become ill. It was clear that the feeling of belonging that these men who had lived in Inga for a long time or who grew up in Inga drastically reduced the feelings of isolation experienced by other men.

The expatriate workers who lived at Camp Plateau in Camp Alstom (Base I and II) and Camp Voight/Elecnor, built by expatriate companies between 2012 and 2016 to house their staff, seemed to care the least about how they were perceived by the local population. These camps that house both the majority of Congolese and international workers contracted by the expatriate companies for the rehabilitation of the turbines are situated on the out-skirts of Camp Plateau. They were often protected by guards, ensuring that no intruders entered the houses of the workers. Most of the camps were also surrounded by fencing, some barbed-wire, giving them the appearance of gated communities. Camp Alstom Base I formed an enclosed settlement with three rows of adjacent ground-floor studios overlooking the same inner square. Accordingly, everyone could see who was coming in and out of other workers' homes. The open side to the square settlement was closed-off by two automatic barriers, one on each side of the cubicle where the security guards who either denied or gave access to visitors sat. At the back of the Alstom flats were windows overlooking Inga's surrounding open space. Although many of the men living there had partners in Kinshasa, they also entertained local women. So despite their solitude, which at times became unbearable and made many workers suffer from stress, they also had more freedom in how they engaged with local women, particularly because it was considered unhealthy and abnormal for young men, whose reputation locally mattered less, to be sexually inactive for such a long time (Pype 2012).

Most of the predominantly European senior staff members were housed in Base II. The other camps built by other companies differed in that they consisted of separate houses, usually housing three visiting expats per house. Some of these houses were newly built, others refurbished SNEL properties. All of them were guarded. Several of these men had local girlfriends who kept them company during the night. All expatriate staff and most Congolese hired from Kinshasa by those companies had the privacy of their own bath-room and warm, running water at all times—a privilege even the most well-off Congolese engineers working for the SNEL did not usually have. Many of the Congolese hired by the foreign companies would engage in sport activities at the local basketball and tennis court or the stadium with a running track that enclosed one of the football pitches where several football teams would train and compete against one another. During the weekends, the expats would leave Inga and either spend time in nature or in Matadi or even Kinshasa, where they could party in a more elaborate manner. In general, these men seemed more at ease, better remunerated than their SNEL colleagues and, due to their temporary contracts, less concerned with the impression they made on-site. This often led to more frustration for the Congolese engineers who worked for the SNEL and had to think about their reputation. There was a certain envy and feeling of inferiority to the expatriates, who were often accused of engaging with local women disrespectfully and of earning a great deal more for performing mediocre work.

The gated camps for non-SNEL workers were male dominated with the exception of a few female expatriates working for Alstom and Elecnor. Only a few Congolese women had been hired by the expatriate companies during the period of my fieldwork, one of whom was married to a local SNEL mechanic and did office work; another had been hired in Kinshasa and helped with the rehabilitation of the Inga II dam as a mechanic. At some point, Alstom hired a female team leader from France. She felt very uncomfortable at the dam, where most men refused to follow her orders. Although the men enjoyed flirting with her and she regularly had to remind them to keep their distance, they struggled with her tone of voice, finding her too authoritarian and incapable of true, compassionate leadership. The female mechanic, who was also welcomed by the men as a pleasant distraction, was criticized for her lack of physical strength and inability to perform certain tasks without the help of men. She herself commented that the men would not even let her try, helping her as soon as she was asked to carry out a more physically demanding task. The men at the dam were not used to have women there, and it was obvious that there was a lot of excess sexual energy, especially for those men who didn't have partners in Inga or were still awaiting their arrival.

INGA AS RESOURCE ENCLAVE

Despite the difficulties of living together, the Inga inhabitants are generally proud to live at the Inga center of technological and intellectual prowess. Having access to electricity at all times enables most inhabitants of Camp Plateau to be permanently connected to the wider world via digital means. In the cities, people speak of returning to the village when there is an electricity outage. And although the engineers will at times complain about Inga's remoteness and its lack of privacy and possibilities for *se distraire* (lit. getting distracted) and therefore define it as a *milieu enclavé* (enclaved environment), it is an urbanized enclave. The notion of being enclaved is used to describe feelings of isolation and the experience of boredom, something observed also in mining or logging industries and historically in colonial concessions and plantations (Adunbi 2020b; Hendriks 2013; Henriet 2021). Nevertheless, comparing Inga to a village would have been an insult to the SNEL engineers for whom the notion carries the idea of backwardness. Through the presence of the multinational companies and the rehabilitation work, Inga was experienced by the engineers as a gateway to the newest technologies in their field, brought to them by experts on-site. Benjamin in particular felt proud to be part of the G24's rehabilitation and to finally see what he had been studying during all those years at university.

For the local people, the distinction between the *mbanza* (pl. *ba-*: big city) and the *bwala* (pl. *ba-*: village, town, home) is made in the Kikongo language and used to define Inga. To the *ayant-droits* of the region and their families, Inga is at times referred to as *bwala*, in the sense of village; sometimes it is referred to as *village modern*. The engineers and other SNEL employees refer to it as *cité, cité particulière,* or *village valorisé*[17] when trying to explain how it takes on an urban form combining both rural and urban characteristics. Inga's urban form is an amalgam of different styles, ever evolving. It contains elements of residential areas, with a differentiation between the areas where detached, semidetached, or terraced houses dominate. Camp Kinshasa and the informal camps resemble the temporary settlements of labor camps, more organized and better equipped than slums despite visible dirt belts and a general lack of well-working sanitation infrastructure. In Kinshasa and Matadi, the *cités* are the areas further removed from the center, itself referred to as *ville* (De Boeck and Plissart 2004). In Inga, the term is used to indicate the urbanized character of the place and its importance as *poumon du pays* (the lung of the country), necessary to bring life to the cities that depend on Inga as provider of electricity for a big part of the country.

Bell and Jayne (2006, 5) argue that being a city is determined by the "urban habitus; it's about ways of acting, self-image, the sedimented structures of feeling, sense of place and aspiration." To them a city is only as small as its inhabitants think it is, or how the other urban centers make them feel (Bell and Jayne 2006). Even though Inga's urban form offers a home to a mixture of ethnicities, classes, skills, vocations, and advanced technologies, it cannot be defined as "post-global." The *Ingatiens* do not identify Inga as a place where "desire, ideas, mobility, and affects" can emerge from a context of a "contemporary tech economy" (Pype, this volume). Even though the workers desire to orient their gaze away from the "colonial city" and have aspirations to become part of the post-global world described by Pype, they experience a powerful global reality in which their future continues to be determined by Western and Chinese global centers and money flows. China's presence in Inga was experienced in a negative way because of the quality of materials and the meager payment received when working for them.

Inga can be better understood as a "resource enclave" (Adunbi 2020a, 39) or "extractive enclave" (Adunbi 2020b, 805), an area where natural resources like water, oil, wood, gold, or diamonds are transformed into commodities.

Inga is part of that global neoliberal system that connects local actors to transnational networks (Adunbi 2020b). For the engineers this meant that they could indirectly partake in a system in which their knowledge was valued over that of local men who did not study. Being part of the enclave meant being hyperconnected in terms of access to knowledge and the things they were passionate about. It also meant that through the experience of working with the expatriates, they could augment their own skills and begin dreaming of a future, perhaps as an employee of an expatriate company themselves. But they did not experience the emotions and feelings of empowerment like those associated with the post-global city (Pype, this volume). The close proximity to the population that had contributed to the building of the dams augmented the feelings of being away from the capital, where the engineers could live a more socially fulfilling life near family and friends but also in anonymity. The engineers were therefore isolated from the rest of the country as well as hyperconnected to "networks of global capitalism," a tension not unlike that experienced in colonial concessions and other extractive enclaves (Adunbi 2020b; Ferguson 2006 in Henriet 2021, 6).

The difference between Inga and the more extractive enclaves is that hydroelectricity is not exhaustive, whereas mines and forests will at some point come to depletion, forcing the companies to uproot and find other areas for their destructive activities. This leads to a very different temporality and resulting forms of habitation, geared toward a greater sense of permanence in certain areas of the Inga agglomeration. The initial wooden houses of Camp Kinshasa resemble the habitations of the more temporary logging and mining camps, built to be vacated once they have served their purpose. Inga is bound to expand both demographically and geographically because of the future phases of the Grand Inga scheme and the industries that hope to be installed within the area (i.e., a hydrogen plant). The urban form is not static; it is ever evolving and more permanent than what one would find in oil, logging, and other more temporary enclaves. Whereas the extraction of oil, gold and other minerals leads to making habitable places inhabitable through environmental degradation and social conflict (Hilson and Banchirigah 2009; Hecht 2011; Martinez-Alier 2002), Inga has become a home to people where it was previously inhabitable.

Historically, human settlements frequently have formed near natural waterways or roads, enabling the exchange of goods and knowledge and more comfortable living conditions. Inga and logging concessions are situated in more remote and harder-to-access localities; their natural environment is less accommodating. Inga was a predominantly forested area rife with *binkofia*, or black flies, known for causing *mbelolo ya meso* (river blindness). It is therefore possible to argue that certain technologies used to extract or transform natural resources are often instigators of artificial living conditions. I use the term "artificial" to denote the kind of living arrangements that have been created in a short space of time in order to provide housing to a labor force. In order to make Inga habitable, it was required to pour DDT into the Congo River to kill the eggs of the *binkofia* and thereby counter the spread of river blindness. The environmental damage caused by the creation of the dam itself is somewhat hidden by the dam itself, its water reservoirs, and the Inga agglomeration. The construction involved deforestation and substantial landscape alterations requiring the use of explosives and heavy machinery. Several of the older SNEL workers recall how trees that were cut grew back overnight, indicating that the ancestors were not happy with such drastic alterations to their landscape. It also shows that the workers themselves felt uncomfortable with such destruction, even if it came with the promise of electricity.

INGA'S SOCIAL GEOGRAPHY AND EMANCIPATORY PROCESSES

Urbanization is the outcome of the dialectical relationship between material forms and social processes (Harvey 1996; Waitt et al. 2006; Walker 2015). Inga's urban form is therefore not only the result of the camps and houses constructed during the 1970s and after but also the result of social processes at play in Inga such as exchange and cooperation but also competition and conflict. These are ultimately the elements that make the engineers feel both part of the SNEL community but also somewhat isolated. The engineers usually have easy access to water, so they would allow local families from poorer areas like Camp Kinshasa to come and use their water. They would also buy local products like vegetables, fish, or meat. But between the engineers and the local population there was also a lot of competition. Despite inhabiting very separate worlds, the envy felt by locals meant that the engineers could never be at ease. Within the camps and communities, there was also a strong sense of competition. A friend of mine told me where to buy beignets[18] and simultaneously accused other women of having added excrements to theirs. Even though these comments weren't necessarily to be taken literally, they did encourage me to stay away from these women's products and buy from women toward whom she felt a certain sense of loyalty. Within the plant, several staff members reported their colleagues of misdemeanors to their *chefs* (superiors) with the hope that they would be reprimanded and less likely to get promoted before them. There was also the existing conflict between the original inhabitants of the site and the newcomers, with several *ayant-droits* claiming to be the one and only *originaires* of the site.

In Inga, the different communities mainly compete over work and land, a clear consequence of the economic and social inequalities existing within the wider country. The original camps, although somewhat expanded, continue to accentuate and reflect difference and encourage elements of separation and abjection between the different communities on-site. Adunbi (2020b) writes that resource enclaves often result in the disenfranchising of local communities whose environmental and socioeconomic loss never outweighs the gains obtained through resource extraction. In Inga too, the local communities experienced more losses than gains; however, a section of the population successfully adapted to the presence of the dam by trading with workers, procuring jobs at the dam itself, or benefiting from electrified housing. The nearby villages were not electrified. Although the *ayant-droits* claim that their ancestors received no worthy compensation for giving the SNEL their land, the SNEL has given them certain privileges in recent years. In 2016 they were given motorbikes and a tractor (although parts appeared to be missing), they have been given an office at Camp Plateau, and several of their family members have been employed at the dam, either by the SNEL or multinationals. This is a direct result of the support local communities have been given by a range of environmental organizations and the Congolese civil society.

The rehabilitations of old SNEL houses and newly built camps for expatriate workers on Camp Plateau can be understood in terms of being inscribed on what was already there before. The SNEL workers reside in comfortable houses owned by the SNEL, whereas the workers who partook in the construction of the dam but were then dismissed are occupying the same wooden houses in Camp Kinshasa that they occupied during construction time. The only difference is that many of the houses are now degraded and occupied by large families instead of coworkers. The spatial division that existed between the homes of the expatriate and higher-skilled Congolese workers and the local Congolese population hired as labor force to build the dams still exists today. But whereas the expatriate workers on-site were predominantly white, today, Camp Plateau is inhabited by a majority of highly skilled Black employees. The separation between the newly built expatriate quarters and the Congolese people resembles that of oil enclaves in Nigeria and even colonial practices where housing classifications were used to differentiate between communities despite the elaborate interaction that existed between them (Adunbi 2015; Henriet 2021).

The social geography in Inga is coproduced by technological expertise, class, education, religion, people's personal connections, but also by people's ethnicity. The majority of managing staff within the expatriate companies were white Canadians and Europeans. They lived in the most comfortable housing on-site. Although they formed a minority, white working-class lives and bodies in Inga were inscribed with more social value than their Black counterparts. The higher-educated Congolese were earning less than the lower-educated expatriates doing very similar jobs. Unemployment within the Kongo Central region pushes people to seek work in Inga, but the majority of Camp Kinshasa's, Camp Makuva's, and Camp Wenze's inhabitants remain unemployed by the SNEL and amid the least formally educated on-site. Although some of these inhabitants have strong technical skills and are at times hired on temporary contracts by the expatriate companies or as *journaliers*[19] by the SNEL, they are usually remunerated poorly for their work. Within the SNEL, the majority of permanent Congolese *chefs* in Inga do not identify as Mukongo despite working in the Kongo Central region. Most lower-skilled laborers and inhabitants of the site do, however. This has also resulted in feelings of resentment toward Congolese *chefs* who have a different ethnic identity and inhabit the best homes and areas on-site. These *chefs* were appointed because the SNEL hired them in Kinshasa, where these young engineers had completed their university degrees in engineering.

Social processes are "always mediated through the things they produce, sustain and dissolve" (Harvey 1996, 61). The resulting inequalities, therefore, are also productive of other social processes and new forms of housing that emerge in new locations, such as Camp Wenze and Makuva and the outskirts of Camp Kinshasa, using materials like stone that aren't authorized by the SNEL. It is outside the control of institutions "in the interstices of that lack of control that all sorts of liberatory and emancipatory possibilities can hide" (Harvey 1996, 63). People continue to add houses to camps where building has been prohibited despite the camp representatives being regularly reprimanded by Inga's private security service, Star Securité, and the local police for not preventing further constructions. Other emancipatory practices have been the connecting of new houses to the electricity grid despite not having official permission, the destruction of water pipes by women who cultivate the land around the Inga dam in order to more easily water their crops, and the conducting by the customary chiefs of rituals for expatriate workers in order to prevent accidents in return for gifts and money.

The spatial divisions are constantly breached by the interactions that the enclave enables between people from a variety of backgrounds, brought together by the existence of the dam. People meet in church or in the local bars and offer each other services to compensate for being isolated from the rest of the country. Expatriates mix with customary chiefs when they conduct the rituals to ensure that their work on the dam/river will be without accidents. This augmented dependency of one group on another means that despite tensions and difference, there is also cohesion and collaboration as a result of being enclaved. Benjamin, for instance, who felt more isolated by the SNEL community due to his religious persuasions and the accusations made by his colleagues, felt great comfort in the Branhamist community in Camp Kinshasa. Despite being from the Plateau, he was more comfortable going to church there, where he found that religion could overcome the existing divisions between him and the locals. Several people from the Plateau also frequented bars in Camp Kinshasa, where they felt they could experience a little more anonymity. It was often in the bars in Camp Kinshasa that locals, expats, and SNEL workers met and managed to overcome their differences and escape the pressures of living enclaved.

CONCLUSION

In this chapter I provided an anthropological lens on the lives of the engineers in the enclaved context of Inga. I have thereby contributed to the understanding of what technology can do when it is the raison d'être of a particular agglomeration. It tells us what kind of urban form has been created surrounding the Inga I and II hydroelectric dams and what kind of social relationships people have formed as a result. I argued that it is the combination of lower- and higher-skilled staff needed for the operation and construction of a hydroelectric dam that has contributed to the particular social lives on the Inga site, different from those usually observed in workers' camps. It is thus the requirement for technological expertise that produces the social geography in Inga and reproduces existing inequalities visible in its built form. By providing insights into the lives of the more highly skilled staff on-site, I tried to explore their cultural style in relation to figures of success. I then showed that despite their seemingly comfortable lives, these men work hard to be accepted and supported by their SNEL colleagues and leaders. Through a careful balancing act, these men must go through hurdles resembling those of the liminal phase within a rite of passage in order to become respectable men. I then argued that both Inga's general mood and urban form, which I described as artificial, contribute to a sense of isolation and entrapment, mainly experienced by the SNEL workers who have lived elsewhere prior to being appointed in Inga. By exploring how the engineers and other young people deal with their feelings of isolation, I further accentuated that it is the bringing together of different communities in an artificial context that leads to feelings of frustration and competition. At the same time this offers opportunities for unexpected meetings, emancipatory practices, and the development of new cultural styles.

NOTES

1. SNEL or Société Nationale d'Électricité (National Electricity Company).

2. The site's director, however, despite being from the east of the country, was highly respected. The workers appreciated that he himself had not been educated as an engineer but began just like them, as a lower-grade laborer, and made his way through the company via his hard work and not his university degree.

3. Lit. "have rights," those who have rights to the land due to ancestry.

4. Camp Plateau is where most SNEL workers and expatriates reside and where the original village of Matselele was situated, overlooking the plains. The remnants of this village are the large baobab trees adjacent to the presidential villa where President Mobutu used to reside when visiting the dams. The village was vacated long before construction of the dam. The two most popular bars are built on its cemetery, considered a sign of disrespect by the elders and a sign for Christians who don't drink alcohol that bars are places of immorality. Within Camp Plateau, there are smaller camps that each have their own representative.

5. Marriage in the DRC is an important social marker of adulthood; otherwise males remain "boys" (Pype 2007, 252).

6. Several Congolese engineers and technicians would complain about the fact that expatriates had local girlfriends despite their families at home, that they paid money to be with women, and that they felt that the expats could thereby live out their sexual fantasies. They also found them controlling in the workplace, arrogant even, displaying behaviors that suggested a sense of superiority felt toward the Congolese.

7. Many of the dam's older engineers, electricians, and mechanics had either been taught there themselves (as family members of SNEL staff) or had taught the younger generation themselves.

8. At the time of writing it was believed that the Grand Inga project would be

developed by a consortium of Chinese and Spanish companies. It would consist of six Chinese companies gathered around China Three Gorges Corp. and AEE Power Holdings (based in Madrid). The engineers were concerned that the materials used by the Chinese companies would be of poor quality. The local communities believed they would receive no compensation in a situation of community displacement. Presently plans have changed again and the World Bank has shown interest once more in a $14 billion project to develop Inga III. This has raised concerns regarding the country's debts and the fear that this will result in a further lack of investment in other highly needed services. There are concerns that the electricity produced at the dam will not improve the existing economic disparities but predominantly serve other countries and the mining region in the DRC. In addition there are profound environmental concerns regarding the Inga III project, as it will contribute to climate dysregulation through its effects on the river's flow and connected carbon sinks.

9. It is prohibited by the SNEL to build houses in stone in Camp Kinshasa or the other informal camps on Camp Plateau. Some of the more recently built churches in Camp Kinshasa are in stone. This leads to conflicts between the elders, accusing one another of having given permission in return for money when they didn't actually have any legal power to grant such a privilege.

10. Camp Kinshasa operates a system of load shedding or *délestage* as the infrastructure is not adjusted to the size of the population connected to the grid. Therefore only half the camp can be electrified at a time.

11. This fear was also experienced of certain SNEL colleagues who might be envious of their special position as engineers. The engineers gave me the example of the local Agence Nationale de Renseignements agent who was believed to be disliked in Inga and to have been poisoned there in 2015.

12. Camp Kinshasa had several free-roaming animals like chickens and pigs. Children often walked barefoot, making them vulnerable to chigoe fleas and other parasites. During 2016, a stone block of public toilets was constructed at the edge of Camp Kinshasa, but the local people complained that it stank and that the lack of water resulted in the toilets not working properly. As a result, people continued to defecate in the nearby forests or dirt belts alongside the camp and the few toilets in Camp Kinshasa dug in the soil by individuals who had the space for them within their compound. The camp had several water pumps, but there was no access to water inside people's homes. Women also collect water in nearby streams or at the taps outside some of the homes at Camp Plateau to compensate.

13. Maman Eugénie traveled with International Rivers to Berlin and Brussels to meet with European policymakers and civil society organizations to discuss the concerns of the local communities about the further development of the Inga dams and the green hydrogen extraction and development plans in the DRC related to this.

14. Staple food made from cassava flour boiled and stirred in water.

15. This was also related to the fear of being poisoned. As a pastor in church, he also

feared that people could try to spiritually target him via the consumption of spiritually contaminated food.

16. At the time, Jerome wasn't married but had been engaged to Regine for a few years. In 2016, Regine was still living with her sister, whose husband, a mechanic, had cut himself in the femoral artery inside the penstock of one of Inga II's turbines. He died in Jerome's arms before Jerome could even attempt to get him out.

17. "Town, city, large settlement of particular importance," "particular city," and "valorized village."

18. Beignets are usually wheat flour-based balls of dough fried in hot oil, though sometimes people use corn flour. They are often sold in the markets in the morning, and many SNEL workers buy them to take to work for their breakfast.

19. Temporarily employed by the SNEL, meaning they can work for one month and must then be off work for two months. This is a system to give more people a chance to work for the SNEL.

CHAPTER 4

Enchanting Urban Futures Through Geothermal Explorations in Nakuru, Kenya

NICK RAHIER

Erik Wamanji, one of the contributors to the first edition of a magazine called *Steam*, published by the Kenyan state-owned Geothermal Development Company (GDC) quarterly, describes Menengai—a dormant shield volcano just north of Nakuru in Kenya where GDC drills geothermal wells—in the following manner:

> Menengai—that caldera in the Rift Valley that is heavily woven in eerie lore and myth—is one of the promising spots that will shed light to Kenya. A product of volcanic activities, Menegai has been popular with legend and tourism in equal measure, but now it will earn another title—the "Caldera of Light." However, from a cursory glance of Menengai, one would be forgiven for dismissing it as nothing beyond the aesthetics it offers. Yet, beneath it, lies a treasure trove that will drive and light our country. Thanks to scientific studies, Menengai is said to boast of a geothermal potential estimated at 800 MW. (Wamanji 2010b, 18)

Wamanji further describes Menengai as the company's flagship project that will "drive and light" the country. The volcano, he argues, "known for its eerie lore and myth is a place of 'great hopes'" (18). "Science will trounce superstition," the article reads, and Wamanji concludes that "no one knows what surprises Menengai will pull next, but for sure its legend would go on and on as the GDC turbines start to roll and the green blurbs glitter" (19).

This description of Kenya's geothermal business in Nakuru, a secondary city approximately 160 kilometers distant from Nairobi, introduces the topic of this chapter: how Nakuru's urban future is enchanted and materialized through technological interventions by the GDC in the Menengai volcano. Before the GDC began activities in Menengai, the place was considered "haunted" and therefore dreaded by Nakurians. Maasai interlocutors argued the name "Menengai" is a reference to the Maa idiom *n'kai*, meaning "corpses," and legends allude to a bloody battle between two Maasai clans. Members of the defeated clan were thrown over the rim and fell to their death. The fumaroles arising from the crater bed were (are) considered to be the spirits of the deceased warriors that roam around the blasted landscape. Some Nakurians argued that odd things still happen within the vicinity of the volcano. An often-mentioned incident among my interlocutors was the suicide of a Catholic priest called Father Kabutu, who drove his car over the edge, plunging to his death. Even internationally, the idea of Menengai as a haunted place drew people's interest. In 2007, an episode of a series called *Destination Truth* that aired on SyFy was dedicated to Menengai's occult stories. It is within this context that the GDC refers to its activity as doing away with "long-standing taboos."

The GDC was brought to life as part of the ambitious "Kenya 2030 Vision," a national development scheme signed by former President Kibaki, which aspires to make Kenya a middle-income country by 2030. The company serves as a special-purpose vehicle, part of massive investment schemes that aim to upgrade the nation's infrastructures (road, railway, ports, water provisioning, electricity distribution, etc.). The GDC's tagline at the time it was founded in 2008 reads "Powering the vision," hinting at the company's embeddedness within the broader phenomenon on the African continent of megaprojects that "promise to radically reshape African cities" (Smith 2017, 31), transforming urban centers into "world cities" through technological and infrastructural transformations. The GDC is a step toward realizing that vision by setting up green and steam-driven, large-scale, renewable-energy plants that should improve the Kenyan electricity grid.

Menengai, as a promising "resource frontier" (Tsing 2003) or "resource enclave" (Abundi, this volume) from where Nakuru's ambition to grow is fueled, recalls recent scholarly attention to the "promise of infrastructure"[1] (Larkin 2018) that sheds light on how, among other things, "oil rigs and electrical wires, roads and water pipes, bridges and payment systems articulate social relations to make a variety of social, institutional, and material things (im)possible" (Larkin 2018, 4). Anthropologists (Fontein 2015; Harvey and

Knox 2012; Di Nunzio 2018; Anand et al. 2018; Beck 2013; Bridge et al. 2018; Ibrahim and Bize 2018; Manji 2015; Trovalla and Trovalla 2015; von Schnitzler 2016) focusing on the interplay between the sociality and materiality of infrastructures argue that "ethnographic attention to infrastructure reveals how politics not only is formed and constrained by juridico-political practices, but also takes shape in a technopolitical terrain consisting of pipes, energy grids, and toilets" (Larkin 2018, 4). Fontein calls this "political materiality," or the way politics and sociality "find traction in their entanglement with materialities of milieu" (2015, 9).

In light of this political materiality of infrastructures, the GDC introduces its activity in Menengai's caldera as a technological intervention that "tames" what the company considers Menengai's "undomesticated" space (cf. Wamanji's remark above concerning aesthetics).[2] The GDC thereby domesticates the volcano through science, embedding the place within broader discourses of renewable Kenyan energy futures that are technology driven. The language the GDC uses—well exemplified by Wamanji's descriptions—demonstrates what Mbembe calls "reason [that] is increasingly replaced and subsumed by instrumental rationality" (2019, 14), leading to *techne* becoming its quintessential language (14).

In this chapter, I investigate how that language is negotiated, how it makes technological interventions fail or succeed at their intended goals, and how it both symbolizes and creates promises. In order to do this, I draw upon Pype's analysis of processes of intelligence and invention in Kinshasa and her notion of the "technology contract" (2018). A "technology contract," Pype argues, is "the outcome of negotiations that speak to a society's acceptance, refusal, or partial acceptance of technological innovations" (4). She further states that careful attention to the discursive realm of such contracts and the various practices related to their negotiation offers a heuristic means to explore the social possibilities and meanings of technology (4). Applying this focus, I look at how geothermal explorations in Menengai came into being and have evolved since their onset in 2008. I investigate how the promise of geothermal technology took shape, how the relations it entailed were negotiated, and how the failure or success of its terms led to a potential ruination and/or celebration of not-yet-materialized urban futures. The notion of "trust" will be key to understanding how the geothermal technology contract is negotiated in Nakuru. By applying this approach, I intend to shift the focus from *what* infrastructures promise to *how* this promise is negotiated and materialized.

I first delve deeper into what Kenya's geothermal aspiration entails and demonstrate how the geothermal technology fuels government development schemes for both the nation as a whole and for the city of Nakuru. I do so by investigating the context surrounding the discovery of Menengai's first geothermal well: MW-01. I consequently elaborate more thoroughly on how the volcano's uncanny nature[3] is "mastered" through various negotiations about and engagements with the volcano's materiality that take place in the process of finding heat. I ultimately argue that the premise (and the promise) of the GDC's technology contract is based on the company's expertise in finding heat that happens through processes of enchantment of the volcano's materiality and the envisioned urban futures the infrastructure stands symbol for. I follow Harvey and Knox's stance on the enchantment of infrastructure based on Bennett's (2001) definition, which considers enchantment "a more generally visceral, affective form of relating to that which is side-lined or cast out of formalised, rationalised descriptions of material and social phenomena" (Harvey and Knox 2012, 523).

My analysis of the negotiations I cover in this chapter is mainly based on participant observation and informal conversations with GDC employees and Nakurians more broadly, which happened in Nakuru's urban center, especially during informal meetings in bars and coffeehouses and during GDC lunch breaks. My interlocutors speculated more openly about the sustainability of the GDC's technology contract during these informal meetings. I also conducted structured interviews at the GDC's main offices in Polo Centre (also in Nakuru). Discourse analysis based on reports or news statements that were shared with me by GDC employees is equally part of the presented data. The "negotiations" appearing in this chapter thus unfolded mainly from information gathered within the city where the GDC's workings were interpreted critically by Nakurians.

GEOTHERMAL ASPIRATIONS

Explorations for geothermal resources in Kenya started as early as the 1950s (Tole 1996; Mangi 2017, 1), yet so far only the geothermal fields of OlKaria (100 kilometers from Nakuru) and Eburru (80 kilometers from Nakuru) in Naivasha are operational. These fields produce approximately 865 megawatts of electricity (Mangi 2017, 1). The anticipated potential for geothermal exploitation in Kenya is estimated at a capacity of 5,000 megawatts by 2030 (Mungi 2017, 1). The GDC introduces itself as "avail[ing] affordable, reliable, green energy to catapult Kenya into a mid-income nation in 20 years time" (Wamanji 2010a, 14). In Menengai, pre-drilling exploration started in 2008, which is around the same time the GDC was founded. After surface exploration, exploratory drilling started in 2010. Since then, the Menengai field has been estimated to have a potential of 1,600 megawatts. Earlier announcements indicated an expected production of 800 megawatts by the end of 2018 (Wamanji 2010b). Ever since, however, the anticipated steam output has been revised several times over the past few years (Eberhard et al. 2017), and only 170 megawatts were realized by the end of 2019 (Geothermal Development Company, n.d.). Several explanations have been given for this gap between expectations and output. Eberhard et al.—economists specialized in energy policy—argue that

> despite a multimillion-dollar investment in the GDC and pressure to meet the power supply targets associated with Kenya's 5,000+ MW program . . . , since its inception the company has been able to source only limited steam. . . . It is important to note the large gap between what was originally [predicted] . . . by the GDC—namely, 1,900 MW of geothermal activity (between 2010 and 2014)—and the 105 MW that is [now] expected. . . . While the initial capacity targets may have been inflated, other issues specifically related to the GDC and its business model may have hampered the procurement process as well. (2017, 114)

Their remark that the GDC's difficulties with sourcing steam has to do with its business model raises questions about what went wrong in negotiating geothermal aspirations. In what follows, I shed light on how these negotiations unfolded, in particular regarding the first materialized productive well in Menengai: MW-01.

Well 1 (MW-01)

In the same *Steam* magazine, the former GDC CEO Silas Simiyu wrote the following to celebrate the inauguration of MW-01:

> We are going to rehabilitate ourselves from the oil intoxication. If the Emirates prosper from petro-dollars, so should Kenya with her geothermal steam-dollars. Geothermal is a heritage that Kenya needs to be proud of. With geothermal, we will shift from instability to stability, from despair to hope, from paucity to riches. (Simiyu 2011, 6)

"Menengai Well 1" (MW-01) was drilled in 2011 after months of preliminary surface exploration by geologists and geophysicists. Drilling operators hit steam on May 12, 2011, and although MW-01 was expected to have an output of only 5 megawatts, it turned out to have a potential energy output of more than 10 megawatts. With a maximum depth of 2,206 meters below the volcano's surface, it was the first concrete opportunity for the GDC to expose the subsurface volcanic rocks and minerals of Menengai, and therefore it was considered of great importance to unearth the volcano's hidden potentials and to shed light on the lithology and stratigraphy of this part of the Central Rift Valley (Omondi 2011, 741).

If the GDC's intent was to master the volcano, then MW-01 was proof it had made a first and unique step in mapping the volcano's uncharted bowels. The GDC's success with MW-01 supported the company's promise that its activities would power Kenyan development. The discovery of steam in Menengai came at a time environmental concerns were high on the agenda of the Kenyan government. Plans to issue a ban on plastics were in the making and *wananchi* (common citizens) expressed their worries about the country's sovereignty and the state depending too much on "toxic outsides" that seemed to seep into Kenya, polluting bodies and environments (Rahier 2021). Following the well's inauguration, MW-01 became symbolic of the country's ambition to move toward a green-electricity-driven economy in which the health and success of Kenyan citizens are pivotal. The Kenyan government strategically introduced geothermal exploration as "power from Kenya for Kenyans" that would bring about change; as former CEO Simiyu argued, Kenyan "steamdollars" would allow a "shift from instability to stability, from despair to hope, from paucity to riches" (Simiyu 2011, 6).

The attention given to MW-01 should also be read against the background of Kenya's electricity market being subject to reforms as part of the 2030 Vision blueprint that envisions electricity for all Kenyans. Investments in geothermal energy caused a welcome shift from hydropower to geothermal energy as the dominant player on the Kenyan energy market (Mangi 2017, 2). Although hydropower is a green resource and was until geothermal energy took over in 2018 the primary source of energy in Kenya (2), it is highly unreliable and dependent on weather patterns. This is the reason why it is not possible to do away with fossil-fuel-driven generators as backup (2), which depend on expensive imported crude petroleum. Kenya produces more energy than it consumes, yet predictions of the Kenyan energy demand forecast a rise from 1,841 megawatts in 2018 to between 2,633 megawatts and 3,348 megawatts by

2030 (GoK 2018, 8). The country's reliance on the international petroleum and coal market to deal with peak demands of electricity is expected to significantly slow down national growth and this while an indigenous unlimited resource of energy underneath the volcanic landscape of the Rift Valley is available to be exploited.

Following MW-01's inauguration, former CEO Simiyu compared geothermal resources in the Rift Valley with the Rhine Valley in Germany:

> Take the example of the Rhine Valley in Germany. Rhine Valley boasted energy from coal and water from the mighty River Rhine. This way, the valley emerged as one of the world's premier industrial zone[s]. Our own valleys and hills teeming with geothermal energy and an equal amount of water have all the makings of a Rhine albeit belated. (Simiyu 2011, 6)

Simiyu's comparison of Kenya's geothermal aspiration with the industry in the Rhine delta in Germany presents the GDC's success with MW-01 as a first step toward an envisioned future of economic growth and progress (*maendeleo*) in which Kenya depends less on foreign fossil fuel imports. The well became iconic for national desires, hopes, and aspirations to evolve into a modern, carbon-neutral state.

The unexpected well output of MW-01 also revealed an incredible untapped potential hidden under the volcano's surface. GDC employees were excited and proud when they shared this first success in Menengai, which surprised experts in the geothermal industry worldwide. For the county government of Nakuru, the news about this unexpected well output confirmed the pivotal role of the highland city in fueling the country's *maendeleo* (progress), supporting the county's desire to obtain "city status" for Nakuru. The GDC's presence in the provincial city was consequently framed as part of Nakuru's urban growth, putting it on the map as an important economic and political center driving the country's wealth. In that regard, Alya commented during a conversation we had about the efficacy of the GDC that the company's presence in Nakuru could become a major gain for the regional economy,[4] allowing for the creation of new business parks and "smart cities" within the vicinity of Menengai's caldera and attracting investors from all over the world. With the prospect of Nakuru receiving city status, Nakurians such as Alya considered geothermal development beneficial for Nakuru's revival after the grand industrial exits from the region that had happened gradually over the last two decades. Nakuru, once the vibrant economic heart of Kenya and the epicenter of the "white highlands" from where colonial rule was executed, lost its glory when the highland center was overshadowed by the metropole Nairobi, with its "worldly" lifestyles and tall buildings as emblematic of *maendeleo* (development). The county's promise as materialized through the geothermal project of Nakuru's becoming the epicenter of cheap and green energy production, fueling "smart" and technology-driven industrial hubs,[5] gave life to futuristic visions of Nakuru's relationship with other regions in Kenya. Some of my interlocutors argued the geothermal project was proof of Nakuru's ability to compete with other cities in the world. When Nakuru eventually secured city status in June 2021, the managing director and CEO of the GDC, Jared Othieno, made following statement confirming the GDC's share in fueling the novel city: "By every measure, Nakuru is unique. GDC and geothermal energy will continue to contribute to the spectacular contours of the city's architecture and by extension the uniqueness of Nakuru City" (gdckenya 2021).

Such urban fantasies about technology-driven futures are not unique but have been flourishing all across sub-Saharan Africa. In Rwanda (Doughty 2020) and the Congo (De Boeck 2011), for instance, governments have invested large amounts of money in megaprojects "as gateways for global capital, forming a new node in a network of hub cities" (Smith 2017, 31). These networks of cities are often located within the Global South, and, in the Kenyan case, they connect Nairobi and Nakuru with places such as—in addition to Iceland as epicenter for geothermal development—Kigali, Kinshasa, Shanghai, Dubai, and Rio de Janeiro. The GDC's ties with Shanghai, for instance, are well established as most drilling rigs are bought from Chinese investors. Countries such as Rwanda and Uganda, on the other hand, are closely monitoring GDC activity with the prospect of potentially exploiting their own geothermal energy. This South–South-based geography echoes yet another promise, what Pype defines as "post-global" cities that symbolize a shift from the colonial dominance of the "world cities" of the Global North to a more postcolonial and post-global network of cities in the Global South that offer "a space of desire, ideas, mobility, and affects that emerges in the contemporary tech economy" (Pype, this volume) and in which affects such as dignity, pride, and self-confidence thrive. With this in mind, the activities of the GDC and the company's unprecedented success with MW-01 should be understood in light of Nakuru's desire to put itself again on the map as an important industrial hub within the country and within the wider region and world. Negotiating geothermal dreams in Menengai is therefore intricately linked to negotiations of Nakuru's urban future.

MW-01's Poetic Mode

The GDC's success with MW-01 was crucial for further geothermal development in the region as it meant the endeavor was worth the investment. When foreign delegations such as consultants from the Philippines or representatives of the German state-owned investment and development bank visited the Menengai geothermal field, Well 1 was often the first stop. I once joined such a field visit across Menengai's caldera.[6] When MW-01 slowly came within sight as we progressed from the entry road at the western edge of the volcano and headed east, the company's community representative, Ochieng, talked with awe about the well. He is somewhere in his mid-forties and has been working for the GDC since the beginnings of the company's existence. He was a real motivational speaker his peers looked up to, and at the GDC he was charged with community relations, which made him a well-known figure in and around Menengai. On arrival at the well pad, Ochieng's body language betrayed pleasurable satisfaction as he pointed out how its success was thanks to minute cooperations between, among others, geologists, geophysicists, and drilling operators who all worked together toward striking steam. "This smells of success," he jokingly alluded, referring to the sulfur vapors that filled the air. He considered MW-01 a symbol of the power of science and an example of what he referred to as "tamed nature." The driver of the company's Land Cruiser we were seated in, a Maasai man and age mate of Ochieng, argued that it was thanks to GDC efforts that "Menengai was put on the map." He explained that the caldera used to be desolate land where only herders came for grazing and herbalists gathered medicine. Thanks to the GDC, the volcano was no longer Nakuru's urban margin but, as he put it, "the city's—if not the country's—engine."

The image of the company "taming" the volcano into the engine of urban growth evoked by MW-01 is crucial for how the GDC negotiated its presence in the volcano. Pictures of MW-01 discharging steam were widely shared among newspapers and television stations with its inauguration back in May 2011. A wellhead discharging a column of white steam became iconic for Kenya's geothermal aspiration, and ever since pictures of MW-01 were first circulated, the GDC has proudly published videos and photographs of discharging wells whenever they struck steam in new geothermal fields, such as in the Baringo-Silali area.

Although at the time of finalizing this chapter no steam had yet been transformed into electricity, such images trigger affective investments that keep the dreams,[7] hopes, and futurity portrayed through them alive. These images demonstrate that the aspirations of the nation-state are on the verge of being materialized. At play here is what Larkin refers to as "the poetic mode" of infrastructure, its capacity to mobilize "affect and the senses of pride, desire, and frustration" (Larkin 2013, 335). The well's affordances transcended its instrumental value. The imagery MW-01 provoked and the discourses of growth, energy autochthony, and expertise that framed the well's inauguration were as important, if not more important, than the well's actual material function. A discharging well—a procedure that is necessary to balance steam output—does not produce electricity yet, as the steam is released into the open air instead of powering turbines. The sight of steam being ejected from the well, forming a huge cloud, had, however, poetic stamina, signaling success that was at that point of greater importance than its material qualities. For electricity to be produced, much more was needed, such as, among other things, the construction of pipelines, the licensing of independent power producers, and the construction of power stations and transmission cables. All of these steps were subject to procedural difficulties whether material, economic, or political. The images of venting steam, the overwhelming sound of the wellhead, and the smell of sulfur Ochieng alluded to serve what Larkin (2013, 334–36) defines as an aesthetic function representing the capacity of the GDC to harvest the power of the volcano and to materialize ideals of energy autochthonous futures powering—in the case of Nakuru—a modern, "worldly" city. The poetic aspects of MW-01 thus prioritized how the company's presence in Menengai was introduced, whereby the GDC engaged in a politics of "as if" (Larkin 2013, 335). MW-01 served "as if" it were the materialization of the company's ideals. If MW-01's gasping steam and unprecedented energy output were proof that Menengai's potential could be harvested by the GDC, then the aspirations to cheaper energy futures and worldly cities that the well evoked were equally feasible. MW-01 thus served as a "means by which [the] state proffers these representations to its citizens and asks them to take those representations as social facts" (Larkin 2013, 335). In other words, MW-01 was "a material experience on which individuals, nations and societies ground[ed] identities, aspirations and expectations" (Di Nunzio 2018, 1).

Cross (2014) calls such spaces as MW-01 "dream zones," technological spaces driven not only by material processes and innovative infrastructures that are sometimes not (yet) fully functional, but also by anticipations, dreams, hopes and emotions these technological spaces (in the making) evoke. Larkin refers to this function as "infrastructures as promising forms," a regard for "expectations, desire, temporal deferral, sacrifice, and frustrations that takes us into the realm of the discursive meanings [of infrastructures]" (2018, 178). The materiality of infrastructure is only one among many qualities, and technologies "are always metaphors as well as technical objects" (179). Infrastructures are thus both fantastic as technological and material: "They are made up of desire as much as concrete or steel" (176).

MW-01 indeed embodied what the Kenyan government desired: lower electricity bills, independence from global energy markets, new job opportunities, Nakuru's industrial revival, and, as Ochieng's bodily language betrayed upon visiting the well, its actual materiality—the pressure of the steam ejected from the wellhead, the smell of volcanic sulfur, and the radiant heat the well emitted—gave rise to all kinds of tactile and sensorial experiences that seemed to make these desires—the dreams, hopes, and promises MW-01 stood symbolic for—realistic.

The well's fantastic and aesthetic affordances—its function as "concrete semiotic and aesthetic [vehicle]" (Larkin 2013, 329) in shaping trust in not yet fully materialized energy futures is also key to how the GDC legitimized its technology contract. It is the entanglement between Menengai's heat, Kenya's energy politics, Nakuru's aspired-for urban future, and the images of gasping steam that forms a delicate balance crucial for the survival of the company's technology contract. MW-01 was in many ways a first installment toward fulfilling the "promise" that the terms of the contract—that is, finding heat to chart a new, imagined, Kenyan future, greener, steam-driven, and based on Kenya's own resources—were feasible. The well seemed to confirm that the intentions of the technology's masters to realize the geothermal dream had been successfully executed, and this while other megaprojects at the time of the GDC's debut in Menengai, such as the contested Standard Gauge Railway and the Lake Turkana Wind Power Station, had become subject to public scrutiny because of government's failure to materialize them and the public's awareness of the huge bills these projects generated.

"MASTERING" THE VOLCANO

NICK: This geothermal endeavor is all about probability, right?

BENJAMIN: Well, it is based on deep science, but eventually what you are going to get nobody really knows. [Hesitating silence] At one point some data was wrongly used by incompetent people and interpreted as if Menengai was not going to produce any geothermal

output. All wells were nonproductive according to their interpretations. That report almost killed GDC. Sometimes wells just have to
warm up. . . . It depends on how far from the heat source you are.
Even the government believed we were doing a bad job. That event
really influenced our funding, our activities, public opinion. Even
consultants came in to make a secondary report.[. . . There was a
time a drilling team at a particular rig hit lava or magma at a certain
depth, somewhere around the 2,000-meter mark. The drilling bit got
stuck. A researcher from Iceland or Germany, I do not remember,
. . . was also present. He requested the data from that specific rig and
consequently wrote a paper announcing the volcano was going to
erupt again because of GDC's activity. You see how such incorrect
interpretations of the data causes these kinds of messages to spread?
Everyone was triggered by this paper. The community, stakeholders,
even pastors started professing about the volcano's eruption.

NICK: But, if I may be that blunt, if you hit magma, can I then assume
you did not really know what you were doing?

BENJAMIN: [Laughs] Well, we had not thought we would reach lava at
that depth. Of course it is not good, because it means the drilling
bit got stuck and will eventually melt. We often think we know
Menengai, but actually we do not know anything for sure about this
volcano. . . . There is so much we do not know at all, I'm telling you.

NICK: So who then actually knows where to drill? Nobody?

BENJAMIN: It is deep science, like I told you earlier. But there is not really
someone that says, "There is going to be steam found there in that
particular spot." It is a whole process of data gathering, probability
calculations. If you want an overview of drilling history, well then I
think you have to sit together with different people involved in the
process and ask them about each specific drilling rig. Every rig has
its own history, its own hiccups and stories. Not one rig is the same,
and there is not one person who knows Menengai completely.

This conversation with Benjamin—a Kenyan drilling expert who got his training in the United States and was in charge of the GDC's drilling operations—
took place on a Tuesday morning on October 2, 2018, at the offices of the
GDC housing scientists from different disciplines, such as geology, geochemistry, geophysics, cartography, economy, drilling science, environmentalism,

and since a few months ago, anthropology. I had gathered several clearances in the previous months to investigate geothermal exploration in Menengai, and employees of the GDC saw me as part of the regular troops of consultants on scientific missions in Menengai. My presence at Polo Centre in Nakuru—the managerial heart of geothermal exploration in the Great Rift Valley—was, however, often received with skepticism. As the above conversation demonstrates, the company had to deal with what Benjamin referred to as data leaks following the inauguration of MW-01 that put the company in a bad light, leading to financial restraints and a loss of trust among the general public. These leaks led to debates among Nakurians, often during after-work drinks, about how drilling in the caldera could trigger new volcanic eruptions and the unproductiveness of certain drilled wells—in geothermal jargon called "dry wells"—that cost the government huge amounts of money for no return.

The conversation also demonstrates how geothermal business in Menengai reverted to roles of dominance: Instead of mastering the volcano through science, GDC scientists argued the complexity of Menengai's volcanic system was unprecedented and that, despite all the science and datafication supporting geothermal exploration, nobody really knew how to figure out exactly the volcano's complexity. Geologists and geophysicists argued there was simply no existing technology that could properly visualize Menengai's complex structures. Kenyan scientists working for the GDC often claimed that the know-how coming from places such as Iceland—the epicenter of geothermal development worldwide—was insufficient to properly deal with the geological complexity of Menengai. The volcano thus dominated the experts. The iconic Well 1's record-setting output was—besides good science—also the result of good luck, Benjamin claimed. Mastering the volcano and finding heat depended on how certain data were interpreted and negotiated. The GDC's scientists thereby acted as mediators in this process, engaging in what they referred to as deep science.

Negotiating Deep Science

The notion of deep science captures well how knowledge about Menengai is produced and processed beyond the established protocols within the field of geothermal development. "Depth" is discussed by Taussig (1999), who links it to notions of "secrecy." In environmental anthropology, a material approach to the topic of "depth" and "surface" only recently gained traction regarding topics such as "deep mapping" (Roberts 2016) and explorations of what is considered earth's "critical zone" (Arènes et al. 2018). In the following, I combine both analytical lines: I look at how the metaphorical meaning of "depth" is deeply entangled with the volcano's material depth.

"Depth" in the case of the GDC is polysemic. GDC scientists used it to refer to the material depth of the volcano, which plays a crucial role in finding heat, and to highlight the scientific complexity of their endeavor, which relies on knowledge from various fields of science such as geography, hydrology, geochemistry, geology, and physics. The quest for heat in Menengai implied minute material engagements with the affordances of Menengai's topography, hydrology, soil composition, and politics, by scientists of all these disciplines. In order to keep viable the desires, dreams, and aspirations the geothermal industry symbolizes, GDC employees preferred to keep this complexity under the radar; borrowing Latour's words, it was necessary to keep the black box closed, in "the way [that] scientific and technical work is made invisible by its own success" (1999, 304). This practice of occulting, similarly observed by Antina von Schnitzler (2016) in regard to prepaid water meters in South African townships, made the highly politicized geothermal industry a neutral, technical undertaking to be treated by a select group of experts. I follow Larkin here, who argues that

> infrastructures represent and are represented in their built forms; the protests that congeal around them; the sets of numbers, graphs, and tables by which they are administered; the budgets that undergird them. These depend on various material and formal devices, each of which invokes specific modes of address, draws together specific sets of actors, involves differing uses of secrecy and transparency, and constitutes the political in distinct ways. (2018, 186)

The GDC invoked a level of secrecy by enchanting its understanding of the volcano as "deep science." Secrecy as "depth" was part of their efforts to master the volcano's complex reality, making their explorations in Menengai and the consequent processes of materializing the aspired greener, "worldly," urban futures opaque and obscure, hidden under a layer of success and scientific expertise. This practice entailed a process of "datafying" the volcano by experts and was to some extent an occult undertaking, not in the sense of the supernatural but as an activity cut off from the view of outsiders and relying on complex understandings of the depths of the volcano; both its complex geological features and the imaginaries the volcano and geothermal infrastructure evoke in light of Kenya's geothermal aspirations.

Secrecy as a form of depth became most noticeable during my presence at the offices of the GDC, which incited mistrust among employees. Ochieng, whom I regularly met in his favorite pub, confided in me that colleague geologists found rather suspicious my presence "for research" shortly after the CEO had paid a visit to Belgium on company matters. In fact, so Ochieng told me, among some of his colleagues there was the belief I had been hired to spy out employees' allegiance to the company, as political reckoning had caused turmoil at the company's managerial level ever since the former CEO had been fired over a corruption scandal. On top of that, regular sightings of my presence among the communities living around the caldera added to the idea I was looking for ways to negatively portray the company's work. Therefore, my interactions with other members of the company besides Ochieng often happened rather tediously and from a distance. I shared this experience of distance with the communities living in proximity to the volcano. Njoroge—a Gikuyu man in his mid-forties living along the volcano's edge—explained that the company's workings remained a rather mysterious and occult undertaking hidden behind scientific reports, administrative procedures, and constantly changing outcomes, processes from which the local community was mostly excluded. For many residents, GDC activity mainly meant SUVs driving at high speed along the dusty roads in the residential areas (which give entry to the volcano's caldera) and, so they told me, false promises about the construction of community water wells and the employment of youths.

The GDC's secrecy and distance caused all kinds of worries among Nakurians about the intentions of the company. This became especially apparent among some of Nakuru's born-again Christians who gathered in caves in the volcano for prayer retreats. As their spiritual practices were organized in proximity to the GDC's working ground, it was not uncommon for them to talk about the company's activities. Ouma and Owiti, for instance, both residing in the caves at the time of my presence in Nakuru, linked geothermal business—and by extension all technological interventions part of the vision 2030 development scheme—to devil worship and Freemasonry. They proved their case through the argument that the company's employees possessed know-how that is limited to a select elite able to enjoy higher education in which, Ouma and Owiti argued, students revert to occult means such as pacts with the devil for their academic success (also see Carbon, this volume, on resistance to—if not hostility toward—foreign tech-experts involved in megaprojects on the grounds of religious and spiritual convictions).[8]

Expertise of "Depth"

In her analysis of the technology contract, Pype argues that in older settings of technological expertise in sub-Sahara Africa the figure of the blacksmith is of importance. The blacksmith, she argues, "produces culture" and "acts as a 'connector' between the undomesticated world and society" (Pype 2018, 5). Blacksmiths often established alliances with the spiritual world, through which they could tame the undomesticated and produce culture. In their case this entailed the manipulation of fire to produce iron goods. Pype further states that "the display of expertise over manufactured objects can induce fear and awe, separate those 'with knowledge' from those 'without knowledge,' and introduce dynamics of power, distinction, and authority" (Pype 2017, 106).

I follow Pype's argument that some provocative parallels can be drawn between blacksmiths and the technology experts in urban society, especially considering the fact the premise of geothermal exploration is equally based on an attempt to master heat. Benjamin's statement that "nobody really knows Menengai" shares resemblances with the workings of blacksmiths who rely on spiritual intervention for their expertise. I certainly do not want to downplay the scientific processes and technological ingenuity that forms the backbone of the GDC's intervention, yet the inability to fully comprehend and systematically predict the workings of the volcano resembles the bonds blacksmiths make with the supernatural or occult to answer the unanswerable (also see Tonda, this volume, on the mystification produced by capitalist technologies).[9] The supernatural in the case of geothermal exploration has to do with the epistemic instabilities of the volcano itself: Its complexity can be researched and translated into data yet never fully grasped in its entirety. The GDC's scientists do not necessarily make use of spiritual connections to go about their daily activities, but their reliance on "deep science" shares similarities with the belief in the power of spirits, as both depend on the agency of the more-than-human to make sense of reality. Whereas blacksmiths consult the otherworldly to establish a diagnosis, scientists mapping Menengai's complex landscape equally rely on deep science and its limits.

In this regard, drilling experts argued Menengai's landscape is so complex to visualize because its structures are buried under the debris of the volcanic eruptions that happened between fourteen hundred and a few hundred years ago (Mibei and Lagat 2011, 2). The technology that exists nowadays is simply unable to visualize at once the various complex dimensions of the volcano's geological structure. "It is as if you try to look at a 3D movie from a 2D perspective"—Mary, a GDC geologist, made the analogy. I therefore argue that the techno-scientific data the drillers believe in are—like the bonds blacksmiths make with spirits—based on a form of alliance between the volcano's material nature and the deep science they rely on, or the limits thereof. One could provocatively ask whether it is not equally spiritual to believe and trust in the agency of various data sets to predict the probability of finding heat and to visualize what is impossible to image.

Understanding and Sensing Multiple Menengais

Occulting, encoding and decoding the volcano's complexity was a crucial part of the deep science. Benjamin explained that almost nobody understands the full extent of the volcano's materiality. Consequently, only a privileged few are initiated into the complexity of the deep science, a kind of knowledge that is volatile, ephemeral, and exclusive. Both older generations of blacksmiths and more contemporary genres of experts such as the scientists of the GDC demarcate "masters" able to cross the boundaries between the visible and the invisible. The GDC's drilling operators and geologists who tried to explain some of the volcano's complexity often ended up referring to vague descriptions of "mental maps" they had, claiming you have to really sense (-*sikia*)[10] what is going on in the bowels of Menengai. What they meant by "sensing" is worth pausing at.

When I visited a drilling operator called Kimutai in July 2017 on Drilling Rig Number 4, he explained that drilling had been paused. It had something to do with the drilling bit hitting a softer geological zone, causing the well chamber to collapse. Kimutai and his colleagues adjusted their actions and guided the drilling bit so it moved away from potential problematic areas, based on the input of geologists. Sensing the problem depended on the experts' minute engagements with the volcano's materiality. For the geologists, visualizing the well happened under a microscope where soil samples were analyzed and ideas shaped about the different layers or cavities the drilling bit was crossing. For Kimutai, visualizing what was going on happened based on how the drilling rig—operated from a control cabin hanging 15 meters or so above the actual platform—reacted to his adjustments of the control panel of the rig. Before a change of shifts, drilling operators briefed one another on the very specific technical encounters they had had, often using language referring to tactile experiences such as areas that were hard to maneuver through, the occurrence of vibrations, and the like. GDC staff also spent a considerable

amount of time in a rig simulator as part of their training. During these sim-
ulations, different drilling circumstances were virtually mimicked. Knowing,
understanding and sensing the volcano imply very specific ways of relating
to it. For geologists, this entails engaging with rocky substances, while, for
a drilling operator, knowing happens through reading the particular ways
in which a rig reacts to the volcano. Kimutai knew how to interpret the rig's
vibrations and sounds in ways that those who had not drilled in Menengai
would not understand. Mary—the geologist—could read rocks and interpret
their shapes and composition beyond what Kimutai could imagine.

These differences in sensing the volcano recall Annemarie Mol's (2002)
work on "the body multiple" that examines how medical specialists enact
different versions of atherosclerosis, depending on their instruments, tools,
and medical backgrounds. Similarly, there is perhaps not one Menengai but
various different volcanoes that exist within the imaginary realm of scientists
of all kinds who try to visualize Menengai's hidden truths.[11] This is also what
Benjamin was hinting at when he explained every drilling rig has its own
history and its own particular way of relating to Menengai. Mastering the volcano entails taking all these variables and possible versions of Menengai into
account and requires individuals—"masters" (Pype 2018)—who can negotiate between various data sets to untangle the deep science and consequently
"tame" the volcano to harvest its heat. The various categories of experts
are not easily definable or stable. They unearth—or encode and enchant—
different, simultaneously existing truths and sciences[12]—compare the different versions of Menengai—that coproduce the various terms of the technology contract that undergirds the geothermal aspiration. All these categories
of experts benefit from creating depth, privileging certain kinds of knowledge
above others. Lucy—the geologist—argued it was common to have heated
arguments among GDC employees about where to find heat. For each one's
sake, it was important, so she confided in me, to keep some data for oneself. When external consultants, for instance, concluded that more lucrative
heat pockets were located just outside of the volcano, underneath residential
areas and property owned by late President Moi, the company's management
tried to keep this news under the radar. Rumors had it, however, that some
employees sold off data sets to the Moi family, which consequently procured
a drilling permit for exploratory well drilling. This led to accusations of sab-
otage among the employees. By actively keeping certain data, decisions, and
processes to oneself (cf. Benjamin's remarks about "data leaks"), workers keep

the company's geothermal aspirations alive and viable. Mastering the volcano thus pivots on processes of occulting, encoding, and decoding the volcano's complexity in ways that articulate certain modes of understanding and sensing the volcano.

Negotiating Masters

I demonstrated that both blacksmiths and more contemporary experts depend on the agency of more-than-human actors to establish their knowledge. In this regard, Pype draws a parallel with divination, yet another activity often performed by blacksmiths. As with divination, technological expertise often hinges on "the handling of materials and communication with the otherworldly in the search for causes of failures" (Pype 2017, 106). Furthermore, one needs initiation to grasp the full extent of the knowledge involved and become a "master." This initiation could be in the form of ritual initiation—as was often the case among blacksmiths—or in the form of education and apprenticeships into the workings of geothermal deep science. As in initiation rituals, the GDC's experts go through transformative stages that allow them to become masters of the volcano. Extended periods abroad for geothermal training, for example, marked an initial step in the process of mastering Menengai's deep science. It often implied passing extensive amounts of time in Iceland, the heart of geothermal knowledge development. Employees belonging to the higher ranks of the GDC company are trained there. Strikingly, the knowledge gathered through this formal training abroad was overshadowed by scientists' pride about the uniqueness of the Kenyan geothermal field that required unprecedented scientific abstractions and insights. Benjamin argued that foreign consultants often learned from GDC employees instead of the other way around simply because the scientific contexts of places such as Menengai were so complex no training abroad was profound enough to prepare for geothermal exploration in Kenya.[12]

Mastering Menengai also implies another level of initiation than training abroad. Latour's notion of "learning to be effectuated" (2004, 205) is here applicable: Mastering the volcano's deep science implied learning to be affected, a process whereby the bodies of GDC employees become sensitized to (affected by) the transformative potential of the volcano's material minutiae: geologists learning to interpret Menengai's rocky substances, or drilling operators learning to sense and interpret the rig's vibrations and movements. Consequently, this "becoming with" (Haraway 2013) the volcano enables modes of viewing reserved for the initiated that create a divide between those who know and those who do not know, much as blacksmiths learned to be effectuated by the fire they used, giving them the expertise to mediate spiritual worlds. Those who lack the expertise to fully grasp the deep science have to rely on trust in the experts, much as sorcery and witchcraft hinge on notions of trust and intimacy (Geschiere 2013), hence the analogy among Nakuru's Pentecostals between practices of devil worshiping, Freemasonry, and technological innovation such as geothermal development.

In regard to who is considered expert or master, GDC employees argued a select number of people had the ability to visualize in its entirety the complexity of Menengai and define spots to drill. Like blacksmiths, these individuals possess the (secret) knowledge—or have the ingenuity—to understand the invisible powers that govern the world. In this regard, Ochieng and his colleagues argued that besides some "luck" involved in the GDC's success with MW-01, its discovery was thanks to a select group of people who were able to understand the volcano's complex materiality. They equated recent failures of the company to live up to its expectations to a change in management as the result of a corruption scandal. The GDC was, at the time of my conversations with employees between 2018 and 2019, having difficulties in obtaining funding, and salary overdraft worried workers at all levels within the company. Discussions over drinks often dealt with the GDC executives being mere businessmen lacking the knowledge to properly interpret the science. This explained how they time and again met difficulties in managing the company's outcomes. The former CEO, Simiyu, was—despite ongoing investigations into tender fraud he allegedly perpetrated—still praised among many of the GDC's employees. Kibichii, who worked on the Baringo-Silali geothermal project, argued that "people were living big. There was money flowing from the treasury and of course from donors. He [Simiyu] was also very smart in finding funding and was trusted because he was a technocrat. The current guy is a politician." Of relevance here is how authority and power are introduced as being based on the "craftiness" of technocrats. These figures possess expertise that enables them to do more than others. In the case of the former CEO, interlocutors often mentioned he could visualize the volcano as nobody else could, as his whole life breathed deep science. Again by analogy with blacksmiths, this ability to tune into the invisible realm of deep science makes the *techne* experts, as Pype (2018, 8) argues, contemporary "cultural heroes" who are celebrated but, because of their knowledge, often also dreaded.[13]

CONCLUDING NOTE

For a technology contract to be viable requires trust in the technology and its makers and producers (Pype 2018, 14). My ethnography shows that negotiating trust in geothermal exploration in Menengai is a volatile undertaking that depends on the endless possibilities and endless interpretations of the technology and its masters' enchanting of the volcanic landscape. For the geothermal technology to be given credence, finding heat is crucial. The GDC's scientists argued this heavily depends on "deep science," or the complex unearthing of the volcano's minutiae, a task dependent on an amalgam of experts and expertise of which only few people within the GDC know the entirety. Well 1 demonstrated that the science could be trusted, as well as the expertise of the many "masters" that operate geothermal exploration. It created desired visibility for the dreams and hopes the infrastructure stood as symbol for—compare the well as a "dream zone" (Cross 2014)—and came to symbolize a kind of Kenyan techno-utopianism the government is heavily investing in as part of the 2030 Vision development plan (also see Tonda, this volume, on dreams). Its success anticipated the "trust" by the general public the company needed to successfully execute its task of "taming" the volcano to generate more affordable energy futures. The well's fantastic and aesthetic qualities—its function as a "concrete semiotic and aesthetic" vehicle" (Larkin 2013, 329)—were thus key for shaping both not yet fully materialized energy futures and the renewed importance of Nakuru as pivotal hub for realizing the geothermal aspiration. The attention given to MW-01 kept the GDC's technology contract alive and served as proof that the company's intentions to find heat were feasible, that the deep science was working. However, this deep science enchanting the volcano also led to doubts about the technology and its masters. These doubts or lack of trust can result in the technology contract to lose its credence and cause the potential ruination of the (not yet fully) materialized techno-utopian urban futures the geothermal technology stands symbolic for.

My analysis of geothermal exploration in Menengai through various forms of negotiations of aspirations, masters, and sciences shifted the attention beyond what technology promises to how this promise is negotiated and consequently materialized. Opening the black box (Latour 1999) of geothermal "infrastructure as a promising form" (Larkin 2018), bringing the technologies various depths to the surface, demonstrates how "socio-technical imaginaries"—or "collectively imagined forms of social life and social order reflected in the design and fulfilment of nation-specific scientific and/or technological projects" (Jasanoff and Kim 2009, 120)—are created and materialized through a delicate balance of various forms of negotiation that undergird the GDC's promise of finding heat to fuel ambitious urban futures.

NOTES

1. Anand et al. (2018, 27) argue that infrastructures are "promises made in the present about our future" and "insofar as they are so often incomplete—of materials not yet fully moving to deliver their potential—they appear as ruins of a promise." This definition of "promise" runs through this chapter.

2. "To tame" is similarly used in an online news report about current President Uhuru's ambition to tackle the high electricity prices in the country (https://www.kenyans.co.ke/news/63855-uhuru-moves-tame-kenya-powers-high-electricity-costs, accessed July 24, 2021).

3. GDC scientists argued that the Menengai volcano is, geologically speaking, incredibly complex because of what they identified as post-eruption lava flows that cover the caldera's surface. This makes a technique called "surface exploration," whereby the various layers and depths of the volcano are mapped through an exploration of the volcano's surface, very difficult.

4. Alya is a Muslim resident of Nakuru whom I regularly met with to talk about Nakuru's quest to obtain city status. She had been working both as a woman's representative for the county government and as an activist engaged in all kinds of civil society projects in Nakuru. She was a well-known figure in Nakuru and often acted as a spokesperson for Nakuru's *wananchi* (common citizens).

5. Such as the envisioned KenGen textile city park, Lord Egerton agri-city, and Kabarak University smart city.

6. In an effort to get formal clearances to conduct research on GDC premises, I was invited on a formal tour around the caldera.

7. With affective investments I refer to the affects provoked by infrastructures in a fashion similar to Larkin's description of how "roads and railways are not just technical objects . . . but also operate on the level of fantasy and desire. They encode the dreams of individuals and societies and are the vehicles whereby those fantasies are transmitted and made emotionally real" (2013, 333).

8. How Nakuru's Pentecostal community moralizes technological innovations and their link with urban change is beyond the scope of this chapter and will be discussed elsewhere.

9. Epistemological continuity between older categories of experts such as blacksmiths and contemporary tech experts shares resemblances with Horton's "continuity thesis," which posits that both rely on evolving "theories" to explain, predict, and control worldly events (1993, 372).

10. "*-sikia*" denotes both "to feel" and "to hear," and in the context of GDC employees refers to the complex interplay of various senses in trying to understand the complexity of the volcano.

11. Other genres of experts exist in Menengai. Njuguna—a healer and herbalist—masters the volcano's heat through establishing connections with the spiritual realm and by combining various herbal shrubs in medicinal concoctions. He similarly creates a version of Menengai that coexists in proximity to the versions of Menengai generated by GDC scientists. His healing work is, however, beyond the scope of this chapter.

12. See also Rahier et al. (2025) for a discussion of inclusive disjunctivity in scientific and ethnographic knowledge-making.

13. This "pride" also affirms the affective properties of the "post-global" network of cities as defined by Pype (this volume) and demonstrates an awareness of difference; the expertise of the Global North is not necessarily adequate for the Global South.

14. Another contemporary example of how expertise can induce both awe and fear is how Covid-19 scientists are both celebrated and mistrusted. All over the world, prominent virologists have been targeted by antivax movements, often linking them to "occult machinations" to control citizens. In Kenya, interlocutors who feared Covid-19 vaccines argued they were a means created by elite circles to dominate and control *wananchi*.

CHAPTER 5

Dreaming About X-Rays in Kikwit

Visibility, Medical Technology, and Fracture Care in an Intermediate Congolese City

TRISHA PHIPPARD

Adrien Ngonga Piakala—usually simply addressed as Ngonga—is the most renowned healer of fractures in the central African city of Kikwit, Democratic Republic of the Congo, where he has been caring for patients with broken bones for more than thirty years. Growing up in the village of Kabombo in the neighboring province of Kasai, he watched his father work as both a blacksmith and fracture healer, treating the local palm oil plantation workers from nearby Mapangu. In 1983, at the age of eighteen, Ngonga moved 290 kilometers from his home village to the burgeoning city of Kikwit to complete his education. Then a provincial market town and administrative center, Kikwit was entering a period of rapid population growth when Ngonga arrived, transforming from a small hub of just less than 140,000 residents in 1983 to a veritable urban center of 1.3 million in 2016 (Bureau de la Mairie de Kikwit 2016). When Ngonga eventually began working as a healer himself in 1990, it was not long before the city suffered a severe Ebola outbreak in 1995 that garnered significant national and international attention and cemented the city's reputation as a place of medical and techno-scientific expertise. Contemporary Kikwit remains an important node in the Congolese health infrastructures and home to a diverse range of healing experts, including *tradipraticiens.*[1]

In many ways, Ngonga's practice as a fracture care specialist has grown alongside the city itself. His care work has evolved from sporadic requests to treat fracture patients in their homes, applying some of the basic techniques learned from his father, to offering a large, dedicated fracture treatment center welcoming both ambulatory and hospitalized patients suffering any kind of fracture, from simple breaks to open, comminuted (multi-fragmented), or infected wounds. He is so well known that his patients travel from as far away as Angola to seek his care, and he has expanded his repertoire of healing tools and techniques through perpetual innovation and the incorporation of biomedical materials and knowledge. Today, he is famous for both his success as a *tradipraticien* and for offering a pioneering hybrid method of therapy—what he refers to as "tradi-modern" care—that combines materials and practices from both biomedicine (e.g., antibiotics and anesthetics) and "traditional" medicine (e.g., herbal medicines and bamboo casts). His unique approach mirrors in many ways the hybrid urban form of the city itself, which residents frequently insist remains a "large village" rather than a "real city." Often these comments refer to the lack of water and electricity infrastructures in Kikwit. Yet, as this chapter explores, medical technologies, too, are imbricated in this field of imaginative city-making.

In the city of Kikwit, medical technology is unevenly distributed across public and private health facilities, including a diverse range of non-biomedical therapeutic spaces like Ngonga's fracture center. These asymmetries and uneven flows in the distribution of medical technologies throughout the city's complex spaces of care have a profound impact on the meanings, practices, and possibilities of care, shaping both patient perceptions of various therapeutic practitioners and the material practices of those engaged in care work in both biomedical and non-biomedical milieus. In this context, the X-ray machine (usually simply referred to as *la radio*) constitutes one of many examples of a medical technology that has come to play an important material and symbolic role in Kikwit's therapeutic landscape—as in many other African urban centers. A powerful diagnostic technology, it is a device with the power to render the invisible visible and to reveal medical pasts while invoking possible medical futures. A testament to the supposed certainties of biomedicine, it represents the technological promise of better health through scientific mastery of the human body. Yet, in practice, interfacing this with technology gives rise to very real uncertainties, be they biological, infrastructural, relational, or political.

Social studies of infrastructure have long demonstrated how the presences, absences, and assemblages of infrastructure shape urban forms and experiences, with the focus frequently being placed on public services such as water (Anand 2017), electricity (Degani 2017), sanitation (Chalfin 2017), waste removal (Fredericks 2018), and roads (Beck et al. 2017), along with particular forms of infrastructural breakdown such as potholes (Solomon 2021). These studies have contributed to an understanding of how infrastructural assemblages and networks blend the social and technical to actively construct urban spaces and lifeworlds (Graham and Marvin 2001; Graham and McFarlane 2015). With respect to health infrastructures and technologies, the disciplines of science and technology studies and of medical anthropology have produced a growing body of literature revealing the many different enactments and emplacements of biomedicine and its objects, particularly the multiplicities, instabilities, and entanglements of medical objects (Langwick 2011; Street 2014), institutions (McKay 2018b; Van Der Geest and Finkler 2004; Wendland 2010; Zaman 2005), and diseases (Livingston 2012; Mulemi 2010; Nading 2014), as well as bodies (Mol 2002) and patienthood (Taee 2017). Beyond a mere recognition of the heterogeneity and complexity of how biomedicine is realized differently across different spaces and times— particularly in dialogue with competing epistemologies and practices of healing in a context of medical pluralism (e.g., Feierman and Janzen 1992; Hampshire and Owusu 2013; Langwick 2007; Olsen and Sargent 2017)—attention to medical multiplicity offers insight into how a singular object or practice comes to be engaged by multiple actors, in multiple ways, to multiple ends (McKay 2018b, 54).

Following the biographies of and encounters with a singular medical object (like the X-ray) therefore offers insight into how these objects transcend the medical and the technological to diverse social and political ends. Yet in-depth ethnographic attention to a particular biomedical technology and its multiplicities is not common, particularly when it comes to considerations of affective as well as material entanglements. Whyte, Van Der Geest, and Hardon (2002) presented one such anthropology of "materia medica," following Appadurai (1986) to tell us about the social lives of medicines. For medical imaging technologies, such endeavors are even more rare, notwithstanding Street's (2014) nuanced analysis of the various meanings and practices surrounding the X-ray in a public hospital in Papua New Guinea, and Kusiak's (2010) historical perspective on the social experience of radiology in postcolonial Senegal. Moreover, despite increasing attention to the dynamics of emplacement in studies of biomedical technology, seldom has the focus on "place" surfaced at the level of the city, rather than on national or broader regional scales. Hence, the specific dialectics of medical technology, the urban milieu, and everyday care work remain relatively overlooked, particularly in sub-Saharan Africa.

The aim of this chapter is thus to explore material and affective entanglements with X-ray technology as it manifests in care work relating to broken bones in the city of Kikwit, specifically asking how the X-ray functions as a technology of the city and what urban practices it generates. I argue, first, that medical technologies like the X-ray open up new spaces for imagination about technology and urbanity in Congo, as Kikwit's liminal positionality as an intermediate city affects both technological expectations and exposures in the medical field. Second, the social performative work of *la radio* in Kikwit highlights the importance of material technologies in care practitioners' efforts to establish and maintain their position in a competitive urban therapeutic market, embodying the nexus of visibility, expertise, and technology that figures in much care work in urban Africa.

Although this chapter discusses moments of technological breakdown, infrastructural shortcomings, and complaints and comparisons made by my interlocutors in Kikwit about various realizations of X-ray technology, the aim of this chapter is certainly not to reiterate laments about technological "backwardness" or reinforce tropes about technological failure or lack so common in writing about technology and Africa (Mavhunga 2017a; Pype, this volume; Adunbi, this volume). Rather, I wish to suggest that close ethnographic attention to the daily realities of work with sophisticated medical technologies in a context of resource scarcity, economic vulnerability, and infrastructural instability—and to feelings of frustration, despair, anxiety, and neglect, as well as those of pride, accomplishment, and optimism—affords insight into the complex interactions between multiple layers of technological cultures and imaginaries in an urban setting. This follows an impulse similar to what Steven Jackson has called "broken world thinking" (2014), an orientation that draws on moments of breakdown and dissolution as entry points into recognizing not only the fragility and limits of the social, technological, and natural worlds we inhabit, but also the ways in which acts of "breaking" can be generative and productive. Hence, taking seriously the social dimensions of both positive and negative encounters with a medical technology like the X-ray—be they real or imagined, in instances of the technology's absence—not only speak to its multiple meanings and enactments in an urban African setting but also offer new perspectives on technology, affect, and urban forms in Africa more broadly.

By developing the concept of "technology of the city," I do not intend to evoke discourse relating to so-called smart cities.[2] Rather, I wish to consider the social and material configurations of *la radio* in Kikwit as an example of the complex dialectics of technology and urban life, wherein technological imaginaries and materialities are associated with urban forms while simultaneously shaping them. In other words, part of what makes Kikwit a very urban place within the Congolese imagination is based on the presence of actual material technologies, including *la radio*, even while its lack of other infrastructures and its liminal positionality as an intermediate city means that this urbanity and characterization as a technical space is fraught with subjunctivity, ambivalence, and contradictory meanings about the technology's role in present and future care work.

Throughout this chapter, I draw on the Appaduraian-influenced concept of "carescapes" to describe the shifting intersections of embodied people, their material surroundings, and broader society that create lived spaces of care (Obrist 2016, 97; see also Eeuwijk 2014). Whereas Obrist (2016, 97) emphasizes the significance of place with respect to the home, I wish to engage with the importance of the city in these intersections, and specifically the scale of the urban setting in which spaces of care are emplaced. Moreover, my analysis emphasizes the role of technology in constructing these carescapes—a material component of this intersectionality that strongly impacts various affects of care. In so doing, this chapter demonstrates how material configurations and flows of medical technology intersect not only with perceptions of the city but also with the personal aspirations and dreams of the care practitioners whose work they figure into, revealing the emergence of new political affects in relation to technology.

On a technical level, the process of developing an X-ray has three steps. First is the initial exposure, where human and nonhuman come together as the body's dense organic tissue absorbs the penetrating rays. Then, in the dark room, chemical conversions from obscurity into light work to reveal the invisible: The radiology technician first submerges the film into a *révélateur* (development) solution, revealing the latent image, before performing a second immersion in the *fixateur* (fixing) bath to make this visibility permanent. This technological process is mirrored in many ways in the broader social universe of the X-ray, as both patients and care practitioners strive for visibility in their therapeutic journeys and care work. The structure of this chapter therefore follows the X-ray's development process to describe how patients and especially care providers live with—and without—this particular medical technology. I focus on the experiences of Ngonga and of the radiology technicians working at a state-run general hospital in Kikwit, as *la radio* figures prominently in the techno-imaginaries of care and expertise among these practitioners and their clients. Although also relevant for other diagnostic purposes (e.g., tuberculosis screening), X-ray technology is central for diagnosing fractures, which constitute an increasingly common affliction in the city, given the dramatic rise in traffic accidents—particularly those involving the city's ubiquitous moto-taxis (Phippard 2023).

The first section considers the dialectics between Kikwit's urban context and the socio-technical forms that arise in this space, illustrating how Kikwit's position as an intermediate city shapes both expectations of medical technologies encountered in the city and the material realities of exposure, with uneven distribution and capacity reinforcing the liminality of this urban technical space. In the second section, I reflect on the broader "revealing" functions of *la radio*, describing how the X-ray is implicated in "visibility work" on both a material and a social level and what this social performative work of *la radio* reveals about the dialectics between urbanity, technology, visibility, and expertise. The final section explores how this technology figures in care practitioners' efforts to make this visibility permanent—what I describe as a process of "fixture" that enables them to negotiate and maintain their position, which not only is an essential practice of survival in Kikwit's competitive urban carescape but also contributes to the emergence of new political affects.

The empirical data on which this chapter is based stems from fourteen months of ethnographic fieldwork conducted in 2015 and 2016 throughout (and beyond) the city of Kikwit, including participant observation and interviews with diverse care practitioners, technicians, and their patients, as well as through continued interaction via telephone and WhatsApp conversations since then. I also worked for a year as an apprentice of fracture healer Ngonga Piakala, learning his practice of *radio à la main*, interpreting X-ray films together, and assisting in the treatment of hundreds of fracture patients. All dialogue has been translated from either Kikongo (the predominant language on Kikwit's streets) or French (commonly used in bureaucratic settings and medical practice, such as in hospital meetings or during X-ray examinations). To protect the identities of my research participants, all names are pseudonyms, with the exception of Ngonga himself.

EXPOSURE TO MEDICAL TECHNOLOGY IN THE CITY

To begin to understand the complex relationship between *la radio* and the city, it is important to note first that the material possibilities of such technological encounters—the very possibility of being exposed to this medical technology as well as the specific limitations of this human-technological interaction—largely depend on Kikwit's urban context. Moreover, the specific medical technologies present (or absent) in the city are a function of the style or scale of its urban form, as well as its epidemiological history. Most obviously, this operates on a material level, with supply chains, distributed health infrastructures, and geographical barriers to access all influencing the flow of medical technologies between urban and rural locales. The decentralized structure of the state health system means that each of the country's 515 health zones usually possesses sophisticated medical technologies (like an X-ray machine) only at a central reference hospital.[3] In practice, many of the reference hospitals outside of cities like Kikwit also lack functioning technologies or even electricity to power them, so many patients must be referred even further to urban centers like Kikwit. However, as I argue here, in addition to the material configurations of technological access, we can identify an imaginative dimension as well, as the scale of "cityness" is entangled with spatial imaginaries of technology and the role of technology in urban forms.

In many ways, Kikwit resists the atmosphere of an urban metropolis. This is in part due to the large parcel size, the many people raising crops and livestock in the city, and the small number of paved roads or multistory buildings, with the urban landscape comprising instead sandy streets and towering mango trees. Despite its large population size, a common refrain in Kikwit is thus that it is not a "real" city because it lacks specific markers of urbanity, usually referring to two urban infrastructures in particular—namely, fixed-line electricity and municipal piped water. Kikwit is cut off completely from the national power grid, even though the high-voltage transmission lines that transport electricity produced at the Inga dam (see Carbon, this volume) all the way to the south of the country pass adjacent to Kikwit's city limits, running almost overhead houses at the edge of the Kazamba district. Instead, residents obtain electricity from a patchwork of *groupe électrogène* (generators, often used for several hours in the evening and shared with neighbors for a small fee, the informally installed cables strung up through trees between houses), and, increasingly, solar panels (usually Chinese-produced and limited in capacity and quality). Municipal water is supplied by a network of community taps, with frequent ruptures in supply and sometimes questionable standards of purification. For Kikwitois, however, these piecemeal technological assemblages fail to evoke the same urban feel they expect from such infrastructures, and hence the lack of water and electricity are cited as one of the main reasons Kikwit cannot be labeled a city.

In other words, in Congolese imaginaries of the urban, these are technologies of the city—and these technologies have the power to define "cityness" or ascribe city status to certain places, signaling urbanity regardless of population size. This resonates with what Hendricks (2022) and Carbon (this volume) have observed elsewhere in the country, wherein the presence and use of technology have the potential to assign an urban character to locales otherwise lacking markers of urbanity. Medical technologies and infrastructures, too, have come to play a role in urban imaginaries. This is especially so in Kikwit given the unique history of epidemiological crises that have made it a prominent site of more than a century of (international) medical and technoscientific intervention—from sleeping sickness control post in 1912 to Ebola "hot spot" in 1995 (Kibari N'sanga and Mulala 2011). The city is thus both imaginatively linked to and full of material remains and traces of biomedical encounters and enactments of scientific modernity (Geissler et al. 2016). The long-standing presence of medical technology in the city has made it a destination for therapeutic intervention, drawing both its own residents and those from the surrounding rural hinterlands to its diverse sites of care. The city's technoscape thus constitutes a pole of attraction in the medical field. As a key administrative and logistical base for NGOs and state health infrastructures for more than a hundred years (but especially since 1995), the building up and regional significance of the city has actually been linked to the presence of these medical infrastructures and technologies. In this sense, the city constitutes a "tech hub" in the medical landscape of the region (and indeed beyond, given the notoriety of its post-Ebola medical science). However, at the same time, the city's medical structures, institutions, and supply chains remain dependent in many ways on the capital or transnational networks, reflecting the city's broader positionality as an intermediate city.

In this sense, it is important to consider how Kikwit is perceived as a kind of liminal or hybrid form—an intermediate city, not just in size but rather in position, how it is perceived in relation to other larger and smaller centers. For residents, the city is thus caught somewhere between *ville* and *village*, not just in the scale of its urban form but also in its role as a node, connection, or stopover point—a *carrefour* (crossroads), as Kikwitois frequently label it—between centers of power, money, influence, and infrastructure in the capital (or abroad) and Kikwit's surrounding rural spaces. My analysis here of Kikwit as an intermediate city is influenced by Harms et al.'s (2014) work on "remoteness" as not just a spatial concept inherent to place but a "relativistic social construct," both a location and a social relation. They argue that "remote" may not necessarily be geographically distanced from the center of administrative, political, or economic activities, but may experience remote-ness as social, economic, or cultural marginalization. Hence, remoteness has both geographic and sociocultural or economic factors and is always a rela-tional construct. This is important for my analysis of technologies of the city, because technologies are also frequently classified relationally, and for Con-golese such classifications are often mapped onto geography in such a way that technological status and sophistication are usually measured in compar-ison to the technologies present in Kinshasa or other imagined centers of urbanity and technology, such as major cities in Europe. I argue that the case of *la radio* in Kikwit suggests that this liminal positionality as an intermediate city is in many ways mirrored in its technological landscape, not least in the medical field. In other words, as an intermediate city Kikwit does not just mediate between urban and rural forms but also constitutes a space where the mediation and comparison between different forms of technology occur.

In her study of radiology in Senegal in the early 2000s, Kusiak (2010) observed that the lack of advanced medical imaging technology like com-puted tomography (CT) or magnetic resonance imaging (MRI) meant that ultrasound and X-ray technology were the most sophisticated medical tools available. Except for expatriates and those with the means to travel to access American or European medical care, *la radio* was the "pinnacle of 'high-tech' medicine" (Kusiak 2010, 234). The same is true in Kikwit today, especially if we consider geographies of technology on a regional scale, in relation to the city, rather than on a national level, as Kusiak did for Senegal. Kikwit's significance as a regional hub and major population center means that it is home to multiple institutions with X-ray technology, and many people from surrounding rural areas are referred to the city for radiology examinations. Yet more advanced diagnostic imaging technologies can be found only in Kinshasa or further afield, accessible only to those with the means to travel and pay to access these exclusive services. Digital X-rays are rare; although a religious hospital outside of Kikwit purportedly has a digital machine, these images are usually seen in Kikwit only for patients transferred from the capital, where digital radiography is more widely available. Hence, both expectations of and actual encounters with this technology for Kikwitois are intimately linked to the city's liminal position as an intermediate city. Even though Kikwit's radiological capacity constitutes a technological pull bring-ing people toward the city, the status of this technology is always qualified against an even more advanced (and more urban) technological pole.

Just ten minutes away from Ngonga's fracture center, the radiology department of the main state-run hospital in Kikwit is one of the primary spaces in the city where one can find an X-ray machine and undergo a radiographic examination. Joseph, the hospital's lead radiology technician,[4] has worked in the service for six years, after completing his training in Kinshasa. Along with the other technicians—who all either originate from Kinshasa or studied there, since such specializations do not exist in provincial cities like Kikwit— Joseph has seen firsthand this geographical distribution of medical imaging technology, and he explained quite directly how different forms of the technology are associated with different places. As he described it, the capital (or overseas) is the place where the most "modern" (digital) technology lives, while in Kikwit they continue to struggle "in obscurity." The technicians are all trained in digital radiography as well as more advanced technologies such as MRI, which they can never use because it does not exist in Kikwit. Instead, Joseph and his colleagues make do with what they call *technologie ancienne* (old or antique technology, i.e., analog machines paired with out-of-date or poor-quality film development equipment), a label also employed by Ngonga and other care practitioners in Kikwit.

Joseph's lament about working in "obscurity" was frequently echoed by doctors in the city (and also in surrounding health zones in more rural hospitals) and applied both in a literal sense, in terms of working in the "dark" without electricity, and in a relational sense, with Kikwit and its technologies seen as provincial, out-of-date, and generally remote from the central techno-hub of the capital, although of course not as obscure as the surrounding villages that the radiology department serves. Technological obscurity can thus be interpreted as a local idiom of "remoteness,"[5] or more precisely as an example of how remoteness plays out in spatial imagination of technology. For Joseph and his fellow technicians, we see this status of operating in technological obscurity as linked to Kikwit's liminal positionality, with the hospital's X-ray technology always being compared with and assessed as inferior to the advanced versions present in the capital. As we will see below, notions of obscurity are also tied to emerging political affects in relation to technology, such as feelings of neglect by the state. Yet, at the same time, the very same technology in question—*ancienne* as it may be—constitutes a significant draw from the surrounding region toward the city of Kikwit and, indeed, toward the hospital itself within this urban space.

Despite the complaints about technological obscurity leveled by Joseph and his colleagues, then, they also recognize that the hospital is lucky to possess *la radio* at all. Access to any form of X-ray technology is indeed the exception among medical institutions in the city, and altogether out of reach for care practitioners operating outside of the biomedical realm. Across the *cité*, Ngonga performs his fracture care work without access to any diagnostic technology[6] beyond the X-ray films brought to him by patients, usually obtained at the hospital. Instead, he relies on a diagnostic technique he calls *radio à la main* (X-ray by hand). In this manual form of *la radio*, he palpates the site of the fracture with his hands to locate and visualize the fracture, often in silent concentration as he creates a mental map of what is hidden below the skin. Within a few moments has a more or less clear diagnosis, confirming the location of the fracture and the position of any bone fragments, which he describes aloud to the patient and his assistants, sometimes with the aid of visual tools. As his apprentice, I sometimes sketched images of these fractures and the position of various bone fragments for patients to see, or Ngonga pointed out the bones in question on his skeleton model, helping the patients and kin better understand their diagnosis. Similar diagnostic techniques have been observed among other fracture healers and bonesetters in Africa (Ekere and Echem 2013; Onuminya 2004) and elsewhere (Lambert 2012). As Ngonga explains it, you can tell if the bones are in place if there is a *craquement* (a distinct cracking sensation when palpating the fracture site); in those cases, all that is needed is to immobilize the broken bones and apply medication to the affected area. However, this *craquement* is often elusive, and hence reduction of the fracture is usually necessary to pull the broken bones back into alignment.

Despite his frequent reliance on such manual diagnosis, however, Ngonga's position as a *tradipraticien* working in an urban center has also brought him many opportunities to incorporate biomedical technologies like the X-ray into his practice—opportunities he has seized throughout the evolution of his craft, especially since studying nursing science in 2009. His main motivation to study nursing was to learn suture techniques and how to deal with septic wounds in open-fracture cases, but he learned about many other biomedical technologies and techniques as well, some of which he has embraced. In a major city, the ease of access to medical technologies like latex gloves and pharmaceuticals (anti-inflammatory medicines and, more recently, anesthetics) and the prevalence of X-ray films mean that he is frequently exposed to these tools and incorporates them into his daily care work, either of his own initiative or at the behest of his patients. With respect to *la radio*, many of Ngonga's patients arrive after already having procured an X-ray, and, if not, then Ngonga always recommends they visit a radiology service before return-

Figure 5.1. *Tradipraticien* Ngonga Piakala examining the X-ray film of a traffic accident victim at his "tradi-modern" treatment center in Kikwit, revealing a complex lower leg fracture. Photo by Trisha Phippard.

ing with their film to begin treatment, if they can afford to do so. Although he is always willing to work with a patient to diagnose by hand if a patient prefers not to or does not have the financial resources to obtain an X-ray, Ngonga has moved toward relying on the X-ray more and more over the years because he perceives the technology ensures a more certain diagnosis and treatment.

Exposure to medical technology in the city has thus been highly influential in the evolution of Ngonga's hybrid tradi-modern therapeutic approach, even though on a material basis he continues to operate in even more extreme technological obscurity than the radiology technicians working in a strictly biomedical context. From this perspective, we see that attention to the urban quality of Kikwit's carescape is important, because it reveals the layers of interaction between technologies, technicians, *tradipraticiens*, the city, and its rural surroundings, and how, within the pluralistic carescape of an intermediate city, *tradipraticiens* like Ngonga interact with technologies of the city in ways that dramatically shape their everyday care practices. Ngonga's tradi-modern method itself thus constitutes an example of how technology—

and specifically the layering of different techno-imaginaries and materials, including both biomedical devices and so-called traditional technologies— can produce new urban forms and even reshape urban livelihood practices (see also Adunbi, this volume).

REVEALING BODIES AND EXPERTISE WITH MEDICAL TECHNOLOGY

Late one morning in May 2016, Ngonga received a new case—one that brought into focus some of the social and material configurations that come together in X-ray technology, as well as how visibility intersects with the medical technology of *la radio*. His treatment center was already bustling with activity, as ambulatory patients arrived to have their bandages changed, alongside patients with more serious (e.g., femur, tibia, pelvis) fractures staying in one of the rooms onsite. The new patient, Justin, had just arrived from Kinshasa. A twenty-six-year-old theology student, he had been involved in a serious motorcycle accident in the capital six days prior. Justin had been transporting his friend while doing the *rodage* (breaking in) of a motorcycle for an acquaintance when they were hit by a truck. The collision was so severe that his friend died on the scene, and Justin's leg was badly mangled. The day after the accident, he had been given an X-ray in a Kinshasa hospital, from an impressive new digital machine—the technicians had even transferred the images to his mobile phone, his father later told me with amazement—which had revealed a comminuted (multi-fragmented) fracture of the femur. His father, a pastor, was aware of Ngonga's reputation and insisted on transferring his son the 525 kilometers to Kikwit.

That morning in Kikwit, Ngonga and his assistants gathered together to examine the printout of the digital X-ray images that Justin's family had brought with them, attempting to devise a treatment strategy, while other patients and their kin crowded around, peering over their shoulders. Crisp, precise images clearly showed the multiple bone fragments, scattered out of place as though they had been casually tossed across the page. Before even commenting on the fracture itself, Ngonga immediately remarked at the quality of the images; they far surpassed the caliber of the often fuzzy and clouded films patients normally arrive with, procured from the general hospital and its *technologie ancienne*. Yet the exactitude of what could be revealed beneath the skin by either digital or *ancienne* X-ray technology also far surpassed any precision Ngonga is able to offer himself when diagnosing fractures by *radio à la main*.

One of the unique powers of the X-ray machine is that it promises to shed light—quite literally—on that which is otherwise obscure, offering a transformative revelation to achieve visibility. To "X-ray" is of course a common metaphor for the ability to see (through); the power to see and be seen are critical to care work for both patients and practitioners.[7] Fassin (1992) has already pointed out the similarities between diagnosis and divination, particularly with respect to radiological exams that make the "inside" visible, just as a divinatory expert may read the entrails of a chicken to reveal illness within an afflicted body. Yet this analysis of the social performative work of *la radio* indicates that this technology has the power to reveal more than just these invisible "insides" within the body. Indeed, as a technology inherently entangled with questions of visibility, the X-ray offers a cogent example of what Street (2014) has called "visibility work," wherein biomedical technologies are tools that can be used to make both patients and care providers visible in ways that enable affective response and recognition, to various therapeutic, social, or political ends. My data show that in Kikwit, the X-ray machine enables visibility work on at least two levels.

Beginning in the dark room, we see this visibility work unfold first on a material level, rendering the invisible within human bodies visible to patients, their kin, and various care providers—with material consequences for therapeutic opportunities and outcomes. Marie, another of the radiology service's four technicians, frequently described it as a process of revealing a "hidden image"—a process with the potential to concretely define medical pasts, while simultaneously delineating potential medical futures. Of course, the X-ray is not the only medical technology that performs this revealing function in biomedical practice; other technologies, like the microscope—ubiquitous in Kikwit since the Ebola outbreak and response—also render the invisible visible. The emphasis on revelatory visibility as an important offering of biomedicine and its technologies dates back to early colonial medicine in the region, where doctors used "seeing" through the microscope as a means to convert Congolese subjects to biomedicine from other ontologies; similarly, surgery was also often performed as a public spectacle, revealing the body's hidden inner properties, the flesh no longer a barrier to visibility (Au 2017). Newer technologies like a Chinese "scanner" that surfaced in Kikwit in 2015 represent a hypermodern/futuristic example of this same revelatory possibility. For fracture care, however, *la radio* is central.

Justin's fracture was hypervisible—a product of the crisp, clean images produced by the digital technology. Before beginning any therapeutic intervention, Ngonga sat in the courtyard of his care center, pouring over the printed-out X-ray images. He carefully examined each image, noting the position and orientation of the fragments. He reflected out loud, pointing out the complications of the case: "The fragments are truly free. How do we put them back in place? This piece—how will we re-orient it? . . . And what's that there? There is a cavity here, where this piece must belong. The difficulty will be placing this fragment back in place." Despite the clarity of the images, the severity of the fracture and the number of fragments involved still cast doubt on the precise method to be used in reducing the fracture. After a moment of silent study, Ngonga announced that he would apply a specific method he developed for a previous case, flipping the patient over halfway through reduction to approach the fracture from behind. Moreover, since the family had said it was an open fracture, he would verify his interpretation of the X-ray once he was inside the cavity.

Once they unwrapped the leg from its bandages and carboard-box-constructed splint, however, Justin's fracture turned out not to be an open fracture, but a closed one, and a truly difficult case for reduction. Yet thanks to the clarity of the images, Ngonga was able to work methodically to locate each piece by feeling through the skin, consulting the images throughout the process as a sort of road map to reduction. Although it took four attempts at reduction over the span of a week, the treatment was ultimately effective, and Justin was able to return to mobility—and his studies in Kinshasa—after several months of recovery. Just two months after the initial intervention, he was taking his first steps, grateful that he had avoided the surgery (osteosynthesis) proposed by the hospital doctors, accompanied by a USD 2,800 bill and the risk of amputation.

Yet, for many patients, their fractures are less visible, no matter how acutely they may be felt. With digital images held primarily only among patients transferred from the capital, the rest of patients suffering a fracture in Kikwit or the surrounding rural areas usually had to make do with imprecise, clouded images—if they could access *la radio* at all. For many patients, the prohibitive cost of medical imaging examinations meant that the more accessible technology of *radio à la main* was the only method of visualizing their condition. Under these circumstances, diagnosis remains possible, but with less certainty, sometimes leading to surprises in the treatment process (e.g., the existence of additional fragments) that jeopardize therapeutic efficacy.

In addition to the material level, the X-ray is involved in visibility work on a social level as well. In rendering visible the patient's physiological condition, the X-ray can also enable a revelation and even validation of a patient's suffering. Patients—as people, not physical bodies—are made to feel visible, albeit some more so than others, depending on the type of (biological and technological) interaction with or "exposure" to *la radio*. As "relational technologies," X-rays transform bodies through the social and symbolic processes they engender (Street 2014, 118). This gets to the very heart of the relational nature of "care work" (for both care seekers and caregivers), as care more broadly can be understood as a relational resource (McKay 2018b). As Street has argued, "In a place where people predominantly imagine themselves to be invisible (to the state, to doctors, to a global scientific community) the hospital becomes an intense site of visibility work where bureaucratic and biomedical technologies are engaged with as relational technologies that can make the person visible in recognizable and affectively persuasive forms" (2014, 13–14). In Justin's case, in addition to this visibility producing a positive impact on the actual therapeutic possibilities and accuracy of his treatment, it also validated his suffering; care providers and fellow patients alike marveled at what a "difficult" and "serious" fracture he had to endure and recover from. As a result, he was perceived as strong and courageous by his doctor and other caregivers, and he was not chastised when the first three attempts at setting the fracture failed; Ngonga blamed the complexity of the arrangement of the bones, and not his willingness to "respect" the healer's instructions and maintain a particular position, as other patients are often blamed when their initial reductions fail to hold.

From this perspective, we can see that well beyond medical diagnosis, the social performative function of *la radio* is grounded in its ability to be leveraged as a tool for achieving visibility, albeit in conjunction with other important social configurations. In this respect it is interesting to consider how Ngonga's *radio à la main* is implicated in visibility work in both similar and divergent ways. While it undoubtedly lacks the precision to enable visibility work on a material level, Ngonga's choice to refer semantically to this modern biomedical technology of visibility suggests that the revealing function of his manual form of *la radio* is still important. In other words, Ngonga cannot offer his patients the kind of material visibility of their fractures that Justin obtained in Kinshasa, or even a certainty in their diagnosis that they may be able to achieve with the *technologie ancienne* elsewhere in Kikwit. He can, however, visualize their fractures in a way that offers meaningful visibility. As such, *radio à la main* can be considered a relational technology just as much as its analog or digital counterparts, in the sense that it too can make an afflicted person visible in affective and persuasive ways, transforming bodies through an assemblage of care, attention, and touch, rather than electromagnetic radiation and film.

Thus far I have been discussing how the various forms of *la radio* are implicated in visibility work for people suffering from fractures, but it is important to recognize that visibility work on the social level does not just apply to patients; just as the X-ray renders certain patients more or less visible, it also renders certain therapeutic practitioners more or less visible as well. Relevant here is Street's (2014) suggestion that what is made visible in medical practice is not individual disease but relationships and the kinds of persons who are involved in them; I argue that this is as true for the care providers involved in this medical practice as it is for the patients who seek their care. Hence, part of what is revealed by *la radio* in Kikwit is in fact not just afflicted patients but relationships among care practitioners in the city—both those within biomedical practice, like the radiology technicians, and beyond it, like Ngonga. I thus return to my provocation that the X-ray in Kikwit can be considered a technology of the city, to nuance this argument further by suggesting that it is in fact the context of a competitive urban carescape that makes visibility work with this technology so essential for practitioners working in the city. In other words, in a pluralistic urban care market that brings together competing therapeutic approaches, materials, and practitioners, achieving visibility and distinguishing oneself from competition is vital to the success and survival of doctors, healers, and medical technicians. The remainder of this chapter will therefore explore how visibility work is essential for care practitioners to gain recognition and obtain a competitive edge, and how these broader efforts to achieve visibility are often enabled and animated by medical technologies like the X-ray.

FIXTURES OF VISIBILITY IN A COMPETITIVE CARESCAPE

The objective of fracture care is to achieve the consolidation of bones, re-solidifying osseous matter into the proper configuration. Yet those engaged in healing fractures are not only pursuing the consolidation of bones in their daily care work but also continually attempting to consolidate their own power and authority so as to ensure a lasting and (financially) successful practice. Being a healer is in many ways a matter of social recognition (Bekaert 2000), and hence this reputation-building work must be constantly reperformed and reinforced. This is true regardless of the location, but within an urban milieu like Kikwit, these efforts to bolster one's reputation and social position—visibility work, in other words—is especially critical. Through proximity to a large number of different therapeutic approaches, spaces, and practitioners, the city creates a competitive environment for those engaged in care work.

The case of *la radio* in Kikwit also demonstrates that this visibility work is not simply a question of negotiating who has the power to see and be seen, but also about efforts to make this visibility permanent. Just as the *fixateur* bath renders "hidden images" permanently visible on film, visibility work with technology and social networks aims to "fix" reputation and authority in the competitive carescape that is produced by Kikwit's urban nature. In other words, for care practitioners, the visibility work described in the previous section serves as a means of "fixture" in a social sense, enabling individuals to capture and hold attention and strengthen their position or reputation. Extending far beyond the work of repair (i.e., fixing something that has been broken), this work of fixture is about establishing permanence, stability, or order—about determining and maintaining position. I argue here that as these practitioners strive for visibility in their care work—negotiating position, asserting authority, and proving expertise—*la radio* is leveraged in different ways to enact or challenge this visibility and consolidate one's position.

From the hand-painted signs advertising various sites of care around the city, it is obvious that technological apparatuses like the X-ray machine are used to achieve visibility and attract patients as they delineate between different care providers and institutions. These advertisements frequently list not only the therapeutic services but also the material technologies present onsite. The narratives of patients' therapeutic itineraries confirm the importance of these devices in the visibility and reputation of various care providers. What is perhaps less obvious is how these technologies—and their different forms, from digital machines to *technologie ancienne*—fuel personal anxieties that stem from such technological competition, inspire career aspirations and dreams for the future, and are implicated in political affects relating to technology, care, and the state.

In his six years working at the general hospital, Joseph has seen the growing importance of different forms of X-ray technology and its impact on the visibility of his service vis-à-vis other care sites featuring an X-ray machine. He and his colleagues are deeply concerned about the poor quality of images produced by their antiquated machine, which jeopardizes the reputation of the hospital, once the most advanced and well-equipped biomedical institution in town but now rivaled by both private and religious-run medical centers in the region. A religious hospital with a digital machine near Kikwit offers the most advanced technology in the region but, being outside of the city itself, poses less of a threat in terms of direct competition. However, even compared with the four other analog machines present in town, the material shortcomings and frequent breakdowns in their technology are cause for concern. As Dr. Kasongo, the radiologist, lamented, when they produce poor-quality images or are unable to provide service at all because of electricity problems or ruptures in the supply of essential materials like film,[8] this "damages the reputation of the institution." The reliability of competing services is perhaps equally contingent—for example, the machine at another prominent clinic in town was not operational for an extended period in 2015 because the technician had died and no one else was trained to replace him. Nonetheless, this perceived threat of competing technologies, as well as the relative scarcity of these materials overall, has shaped the technicians' perception of their work and their place in both the hospital hierarchy and the broader carescape in the city.

In late 2015, the status of technological "obscurity" marked by antiquated equipment that Joseph had complained about seemed poised to change for him and his fellow technicians. The radiology department received a new digital machine within the framework of a government program meant to reinforce the capacity of reference hospitals throughout the country. Programs to distribute such donated medical equipment are a common feature of the Congolese medical supply chain, usually with the involvement of non-profit partners, and are essential for the continued functioning of basic health services where the government lacks the means to provide them.[9] In this case, the "new" (yet still secondhand) machine had come from Germany—with instruction manuals in German only—but Joseph was optimistic. He and the other technicians were proud of the new apparatus, an imposing, modern, white beast stretching its arms out to fill much of the examination room, its older counterpart pushed to the side. Yet many months after the machine arrived, it remained *en panne* (broken down), waiting on engineers to arrive from the capital to repair its power source. For the technicians, this new arrival was supposed to have brought renewed medical authority to the hospital, replacing the ancient machine's fuzzy images with crisp new revelations. Yet technical problems meant that the machine was not operational until mid-2016, and even then, it did not function as intended, due to power problems and missing components (e.g., an interface for digital output).

Figure 5.2. A radiology technician processing an X-ray at the state-run general hospital in Kikwit obtained using its *technologie ancienne.* Photo by Trisha Phippard.

"We have serious problems with the new machine," Joseph explained, "so for now, we have to continue with the manual system." The newer machine still offered a marginal improvement in image quality over the old system, but without a connection to a computer interface (and printer), the device could only be used together with the existing film development equipment. As a result, the X-ray images produced continued to appear somewhat murky and unclear, a product of old films and chemical agents. Moreover, the functionality of its sophisticated presets (preprogrammed to optimize kVp and mAs settings for each type of examination) was crippled by the hospital's feeble power source. Reliance on petrol-guzzling generators meant that the hospital was only "illuminated" a few hours each day, and the strength of the power was limited. As a result, Joseph and his fellow technicians frequently complained that the machine "refused" each time they pressed the buttons, and they had to devise manual workarounds. Often it was simply pushed aside, the familiarity and reliability of the deteriorating old machine with its fuzzy images preferred to this uncertainty and struggle. The repeated "refusal" of the machine is significant, in that this kind of anthropomorphizing language was common among Joseph and his colleagues, frustrated with a machine that seemed to be beyond their control—much like the underlying infrastructural and governance shortcomings that undermine their work.

In many ways, the story of the new X-ray machine is the story of the contingencies of practicing biomedicine in a place where there are some parts but not quite all, and where machines do exist but are almost always old, secondhand, and often *en panne*—in fact a popular refrain in Kikwit relating to technological infrastructure of all types, not just medical. Larkin (2008) has argued that a sense of lack with respect to technology and infrastructure can be productive of political affects such as resentment toward the state. Whereas Larkin described how the excess of meaning produced by degraded media (images and sounds) offered a critique on the Nigerian postcolonial state, we can see that the hospital's *technologie ancienne*, including the way it restricts newer technologies, performs a similar function for Joseph and his colleagues. The fuzzy images produced by their X-ray machine are also a source of political critique of a Congolese state that is expected to provide for its citizens through a national health infrastructure and a network of state hospitals throughout the country yet fails to do so in dramatic ways, not only failing to provide the basic necessities to enable hospitals like the one in Kikwit to function (e.g., water, electricity, soap, medicines, technologies) but also failing to pay its employees in these institutions a living wage (if it pays them at all).

From this perspective, the idiom *technologie ancienne* (especially in this context, when it is articulated by employees of a state hospital) is not just about comparing different forms of radiographic technology, but it actually a critique of the status quo, and indeed, the (absent) state. Calling attention to their *technologie ancienne* is therefore also a political statement highlighting the failure of the Congolese government to provide what the technicians deem "modern," functional, reliable—in other words, acceptable—material technologies necessary to do their jobs of caring for the population. In this sense, the idiom is also often applied in a context of anticipation, suggesting that while they do not possess such acceptable technologies, it is a sentiment of "not yet," as they expect and even demand to have them in the future. Such anticipatory affect is common in relation to techno-imaginaries (see, e.g., Pype, this volume, and Rahier, this volume).

Carbon (this volume) has highlighted the contradictory affective responses that technologies sometimes produce for the experts who work with them—engineers, in her case—who balance feelings of distress, boredom, and frustration with sentiments of pride, prestige, and success. For Joseph and his colleagues, too, the new machine produced conflicting affective responses. He felt pride in having access to what he described to be a "modern" device, reinforcing the technicians' prominent position in the hospital's social hierarchy. It indicated that his institution was still being supported by the state—more so than other state facilities in the region—and that at least some of the promises of equipment and support would in fact materialize eventually. As a result, he remained hopeful that the situation would improve and eventually they would have a functional digital interface to realize the machine's potential. However, at the same time, the realities of the technical problems, missing components, and insufficient power reinforced long-standing feelings of frustration and powerlessness in the face of state ineptitude, neglect, and even abandonment. Sometimes, the agony was palpable. One morning just before lunch, after laboring for more than thirty minutes to get a clear image on man requiring a spinal X-ray and after multiple failed attempts due to insufficient power (weak X-rays) producing cloudy images, Joseph finally and painstakingly arranged the patient in the precise position once more, only to realize after pressing the button on the machine that the power had gone out. Storming out of the office, he sent one of the other technicians to see what had gone wrong. Learning that they had simply run out of petrol, he shouted in desperation, "How can we function like this?"

Despite these frustrations, the radiology technicians are well aware of the importance of the hospital's X-ray machine for its visibility and appeal in Kikwit's carescape, and they have actively worked to leverage this technology for both institutional and personal gain. During my fieldwork, many complaints were leveled against the hospital's radiology service by patients who had undergone radiological exams, but when they returned the next day to collect their processed films, the technicians refused to hand them over, insisting they stay at the hospital and be treated onsite. For patients, this was seen as a violation of their freedom to choose the therapeutic practitioner of their choice, and unjust seizure of a technological product they had paid a significant fee to obtain. For the technicians, however, they saw the power and desirability of the product of their machine, and they did not want this (medical) image being brought to *tradipraticiens* (especially Ngonga, the primary competitor of the hospital in the realm of fracture care), whom they saw as non-experts in applying this technology (i.e., interpreting the films). This example speaks to the complex flows of *la radio* (and its products) throughout the urban carescape, and ultimately the technicians' inability to fully control the end use of the technology, despite feelings of ownership over the machine itself. More importantly, it also hints at the link between perceptions of prestige of X-ray technology and future-oriented thinking about economic security, both for oneself and for the hospital.

Another example illustrates this point even more clearly. In 2016, the X-ray became a political object within the institution of the hospital itself. State neglect has long meant inadequate or altogether absent pay for the hospital employees, especially for the younger/more recent hires, so the hospital always supplements with a *prime*—an additional monthly premium of USD 20–50—based on their revenues. Individual workers also employ diverse strategies to complement this official income with other means of earning money at the hospital, from demanding petty bribes from patients before treatment (e.g., asking for FCFA 1,000 for "gloves" with no intention of purchasing or using gloves) to selling products like clothing or shoes to patients and other hospital staff during the workday. The radiology service and the pharmacy are the two highest earning departments in terms of revenue (enabling the hospital to pay all workers their *prime*), a fact that is public knowledge among employees, as each department reports its total weekly receipts at the Monday morning staff meeting. The radiology technicians were not shy about reiterating at these meetings the importance of their service and the technology they offered that was not widely available in the city—both in terms of revenue and in terms of attracting patients to the hospital to begin with.

Galvanized by the prestige of their technology, the technicians spearheaded a campaign in 2016 to lobby the hospital's administration to change the structure of the prime payment. Marie felt particularly strongly about this, and every week over a period of several months she stood up and argued that rather than dividing the surplus profits equally among all departments, it should be based on "contributions" made by the service—if she and her colleagues were bringing in a large percentage of the hospital revenue, why should they not be compensated accordingly? Moreover, she reminded her fellow hospital staff that they had specialized training and were not easily replaced, and they undertook great risks of exposure to radiation and toxic chemicals that other departments simply did not have to deal with. The lower-income services were outraged by Marie's persistent lobbying, and every staff meeting during that period devolved into heated arguments followed by appeals to calm, collaboration, and a sense of unity from the hospital director.

The administration never gave in, but this moment in hospital politics is important because it shows how technicians perceive their proximity and access to *la radio* as presenting an opportunity to leverage this prestigious technology to advance and cement or "fix" their own social position in the hospital hierarchy, not to mention the broader carescape. In this sense, visibility work with the technology was directly linked to technicians' personal career aspirations and the means to secure financial stability for themselves and their families, in a state that does not (regularly) pay its public employees. The moment when the electricity went out that led to such palpable frustration for Joseph can also thus be interpreted as not only a technical frustration but a social and political one, because moments like this also jeopardized the service's reputation and revenue, and he and his colleagues had a personal interest in what the technology and its underlying infrastructure meant for their own individual social and economic status.

Ultimately, this example speaks to the ambivalence and at times contradictory affective responses to the technology for practitioners who interface with it in their daily care work. For the technicians, association with *la radio* is empowering, adding value (also economically) and enabling mobilizing and resistance discourse (i.e., resistance to a state that does not pay, as technology empowers them to circumvent, resist hospital/state structures of an "egalitarian" approach). However, at the same time, the director's refusal to give in to the technicians' campaign ultimately produced feelings of boredom, frustration, and despondency over the hospital administration—a stand-in for the broader Congolese state, since it is a state hospital—and its unwillingness to recognize their expertise and prestige in relation to this technology in (economically) meaningful ways. Regardless of these political affects, this example demonstrates the complex entanglements of technology, visibility, and expertise in contemporary care work.

However, the importance of *la radio* in practitioners' visibility work and personal anxieties and aspirations in relation to their position in Kikwit's carescape is not limited to those who (currently) possess the technology. At Ngonga's care center, too, moments of exposure to the products of X-ray technology (as in the case of Justin and the analysis of his digital X-ray) tend to crystallize and lay bare the multitude of dreams, desires, anxieties, and frustrations relating to this technology—and, in this case, the implications of its absence. Such encounters thus frequently lead to discussion of the technology itself and the possibilities it confers—both for care practices and for personal aspirations. Part of Ngonga's frustration with the sharply felt absence of this technology at his fracture center is pragmatic. As he explained, "We lack this technology on-site. If only we had this device here, then we could immediately do everything ourselves, without having to wait or refer the patient." The lack of radiology equipment is a barrier to his ability to offer what he perceives to be both optimal and efficient care, but he acknowledges that it also jeopardizes his business, as there is always the risk that, when he refers his patients to care sites possessing *la radio* for diagnosis, they may not return for treatment. Hence, possessing the technology himself would improve not only his practice in material ways but also his visibility in a competitive market, retaining his patients on-site throughout the entirety of the therapeutic process, and even drawing in new patients seeking access to the technology, even if they were not familiar with his practice.

Yet Ngonga does not just dream about the X-ray machine his main competitors have, or even the digital machines from the capital with super-crisp images that he sees from time to time with patients like Justin. Rather, he dreams of a technology that does not yet exist, a handheld device to instantly reveal fractures, making visible what is beneath the skin in real time.[10] After discovering Justin's fracture was not, in fact, an open fracture as his family had mistakenly reported, Ngonga began to describe his vision of such a device: "If we could have *la radio* here, things would be much better. One day I will have *la radio*. But I need a small machine, so I can hold it over the leg here and directly see what is inside. And then everyone can see." This was not the only time Ngonga discussed his longing for such a machine, and it regularly made its way into narratives about how he saw the future evolution of his practice.

It is worth noting that what "everyone" would be able to "see" with such a device is not just the bones underneath the skin, but also Ngonga's expertise and the technological sophistication of his tradi-modern practice. Describing his dream of such a futuristic version of *la radio* during routine moments of care work, he brings the listeners (care assistants, patients, and their kin) into a shared vision of a not-yet-materialized future that challenges the assumption that sophisticated (new) medical technology belongs to the realm of (Western) biomedicine. Beyond his innovative practice in general and his steadfast dedication to advancing what he calls the "two sciences" (i.e., "tradition" and "modern medicine"), these visions of the future present a possible world with alternative technological and power formations, an alternative modernity of *tradipraticiens* grounded in superior technological mastery. On that morning in Kikwit during the treatment of Justin's fracture, it was Justin's father, a pastor, who summarized this sentiment clearly. After listening to Ngonga's discussion of the X-ray, his vision of the future, and the techniques and "traditional" medicines he would use in this case, he declared with great pride and excitement to the crowd of onlookers assembled that Ngonga's work is a testament to "African knowledge," "intelligence," and "innovation"—a method that should urgently be brought to Europe so students there could learn from the healer's expertise. In this vision, Kikwit could be seen as a medical tech-hub not just in its hospitals, NGO offices, pharmaceutical distribution centers, and provincial health units—but also in the compounds of *tradipraticiens*, with their own cutting-edge technologies.

Accordingly, Ngonga's "design fiction"[11] style vision of future—himself as central protagonist in a new model of advanced expertise accompanied by a reconfiguration of the distribution of medical technology—can be considered an example of Geissler and Tousignant's provocation that dreaming is a crucial rubric for understanding the "emerging present" of care and medical science on the African continent (2020, 6). They argue that dreams like Ngonga's are often centered around transformation, simultaneously critiquing present configurations and articulating alternative (if sometimes impossible) futures of knowledge, expertise, and care. For both Ngonga and the radiology technicians, we can see that these dreams have a performative function. Beyond mere "dreaming-as-hope," these dreams can be seen as a form of work in and of themselves, "through which people make the world they live in and the world they live for, through which they constitute themselves and trace possible futures" (Geissler and Tousignant 2020, 5). The varied dreams and imaginaries of X-ray technology that I have presented here are intertwined with strategies to achieve and maintain visibility in Kikwit's competitive carescape—tracing possible futures linked to their social position being enhanced through access to *la radio*.

Ngonga's imaginary future version of *la radio* is also significant in that it reveals how, as with the radiology technicians, political affects emerge in relation to the technology, in this case challenging the state-supported biomedical system in favor of customary knowledge and expertise. Various types of *nganga* (especially *tradipraticiens*) frequently complain that the state does not support them, pursuing a strictly biomedical state model and even actively undermining them through systems of taxation/extortion. What is new with

Ngonga's dream device is the appropriation of biomedical technology to support these claims to authority and suggest alternative formations of technological expertise.

Ngonga and the radiology technicians are rivals in many ways, competing for attention and validation of their authority by care seekers in a pluralistic urban care market. Despite the fact that they are working on fundamentally different projects—Joseph, Marie, and their colleagues using their access to scientific knowledge and a technological apparatus to seek validation, privilege, and security within the state biomedical system, while Ngonga uses innovation, care, and appeals to "tradition" to challenge the hegemony of this very system—both leverage *la radio* in different ways to meet their ends, stoking their personal ambitions and dreams for the future. Given the significant impact of the urban context and Kikwit's competitive carescape in shaping these dreams, it is clear that the X-ray creates a new space for imagination not just about the city itself but about the dialectics between technology, urbanity, care, and expertise.

CONCLUSION

In this chapter, I have considered the significance of various forms of X-ray technology—ancient monoliths, new digital devices, imagined, future, handheld inventions—in Kikwit's therapeutic landscape and asked how the various presences and absences of this technology produce material and affective implications for practices of care. My analysis of the social worlds of *la radio* in Kikwit has demonstrated that material technologies like the X-ray not only constitute important medical infrastructure shaping therapeutic trajectories and experiences of care toward/within the city, but also create new spaces for imagination about how technology intersects with urbanity in Congo more broadly. The X-ray is thus a part of imaginative city-making in Kikwit, associated with its liminal urban scale and positionality—an urban space associated with technological access, while simultaneously a not-yet-city with deep associations to more rural and so-called traditional practices, epistemologies, and materialities of care.

In considering the ambivalent relationships between this medical technology and the urban residents who interface with it, this chapter has demonstrated how technological flows, presences, and absences intersect with imaginaries of what makes a "city," while also simultaneously being linked to emerging political affects and individual dreams and aspirations. This perspective presents cities like Kikwit as places where competing and contrasting forms of technology give rise to a variety of affective responses and shape contemporary care work in material ways. Attention to both the material and the affective dimensions of various forms of X-ray technology therefore helps us to understand how the social and the political—as well as the "hidden" or "invisible"—aspects of urban living are deeply imbricated with the actual materiality of medical technologies like the X-ray machine. Hence, the absences and various forms of lack relating to the technology are also critical for understand the link between the urban context and the visibility work it necessitates for care practitioners, as are alternative propositions and imagined futures like Ngonga's *radio à la main* and his imaginary future device.

Finally, this chapter has emphasized the dialectics between visibility work and the urban context, as for both *tradipraticiens* like Ngonga and the technicians at the hospital, visibility work relating to the X-ray reveals the importance and productivity of such technologies in a competitive urban carescape. First, Ngonga's innovative tradi-modern assemblage of different technological cultures illustrates the potential of technology to produce new urban forms and practices. Second access to medical technologies, as tools of visibility, is perceived to have the potential to be leveraged by practitioners to establish, reinforce, or transform one's reputation, position, economic prospects, and future security. Even if these strategies are not always successful, they offer new insight into how technology, urbanity, visibility, and expertise intersect in contemporary care work in African cities.

NOTES

1. Non-biomedical healers are referred to by the general term *nganga*. Encompassing a wide variety of epistemologies and practices, these healers include both *nganga ngombo* (spiritual healers or divinatory experts) and *tradipraticiens* ("traditional practitioners" such as bonesetters or herbalists). The city is also home to many prophets, exorcists, and healing churches offering various forms of care. For broken bones, a spiritual cause is rarely suspected, and most care-seekers turn to biomedical options or *tradipraticiens* like Ngonga.

2. For a relevant critique of "smart city" narratives in the Congolese context, see Pype 2017.

3. These reference hospitals are located in the largest village or town of the health zone. Peripheral village health centers serve as a first point of contact for much of the rural population but offer only essential medicines and a nurse or doctor who must refer patients in need of more advanced diagnostic tests or treatments.

4. The hospital also had a radiologist, who held a five-year (license) qualification, in comparison to the technicians' three-year (graduate) degree. However, he rarely came to the hospital, as he preferred to work off-site and send the radiology reports daily after analyzing the films at home. This meant that on a practical level, Joseph was in charge of the daily operation of the service.

5. A related Congolese idiom, of places being either *enclavé* (isolated, enclosed) or *désenclavé* (open, connected) is frequently used to describe cities, but not technologies, which is why I focus on the idiom of "obscurity" here.

6. He also has a simple blood pressure monitor, but the device offers nothing in the way of diagnosis, only helping to determine whether patients are in a suitable state to undergo the painful reduction intervention.

7. See Kusiak 2010 for an exploration of how the broader meanings of radiology can be understood through the related rubric of "transparency."

8. For example, in June 2016, an "administrative delay" in the supply chain resulted in the radiology unit being unable to perform any X-rays for several days because it had completely run out of film—except for a handful on reserve for potential emergencies with high-status patients: as Dr Kasongo explained, "They can't very well have the *médecin directeur* come in with a broken femur and have no films to X-ray him!"

9. This is reflective of the increasing role played by nonstate actors in medical research and treatment in Africa more generally, as public health has been transformed by political and economic liberalization and globalization across the continent and local medical infrastructures are now inextricably linked with transnational flows of research money, medical technologies, scientific knowledge, and the politics of "global health" (Crane 2014; Dilger et al. 2012; Geissler 2015; Nading 2017).

10. Portable X-ray machines do exist, particularly oriented toward veterinary medicine, but not the sort of "X-ray vision" that Ngonga describes.

11. Design fiction is an emerging area of design situated somewhere between science fact and science fiction; through "creative provocation, raising questions, innovation, and exploration" (Bleecker 2009, 7), it enables the exploration and critique of the implications of existing and emerging technologies, presenting alternative technological futures without being grounded in the "realism" of (current) design constraints.

CHAPTER 6

The "Bend-Skin"

A Connector in and Co-Constructor of Mbouda; or, How Post-Global Flows Enable Urban Mobility

VIVIEN M. MELI

TRANSLATED BY VICTORIA BERNAL AND KATRIEN PYPE

Around the world, and also in urban Africa, the four-wheeled car is considered the technical and symbolic embodiment of modernity and modern, urban life, even though it causes traffic congestion and climate and environmental crises (Stefanelli 2021). Far more than motorbike ownership, car ownership is an outward sign of well-being. Traffic jams in cities, though, do not tally with various representations of cars and urban mobility. They combine problems of urban governance, infrastructure, technology, and citizen education. It is in this context of increasing traffic jams that motorbikes have come into more use in many African (but also Asian) cities, where they facilitate mass transport and mobility (Peters 2020; Akmel Meless 2017; Kalieu 2016; Keutcheu 2015; Djouda Feudjio 2014; Tublu 2010; Marchais 2009; Kaffo et al. 2007).[1] In large cities cars and motorbikes share the space with mass transport, such as cars, buses, trams, and sometimes even underground transportation infrastructure. In some small and medium-sized towns, such as Mbouda in Cameroun, the ethnographic terrain for this chapter, motorbikes dominate the transport sector.

This chapter is concerned with the dialectics between urbanity and motorbike performativity in Mbouda, where, since the 2000s, the moto-taxi, popularly called the bend-skin, has become the main means of transport. With its 175,986 inhabitants, Mbouda is one of Cameroon's ten largest cities.[2] Mbouda district, which comprises both the city and a rural hinterland, is home to the Bamiléké people and other ethnic groups of the Ngiemboom language group.

It has the highest annual population growth rate on the African continent at 7.8 percent, and has a population density of almost 734 inhabitants per square kilometer. Anyone crossing the town is impressed with the coming and going of bend-skins. These are parked at various pickup points, where passengers disembark, or drivers wait for users along the roads. The moto-taxis are on display for sale in front of stores and in open-air repair shops. Spare parts for motorcycles are highly visible as well in technological production units for motorcycles. All of this means that the motorcycle and its accessories are everywhere present in the city of Mbouda.

Most shops consist of motorcycle repair and maintenance units. These include what are commonly referred to as *garages*, of which there are thirty-three in Mbouda (figure 6.2). Another type of repair unit is the motorcycle wheel repair and sales unit, of which there are five in town. Other repair shops are only concerned with motorcycle engines. Mbouda counts also three rubber motorcycle parts-manufacturing units and two upholstery units, twelve main bend-skin parking and loading points, and eight points where they can be washed. All these locations make up the bend-skin logistics network in Mbouda. They are products *of* the city, that is, the outcome of a local appropriation of motorcycle technologies for specific bend-skin needs and services in Mbouda. In these spaces, the bend-skins are also adapted to the context of Mbouda, ensuring the circulation and accessibility of goods and people amid limited transportation infrastructures that enable movement between the city and the rural hinterland.

The bend-skin is at the center of an urban socioeconomic world, as it is a source of new jobs. Through the connectivity it ensures and the urban interactions it facilitates, the bend-skin is also a producer of urbanity. The main question in this chapter is, *How* do the bend-skin and the city of Mbouda work to produce each other? Mbouda's urban fabric consists of bend-skin parts; actors such as bend-skin assemblers, sellers, repairmen, drivers; their clients, passengers, and people in the rural hinterland; and Chinese factories and traders.

The chapter is fully in line with Akrich's (1989) observation that city life is produced by technologies in the city, while also building on literature that emphasizes how urban borders and urban margins constantly re-make cities (Sierra and Tadié 2008). In Mbouda, as I will show, the bend-skin and the city co-shape one another: The motorbike is an urban connector, while the bend-skin itself is an outcome of Mbouda's urban context, characterized by uncertainty. The latter is a consequence of the illegality and bottom-up character of the bend-skin economy and of the urban planning crisis in Mbouda. Furthermore, Mbouda's motorcycles are imported from Asia, particularly China. This can be drawn back to diplomatic policies between Cameroun and China (see below). Thus, the bend-skin's connectivity, through which it facilitates connections between Mbouda and the rural hinterland, depends on transnational flows between Mbouda and Chinese factories. The various socio-technical practices (Sheller and Urry 2006) that I will discuss are dialectically related to these two different scales of connectivity.

Although motorcycles are still marginal in the study of urban life, several scholars have explored their worldmaking effects. Peters (2020), for example, describes the performativity of motorcycle cabs in the economy and movement of people in the Indonesian city of Surabaya. Motorcycles in cities in developing countries operate as both transporters and employers (Peters 2020, 477). Following work by Star (1999) on the methodological perspectives of infrastructure ethnography and by Larkin (2013) on an anthropology of infrastructure that combines technopolitics, biopolitics, aesthetics, and technology, other works have emphasized the anthropological perspective of urban infrastructure and technologies in general, and of urban transport in particular. Basri (2012), for example, describes the dynamics of the *ojeg* (moto-taxi) through the young moto-taximen on the island of Ternate in Indonesia. The *ojeg* enables the young to be social actors, represents freedom in the public space, and, at the same time, constitutes an attractive economic activity, generating income while also functioning as political instrument. In similar vein, Bedi (2016) and Peters (2020) consider moto-taxis to be a bottom-up infrastructure, used against systematic traffic jams, that fills urban transport gaps and ensures people's interaction with the city. During these moments of slow movement or even of blockage, motorbikes facilitate faster mobility. They pass between the cars and allow passengers to continue on their way. Mutongi's (2017) historical account of the *matatu* in Nairobi, Kenya, is even more revealing of the social work performed by the motorcycle in society. *Matatus* appear to regulate sociopolitical, economic, and cultural life in Nairobi, while giving the city its vitality. Sopranzetti (2018) draws attention to the civic and political engagement of moto-taxi drivers in Bangkok, where the motorcycle was used to help leaders of the "Red Shirts" escape police and military violence during the May 2010 protests.

The scholars mentioned attend to the life of infrastructures in the city but do not reveal the intimacy between infrastructure production and its milieu. This chapter, zooming in on the technological interactions of bend-skins and the city of Mbouda, will explore this intimacy. As Pype (2017, 114) has noted in her call for a study of technology cultures: "The challenge is to remain attentive to the polysemy of technology, innovation, and creativity, as well as the contiguity of meaning, practices, and experts."

This chapter is organized around three main axes: (a) the urban connectivity produced by bend-skin technology and how this connectivity makes the city; (b) the post-global flows and the adaptations and repairs on which this connectivity is based; and (c) the techno-sociability of the bend-skin in the city. I start with a brief historical overview of the bend-skin economy and then move on to the transnational connections along which bend-skins travel. In the following parts, I explore the "connecting" work of the bend-skin, that is, bringing together economic entrepreneurs and clients, bridging the distance between the rural hinterland and the city, and reassembling economic and state operators in Mbouda.

Since 2007, I have carried out research on transport conditions,[3] urban-rural transhumance (Meli 2011), and transgressions of norms in transport (Meli 2014) in Mbouda. Data collection was carried out between September 2020 and February 2021, then again in June 2021, and followed two procedures. The first consisted of semi-structured individual interviews with the main bend-skin artisans (bend-skinners and bend-skin repairers) in Mbouda and of direct observation of transport practices, technological production units, means of transport, and adaptations and modifications made to motorcycles. The second procedure involved mapping urban connectivity and the distribution of motorcycle technology production points. Observations focused on social services, road infrastructure, and the rural transport supply radius in the city of Mbouda, as well as on activities within motorcycle technology production units.

TRANSPORTATION IN MBOUDA

The moto-taxi dominance in Mbouda's transport sector (Kaffo et al. 2012; Djouda Feudjio 2014) is part of an international dynamic that has developed in Cameroon, with four major spatiotemporal foci. The first event occurred in the towns of Maroua, Garoua, and Ngaoundéré in the 1980s, where people benefited from smuggling practices and the porous border between Cameroon's northern regions (Far North, North, and Adamaoua) and Nigeria. The second focus, once again in the 1980s, was the Eastern Region, particularly in the towns of Bertoua, Batouri, and Yokadouma. This region is geograph-ically adjacent to the northern part of Cameroon. In the National Devel-opment Strategy document for the period 2020–2030 (2020), these regions are presented as those most affected by poverty. Their proximity and porous borders with Nigeria, from where motorcycles were imported by smugglers, facilitated the development of the moto-taxi business. Today, with a secu-rity crisis due to the terrorist exactions of Boko Haram, imports have been completely halted. But the moto-taxi business is still alive and kicking, as the new focus of motorcycle imports, China, supplants the earlier importation of Japanese motorcycles. The third focus, from the 1990s onward, was the Littoral Region, particularly in the city of Douala. It was here that the name "bend-skin" emerged (see below). From then on, Douala became the center of expansion for urban public transport by motorcycles in Cameroon. The fourth focus, from the beginning of this century onward, was the Centre Region, in the city of Yaoundé, the West Region, in the cities of Bafoussam, Mbouda, and Dschang, and the North-West Region, in the city of Bamenda. As a result, all of Cameroon's main cities depend on bend-skin mobility nowadays.

The entry of the bend-skin into Mbouda's social universe occurred at a moment of tense political crisis in the 1990s, also called the "democratic spring" (Smith 2013), which was characterized by "dead city" (*villes mortes*) days. The protests were civic responses to the economic crisis since the sec-ond half of the 1980s. During such days, protesters refused to engage in any economic activity and use of mass public transport was forbidden. Yet owners of motorcycles facilitated residents' mobility. Their intervention during such days of political immobility resuscitated urban life in Cameroon, and grad-ually expanded the sector of moto-taxis. Today, Mbouda is the fourth larg-est bend-skin producer in Cameroon. Mbouda natives are even considered among the pioneers of the bend-skin economy in Douala, Cameroun's largest city (Kalieu 2016). Traders from Mbouda but based in Douala provided pur-chasing benefits to other residents in Douala with a Mbouda background.

The name "bend-skin" draws on the bodily praxis of moto-taxi drivers: Drivers and passengers have to "bend" their body ("skin") as they go over potholes, holding tightly their belongings and their hearts even tighter. The label "bend-skin" has become a cultural and historical-contemporary cate-gory thanks to a folkloric and popular dance among the Bamiléké. The very popular musician André Marie Talla, a blind singer, guitarist, and songwriter, started the craze with his hit "Bend Skin."[4] The idiom of "bend-skin beats"[5] refers to music for riding motorbikes through the crowded and unpaved streets of the city; it also provides the rhythm for a dance that imitates the way one rides that motorbike, slinging one's leg over the seat, adjusting one's weight—shoulders forward, butt back—and holding on for dear life. Bend-skin beats were the sound of Douala, Yaoundé, and other Cameroonian cities in the 1990s.

CHINA-MBOUDA

In the first decade of the twenty-first century, the Chinese market opened up. From that moment on, the cost of products in general, and motorcycles in particular, from China became significantly lower than from Japan, which has a longer history of importation into Cameroon. The November 8, 2012, issue of the journal *Jeune Afrique* wrote about the history of bend-skin in Douala and Yaoundé:

> Senke, Sanili, Lifan, Nanfang, Jincheng, Sanya, and Skygo . . . Massively imported for ten years. Chinese brands are omnipresent. . . . More than 95 percent of motorcycles circulating in these two cities [Douala and Yaoundé] are made in China. . . . These days the dealers—Moto-Sanili, Cocimecam, Grand Bazar, Business Link International, etc.—order directly from China. . . . Today the price of Chinese motorcycles varies between FCFA 300,000 and 490,000 FCFA (between 450 and 750 euros), half that of a Japanese Yamaha, Suzuki, Honda, or Kawasaki. Before the 1990s, the latter cost between FCFA 950,000 and 1.2 million FCFA (between 1,460 and 1,850 euros). Today, the same machines can be bought for less than FCFA 800,000 (around 1,230 euros). The rise of Chinese motorcycles has driven down prices across the whole market.[6]

The importation of motorbikes from China is carried out by dealers approved by the government of Cameroon. They have their headquarters mainly in the city of Douala (the port through which the motorbikes arrive) and have representatives in several localities in the country. The imported motorcycles arrive in Mbouda in crates and are assembled by local crafts-men, trained on the job in garages or for the specific needs of a motorcy-cle sales outlet. Assembly points often double as sales outlets. These spaces are rather unassuming in outlook: They are often only verandas in the commercial buildings and/or motorcycle sales rooms, with no other specific fittings. Local craftsmen manage to manufacture or substitute parts themselves in order to obtain a desired functionality and satisfy needs. When placing orders, importers specify the local uses of motorbikes in Cameroon, and these are manufactured accordingly, thus linking the territories and allowing particularities. Replacement parts may be new, sourced from the motorcycle parts-manufacturing industry in China, or secondhand, coming from other motorcycles already discontinued.

Bend-skin mobility, so characteristic for Mbouda's urbanity, thus only exists *because of* Chinese devices. Here lies the novelty of this chapter: An ethnography of the bend-skin economy allows us to rewrite African urbanity from an assemblage perspective that combines Chinese and Cameroonian objects, ingenuity, desires, and experiences.

THE BEND-SKIN: AN URBAN ECONOMIC CONNECTOR

Margier and Melgaço's (2016) description of a panoply of "urban actors" includes the homeless, prostitutes, street vendors, beggars, young people, elderly women, protesters, and graffiti artists. An overview of urban actors in African cities would certainly include moto-taxi drivers. Their appearance and role in Mbouda society is intimately tied to the urbanization process with its specific challenges for the transport infrastructure and delivery of services. While much research has already been carried out on inadequate urban planning and poor urban governance (Sietchiping et al. 2012; Kurt 2009; Perseil and Pesqueux 2014; Sahabana and Godard 2003), hardly any attention is given to how residents respond to outdated urban transportation systems. This responsiveness provides a more constructive lens on urbanization processes, beyond the common categories of "failure" and "crisis." Guma (2020) questions the well-known narrative of African cities in crisis and the diagnosis of anomic urban infrastructures. He postulates a paradigm of incompleteness and proposes we understand urbanization as a constellation of multiple processes of building urban infrastructures (not only in Africa, but globally). Cities are continually "under construction," so Guma reminds us. They are being built in space and time, very often in a dialogue with arising opportunities and possibilities.

The bend-skin economy constitutes an opportunity within Mbouda's urbanization process that has arisen since the mid-1990s. The economic potential of bend-skins in Mbouda[7] explains the enthusiasm of Roméo, a motorcycle craftsman. At the time of fieldwork, Roméo had sixteen years of experience in the bend-skin economy. Thirty-four years old and married with children, Roméo was the owner of a garage located opposite the municipal soccer stadium in Mbouda. At the time of the research, the garage was situated amid other economic facilities: There was a metal-welding shop, a telephone repair shop, a mobile phone booth and a shop, which also hosted a bar and a restaurant. Roméo's attire hardly suggested that he was a garage owner. At one of our meetings, he was dressed in a boubou with a jacket over it and matching trousers. Even during the rainy season, Roméo works in the open air space of his garage. The garage showed wear and could only be characterized by disorder, yet it was full of social and economic significance. Roméo stated:

> ROMÉO: I make motorcycles, I skin them.
> VMM: You yourself?
> ROMÉO: Yes, yes! I fix them up and sell them afterward.
> VMM: Really? Explain that to me. That's new.
> ROMÉO: Yes! [Laughs] When I buy a motorcycle that is very old, I think about how to modify certain things to bring it up to date. To attract the customer too.
> VMM: You rebuild it?
> ROMÉO: Yes, I rebuild it! Well, I'm replacing everything that's spoiled. Anything that needs changing, I change. I bring it up to date.
> (December 3, 2020)

Roméo engages in a wide set of bend-skin activities: he repairs, maintains, adapts, modifies, transports, and also resells as a secondhand salesman. He furthermore manages the garage and trains future bend-skin professionals. This diversity of practices fits very well Mavhunga et al.'s description of Africans as "makers, hackers, and disruptors of incoming technologies and installers of new meanings, forms, and functions of the technological" (2016, 47).

Essentially informal (Kurt 2009) and implemented by private operators, urban public transport is dominated by bend-skins. In the context of deeply experienced urban poverty, this means of transport represents an opportunity and an attitude of resilience toward what Ela (1998) calls "the challenges of the world below." Contemporary populations in the South are confronted with often unremarked levels of precarity. Poor rural populations migrate to the city and find themselves hemmed in by urban poverty. It is through the bend-skin that they confront their situation of precariousness (Sop Sop et al. 2000). In such a perspective, the bend-skin worlding provided a means of resilience in the face of the urban crisis in Cameroon in the 1990s (Djouda Feudjio 2014).

Mbouda's residents divide the world of urban bend-skinners into two main categories: professional and nonprofessional. The first category, like Roméo, have bend-skinning as their main professional activity, though one of the most obvious features of the bend-skinning economic system is the diversification of sources of income. Each main income-generating activity is usually supplemented by secondary activities. Farming, particularly non-mechanized subsistence farming, is the main secondary source of income for local residents, bend-skinners included. For nonprofessionals, bend-skinning is a secondary source of income. This category of bend-skinner takes advantage of bend-skin income to make ends meet. Within this category, several subgroups can be distinguished. First are the *periodic bend-skinners*: They are primarily motorcycle owners and perform various trades and activities in the private, informalized sectors. They bend-skin in their spare time, according to their own schedule, and thus blend into the anonymity of the city. Then there are the *vacation*, *weekend*, and *bank holiday bend-skinners*: these can be owners, tenants, or drivers employed by a motorcycle owner. The latter pay rent to the owners. Pupils and students, during school and university vacations, are particularly numerous in this category. Finally, there are *occasional bend-skinners*: These are drivers and/or owners of motorcycles, for particular uses, like business services and/or personal uses. For the benefit of their journeys, they transport passengers for payment. They do not deviate from their planned routes and seize the opportunity of a user whose destination is on their route.

The bend-skin profession is at the heart of urban activities, without which many urban activities could not be performed. Peters (2020, 475) made a similar observation in Indonesia, arguing that the motorcycle cab is a major urban infrastructure, bringing together the different parts of the urban economy. Obviously, bend-skinners ensure daily and permanent urban connectivity, day and night, according to their own schedules, particularly in terms of time and place of work. Usually at dusk, most bend-skinners return to their respective homes. The city wakes up to the rhythm of the bend-skinners, who usually begin work at 3:00 a.m., along with *bayam-salams* (resellers operating on the pavement). The bend-skinners set off from the neighborhoods toward the city center and then turn toward the plantations and rural markets before sunrise.

Bakoum, a thirty-year-old bend-skinner, described the importance of the bend-skin: "Without lying to you, . . . I'm here as you see me here. I only have this bike. It's everything to me. The bend-skin is the mother of the orphan" (December 29, 2020). This metaphor of "the mother of orphans" is significant, as the orphan is the image of weakness, of socio-affective vulnerability, and material and economic destitution. The image of the "mother" is protective, caring, nourishing, reassuring, and is of a person providing capital. The comparison is an appropriation of a locally well-known saying: "The market/commerce is the mother of the orphan." This ties in with the Mboudas' long-standing reputation in Cameroon for excelling in commercial activities. Through their dynamism in commercial activity (Champaud 1981), the Bamiléké people embody economic entrepreneurialism, both in agriculture and in the urban economy (Pain 1984; Dongmo 1981). Bakoum's comparison between a mother, the market, and the bend-skin is also illuminating in terms of connectivity: The mother is another connector, in contrast to the figure of the orphan, who is a socioeconomic and financial disconnector. Like the mother, the bend-skin is a social mobilizer, a social resource, and a source of capital.

URBANITY THROUGH THE BEND-SKIN

Cameroonian cities, as in most African countries, are experiencing the pains of galloping and poorly controlled urbanization. They are welcoming large numbers of people for a wide variety of sociocultural, tourist, and economic reasons. Mbouda's urbanization process corresponds with the sprawl model, which is characterized by the devouring of space, following the influx of rural (Yemmafouo 2017) and "poor" (Plat 2003; Diaz Olvera et al. 2002; Agier 1999) populations. Migration between town and country is permanent and increasingly dense. The challenges of this reciprocal interpenetration are sustained by the necessary food requirements of urban populations vis-à-vis the rural world on the one hand, and the identity links that city dwellers have with their villages of origin on the other.

Urban poverty is a consubstantial reality of urban development. UN experts write that "poverty of income at the individual level, but also in terms of socioeconomic deprivation and vulnerability [is] associated with its spatial manifestations in the city" (Commission économique des Nations Unies pour l'Afrique 2016, 23). Spatial manifestations of poverty include settlements in the countryside or close to the city, and frequent flows of the rural population to the city. Urban sprawl helps optimize "rural-urban transhumance" (Meli 2011) by bringing the city closer to the villages. The bend-skin plays a prominent role in the shrinkage of the movement to and from the city. The various bend-skin practices offer maximum opportunity for urban social and spatial connectivity. They help to extend the city beyond its boundaries and, at the same time, replenish it with potential resources from its surrounding rural localities. Like the young *ojeg* drivers in Ternate mentioned earlier, Mbouda's bend-skinners ensure urban social and spatial mediation (Amin 2012). Unsurprisingly, several bend-skinners live in the villages surrounding Mbouda but work in town.

The links that bend-skinners establish not only are the literal paths between different points in the city but also combine technological opportunities and the sociohistorical context of the bend-skin economy. The road is often a translation of a state institutional project, and its significance thus goes beyond the material dimension of facilitating the mobility of goods and people (Harvey and Knox 2015). De Bruijn and Van Dijk's (2012, 1–3) analysis of the Faidherbe Bridge in Senegal goes along the same lines: This bridge connects the locality of Saint Louis to its social, economic, and political dynamics, both historical and contemporary. In the same vein, Pype (2016: 250–251) describes truck drivers as one of various connectors between Kinshasa and the hinterland that appear in the ecosystem of two-way radio communication houses in Kinshasa. The communication tool facilitates social, monetary, and informational exchange between Kinshasa's residents and those in the interior of the Democratic Republic of the Congo, and thus does more than merely help transcend distances in a context of outdated (and sometimes absent) transportation infrastructures.

As for the physical connectivity in Mbouda, it is exactly the poor quality of the road infrastructure that inspires alternative connectors. Only Mbouda's main road, National Highway 6, and the road connecting Batcham Subdivision are paved and in relatively good condition (see figure 6.1). A geospatial assessment based on satellite images and empirical verification in the field shows that almost 92 percent of the city's roads are unpaved and in poor condition. Mbouda's secondary roads, located in the residential areas, are unpaved, making mobility and accessibility by city cabs impossible. With their two wheels and slick design, bend-skinners do not face the same lim-

Figure 6.1. Makeshift assembly site in one of the city's motor-taxi shops. Photo by Vivien M. Meli 2020.

itations as taxi drivers, who usually do not have four-wheel drive. People in services and administrations, schools, health services, administrative services, religious services, and places of commerce depend on the bend-skin (see figure 6.2).

The transport fees are relatively low (from XAF 100, which equals USD 0.16) and meet the spending capacities of both Mbouda's population and those in the rural hinterland. The large number of bend-skins available in Mbouda creates a competitive edge among bend-skinners.

Bend-skins connect Mbouda's town center, its periphery, and the rural localities around. The latter make up the agricultural basin that surrounds the town, making bend-skins the arteries of the local economy. As in many other African cities, Mbouda's population depends on rural areas for food. And here bend-skins and their drivers are vital.

Bend-skin drivers furthermore perform the "right to the city" (Lefebvre 1968) insofar as bend-skins have replaced other forms of access to Mbouda such as walking to the city, taking a bike, or hopping on a truck (driving with food or stones to the city). I therefore argue that the bend-skin democratizes urban space, making it more inclusive. Komba, a bend-skinner, put it this way: "I'm everywhere. In town, in the village, I'm everywhere. Everywhere I go—[including] Babadjou, Batcham, Bangang, Balatchi" (interview, December 29, 2020). Bend-skinners thus can be added to the growing literature of "connectors" in African societies, like the Shona hunters who connect their villages with the animal and the spiritual worlds (Mavhunga 2014) and Kinshasa's radio-telephone operators who connect people in Kinshasa with their families and acquaintances in remote, landlocked rural localities; or truck drivers and sexually active girls with multiple partners (Pype 2016).

ASSEMBLING

The assembling of motorcycle parts from China in Cameroun corresponds to a need expressed by Cameroonian dealers for the local market. The first concessionaires from the 1990s, notably Cocimecam and Grand Bazar, were from Mbouda, which facilitated the introduction of motorcycles. The Mafouoka cinema hall in Mbouda's town center had also been transformed into a store selling motorcycles and spare parts (Kaffo et al. 2007).

Pieces of the bend-skins may be imported from China, but they are also very much a product of Mbouda's moto-taxi experts and of the local population. The spare parts market is supplied not only by imported products but also by locally manufactured equipment, most of which is salvaged. Recycled spare parts are very often salvaged from disused mechanical equipment and motorbikes. Locally made rubber parts are produced mainly from used tires from lorries and tractors. Iron parts are forged locally to meet specific repair, transformation, and adaptation needs. Adaptation and modification materials can be found in various commercial outlets such as hardware stores. The bend-skin thus combines various technological contributions from industry and craftsmen, both international and local, urban and rural.

Once the motorcycles arrive in Mbouda's workshops, where they need to be assembled, they are subject to various modifications to optimize their operational efficiency. In line with Mavhunga (2017b), I wish to draw attention to contextualized knowledges involved in technology production and deployment in Africa. Urban transport practices respond to the specific needs of its environment. Yet when technological tools are imported, these products do not always meet the needs of their users. When they are adapted to local users' needs and desires, the mechanical object becomes a social object. Obviously, this is not unique to bend-skin motorbikes but is also the case for the Faidherbe bridge in Senegal (Bruijn and Van Dijk 2012) and the radio-telephone booths in Kinshasa(Pype 2016). Yet the bend-skin differs from bridges and radio-telephony because the device itself changes. Immediately after the purchase of a new motorcycle, the bike is modified. As Roméo showed, he often needs to reinforce and lengthen the chassis and exhaust pipes, stiffen the shock absorbers, and extend the chain. The most common requested modification is the optimalization of the motorbike's load-carrying capacity. Ancien, a man of around fifty years, and a professional bend-skinner for thirty years, admitted that he was used to carrying "heavy loads":

ANCIEN: Yes, for carrying loads from the villages. . . . I carry two bags of tapioca. . . .
VMM: And you're used to carrying heavy loads?
ANCIEN: Yes, of course. There are things I carry here that can even fit in a cab. I carry on the luggage rack, I carry on the sides, at foot level. You carry things and attach them where you put your feet down. (Interview, December 29, 2020)

Apart from the bags, Ancien usually also transports the client as well. The motorcycles are designed to carry two people (including the transporter), that is, an average of 150 kilograms for two adults. In practice, however, bend-skinners are regularly asked to carry even more people, and to exceed the authorized load capacity of 200 kg. The size of a bag can be up to 1.5 meters long and almost 50 centimeters wide. Each bag can weigh up to 120 kg. With two bags and the rider, a total of 390 kg might be carried on a motorcycle from rural areas to the town of Mbouda.

Given such practices of overloading in a system of unpaved roads, it is not surprising that the bend-skin very often needs to be repaired. This may be much to the frustration of the bend-skinners themselves, though it reminds us that the bend-skin is not inert. These observations remind us that the bend-skin is, in a sense, alive, just like the human being, and is endowed with intentionality, projection, and action (Latour 1984, 1993, 2006). It is an actor involved in a diversity of interrelations and a producer of diverse urban representations. As a "living" object, the bend-skin deploys, compromises, subverts, modifies, and thus contributes to the order of things.

Bend-skin assemblage also occurs on the level of bringing people together and weaving new ties with the state. Some bend-skinners organize in unions or associations, which at times collaborate with administrative authorities (national and municipal), the police, and other organizations, notably political ones. Nevertheless, bend-skin driving is not part of a regularized transportation system. Bend-skinners are not registered with the social security

Figure 6.2. Modifying a motorbike. Photo by Vivien M. Meli.

system, even though they pay taxes; their operating conditions are often not formalized; access to the activity is open and free; and their transport practices are sometimes unorthodox. In Mbouda, bend-skins have no qualms about ignoring traffic lights, putting pressure on pedestrians in pedestrian crossings, or even driving against the flow of traffic by swerving to the opposite side of the road when traffic jams are particularly dense. These acts of urban disorder often take place in the presence of the police, who not only tolerate but sometimes even allow bend-skinners to break traffic laws. As mentioned, they are often overloaded with people and goods, but they are also fast, occupy unauthorized urban spaces and often lead to congestion in public places. Even if certain bend-skinners wear an outfit enabling them to be identified, the idea of clandestinity and informality "sticks to them." Furthermore, their organization is poorly understood. For all these reasons, Mbouda's administrative authorities fear the bend-skin.

The bend-skin is therefore, unsurprisingly, also often dubbed a *moto-clando* or *clando-moto* or *opep* in Cameroon. The suffix *-clando* refers to "clandestine," indicating that motorcycle transport is a parallel practice that does not obey traffic laws, which the yellow cabs approved for urban transport in Cameroon are obliged to comply with. If they collaborate with administrative authorities and the police, then it is based on an effort to maintain order and security. Mutongi (2017, 12), in a historiography of the dynamics of the *matatu* in Nairobi, perfectly translates this relationship to the informal and shows "how informal businesses succeed and evolve, and how they are, over time, incorporated into regulated marketplaces."

Bend-skin connectivity is tied to this informalization. The above-mentioned urban planning crisis in Mbouda has created a laissez-faire disorder. Given that nothing in driving is—a priori—prohibited, the bend-skinners give themselves the right to set up anywhere in the city and make their own driving rules. Ancien, already cited above, gave a striking example of the use of turn signals in the driving practices of bend-skinners in the town of Mbouda:

> ANCIEN: Here turn signals are of no use to me because when you're a driver, when you've already been riding a motorcycle for a while, you already know how you're going to get around. And when you want to stop, you know how to stop. You see, it's those little, little guys who still drive with the blinkers on because they don't yet know how to drive like those who have already lasted like me. Because when I want to stop, I first look behind before turning or before stopping. I can't just stop any old way or cross any old way. When I want to cross, . . . I look behind to see if someone's coming or not.
>
> VMM: Is that why you take off your blinkers?
>
> ANCIEN: Yes, yes, I've removed them. They don't help me at all. (Interview, December 29, 2020)

These practices defy the rules of automobile driving. Ye, bend-skin drivers respond to the urban crisis by improvising and by being unpredictable themselves.

SUMMARY

One cannot imagine Mbouda's urbanity without the bend-skin. Bend-skin connectivity makes up Mbouda's urban character because of the numerous local technological production units found there, and its larger logistical network. Yet the worlding of bend-skin goes beyond mobility per se and contributes to the dynamics of new forms of urbanization thanks to a mesh of local technologies, their intimacy with the rural world, and post-global materials. Indeed, this chapter has shown how urban connectivities performed by the bend-skin in Mbouda are only possible thanks to the modified Chinese motorcycle. The case study illustrates how a study of the dialectics of technology and the city turns into a complex analytic that brings together histories of technology, experiences of uncertainty, and desires for mobility. Just like any other technology, the bend-skin generates sociability.

Furthermore, the bend-skin is composite, as is the city. Both are itinerant and strategic constructions. Bend-skin urbanity, then, is both the product and the generator of the city, constantly subject to new global movements of objects from within and from outside. This production of urban techno-sociability brings together the global and the local, thus deploying the complexity of the democratic rationality of actors and systems in social production. Without the city, the bend-skin cannot be produced either, as it generates, through its urbanity, a network of local technological productions essential to its operationality. The deconstruction and reconstruction of Chinese motorcycles in Mbouda makes them a local technological production that frees itself from any technological determinism, even in environments where formal skills are absent.

From the above thus emerges an image of intimacy between the bend-skin and the town of Mbouda: They are mutually dependent. If city of Mbouda produces the bend-skin, the bend-skin is its spatial, financial, and economic connector. The described resourcefulness and disorder draw on the informalized economy and thus turn the bend-skin into a key figuration of "Bamiléké dynamism" (Ndongmo 1981). As such, the bend-skin is a producer of urban life and livelihoods.

NOTES

1. The appearance of the moto-taxi in the urban economy is not unique to Mbouda (Kaffo et al. 2007; Djouda Feudjio 2014, Keutcheu 2015; Kalieu 2016). Rather, informalized transport practices in different countries and regions of the world get various kinds of labels, ranging from *boda-boda* in Uganda to *matatu* in Kenya, *zeminjan* in Benin (Marchais 2009; Tublu Komi N'kégbé Fogâ 2010) and Togo, *Jakarta* in Senegal, *Okada* in Nigeria, *Gbakas* and *Woro-woro* in Côte-d'Ivoire (Akmel Meless 2017), *habal-habal* in the Philippines, *rickshaw* in India, Thailand, Bangladesh, and Sri Lanka, and *moto-clando* or *clando-moto* or *opep* in Cameroon.

2. https://www.populationdata.net/pays/cameroun/aires-urbaines

3. https://www.ssatp.org/sites/ssatp/files/publications/ConferenceWorkshopMaterials/RoadSafetyConf2007/DayTwo/IFRTD/ifrtd-CameroonWomenRSafety_Fr.pdf

4. By then he had been a hit-maker for twenty years.

5. https://www.forcedexposure.com/Catalog/tala-andre-marie-bend-skin-beats
-cd/RETRO.023CD.html and https://afrolegends.com/2012/06/05/bend-skin-or-moto
-taxi-a-way-to-avoid-traffic-bend-skin-ou-moto-taxi-un-moyen-deviter-les-embouteil
lages/

6. https://www.jeuneafrique.com/24691/economie-entreprises/les-motos-chinois
es-envahissent-douala/

7. The bend-skin reflects the contribution of the motorcycle to the culture of the
Wichí fishermen on the Pilcomayo River in Paraguay (Preci 2024), accommodating the
economic practices of the city and the hopes of populations in search of urban rent.

CHAPTER 7

Technicity and Co-Citizenship

Campus Connectivity in Tanzania

KOEN STROEKEN AND MOHAMED GHASIA

This chapter contrasts the technological survival mode we call technicity with citizenship, the acquisition of rights. Cities epitomize settings where those without technicity live their lives in jeopardy. Technicity compensates for lack of citizenship, without remedying the lack. Together, our ethnography of city life and our survey on mobile learning illustrate this ambivalent situation. The data also point to a "new" strategy of solidarity that we term co-citizenship.

Technicity is the practical ability to make the most out of a situation where state-guaranteed rights and corresponding duties are absent. By "the most" we should think, first of all, of personal benefit, which comprises plain survival. "A situation where" refers in practice to the "technicities" of East Africa requiring urban cunning for survival. Despite its professed claim to the opposite ethos, the Tanzanian university campus appears to be a microversion of such cities where success depends on the ability to gain access to an existing field of opportunities. Universities try to incarnate the idea of citizenship and equal rights in their approach to students. The data, however, show universities struggling to ensure technological citizenship and failing to do so. The materiality of lack plays a crucial role in this struggle, but also the affect that both students and staff attribute to optimal or degrading infrastructure. Affect is determined by cultural expectations. Hence, before zooming into the use of technological infrastructure in a sample of Tanzanian university campuses, we look into the affective urban context wherein those universities are set.

The first half of our chapter therefore synthesizes qualitative and quantitative data on (political) distrust, technicity, absence of citizen rights, and urban trends, mostly in the field of communication technology. Participant observation was done in urban neighborhoods of Dar es Salaam, Nairobi, and Morogoro and peaked for the first author in early 2021. He has coordinated since 2012, several times a year in situ, academic exchange between Flemish universities and a Tanzanian institute of higher learning. The second author is a Tanzanian educational technologist who grew up in both rural and urban settings and conducted the survey on mobile learning.

Based on current developments of technological culture in East African cities and university campuses, our analysis will come up with a third, hybrid condition between technicity and citizenship. The urban neighborhood, such as an inner city's set of streets, and the enclave that is a campus seem to paradoxically give way to an orientation on rights, albeit collective rather than individual rights. For this (post)global urban condition the chapter proposes the term "co-citizenship." The medieval guilds were an example of such indirect citizenship, in another time and place, although no less in a context of urban technology-based business and financial insecurity (Weber 1998). Guilds organized technicities (skills, tools, networking) to guarantee their members' livelihood and attain a kind of citizenship in the city. New forms of indirect citizenship have to be considered today that defy the binarities of modern and traditional, global and local, urban and rural. Tanzania's recent history and shift in political culture help to explain the lesser probability of a citizenship in the strict sense.

TECHNICITY: A PLACE WITHOUT RIGHTS?

Walk the streets in the densely populated neighborhoods of Nairobi and Dar es Salaam, or the smaller cities of Mwanza and Morogoro, and every sound, smell, and view will exude technicity. Each dweller attempts to squeeze his or her presence in. The numerous bundles of electricity cables spanning the intersections attest to the absence of a bigger plan anyone could fit into (figure 7.1). A line is added with every newcomer to the neighborhood. Nobody uses a map (*ramani*, Swa.) to go from A to B. One follows roads and moves between intersections. Policymakers in Nairobi apply the same logic by building apartment blocks one after another to win terrain back from the slums, or "informal settlements," that used to be there. The builders win by force of "concrete" presence.[1] It is a war out there, technicities colliding.

One technicity is that of the vagrants. The other is that of the top dogs.

Figure 7.1. A tangle of wires in Dar es Salaam. Photo by Koen Stroeken.

The layers never meet yet share the lack of a concept, it seems, that of citizenship. That's "Kanairo for you," the inhabitants say, 'little Nairobi," a place supposedly without rules or rights. Another slur is "Nairobbery." "Kanairo" is the subtitle between brackets of the song "Tabia za WaKenya" (The characters of Kenyans) by the artist Mejja, who illustrates the absence of rights through the hyperbole of someone seen entering a toilet and still having the door pounded, to be asked if it is occupied (*Mkenya akienda choo na aone kuna mtu, bado atabisha na aulize "Kuna Mtu?"*).

In between the two layers, members of the lower middle class have no qualms about paying high rents for those apartments in a midlevel high rise. Every working day they walk across the "dangerous" neighborhoods surrounding the buildings because the time and place at which they pass as commuting pedestrians is theirs. They are lucky enough to have no map in mind of the slum that could scare them. A citizen in the true sense, relying on equal rights and duties, might be alarmed because of the threat mapped at macroscale and the absence of externally organized order that guarantees rights: All things considered, anything could happen when crossing the slum.

In technicity, there is no scale at which people have rights, and "all things" can be considered. One goes from A to B. As my Kenyan friend and I observe life in the informal settlements along the Mathare River in Nairobi, we note how the commuters conquer their place and time through habit of passage and speed of pace. When asked directions to a place nearby or information about a pending event such as a football match, they quickly signal that they do not know. They know A and B, that's it. Why indeed not remain blissfully ignorant about the volatile surroundings? Street vendors and slum dwellers for their part cannot count on keeping their integrity, their privacy, a moment of peace, a safe place. Nor can they take a rest in the assumption that the field of opportunities sleeps too. Sunday exists only for the center's fancy shops. In the narrow streets the bustle dies out slowly around midnight to start again before sunrise. Every day.

"Mjini ni mjini" ("The city is the city"), says the cabdriver in Dar es Salaam stuck in traffic. Any free space will be filled by other cars lying in wait behind and beside him. The jam and the intensity due to density defines the city and its technicities. The urban setting has a technical aspect in that inhabitants need to bridge distances between places that depend on each other for production and consumption. Hence, traffic and communication are pivotal and remain unaffected by a slumbering economy. Hordes of taxi motorcycles (*boda-boda*) with one or two passengers sitting behind the driver are in continuous movement. Others wait at intersections, their engines roaring in anticipation.

On the road the rules are simple: *The larger vehicle has priority*. Bicycle and pedestrian must fend for their lives. *Bajaji* tricycle-taxis irritate because they occupy an intermediate place. They drive very close to the larger vehicles, like agile pedestrians crossing traffic, and maneuver themselves out of the traffic jam, yet are almost as fast as cars that have struggled themselves free through a shortcut. "Ujanja" (cunning), the cabdriver remarks. This city knows no citizenship in the strict sense. But it has institutions (established practices) that naturally grow out of the interaction between technicities. With these institutions come rules and privileges, which brings us back to rights. The car can count on the motorcycle ceding passage. Is that not a right implying a duty for the motorist? Not legally enforceable, some guarantee persists.

Consider a handful of examples, ethnographic vignettes, illustrating the collision of technicities by the unsteadily employed youth in the city. Have the street struggles of these millions of landless not generated together an indirect form of citizenship in the city?

Figure 7.2. The booth of a *fundi* in Mwanza. Photo by Koen Stroeken.

A shoe-seller on the market tells us that he has an established business but that he began one day with displaying a few secondhand shoes on the street. After a while he had his spot secured because the totality of vendors condoned his daily return there. This was no minor feat, reproducing an event that has happened to the daring enough on so many street corners for decades. The guarantee by community hall came later as his shifting locations climbed the hierarchy to get a spot on the market.

In the village too, the one who owns no chicken can catch a few pigeons first. Once these are sold, a hen is bought. In time follow goats and eventually perhaps a cow or two. The taxi owner started by driving someone else's car using Uber and Bolt. Opportunities are out there and quite reliably so, because steps toward improvement got fairly institutionalized in the shadow of the formal market's regulations. Far from an individual enforceable right, something of a guarantee does hover loud and clear at the horizon.

Official sellers of communication technology are only allowed to sell certain spare parts to repair iPhones, but a *fundi*—an artisan or technician such as a mechanic—has no limits save talent and need not obey the company's rules, so he (usually a man) will have his small booth just outside an official shop, lying in wait to squeeze in his technicity, often with much higher efficacy (figure 7.2). The *fundi* started off on a chair behind a box under an umbrella at the street corner. Like a guild in its nascent stage, the group of vendors or artisans in this case guarantees the process, an informal, collective right to a place in the street and concomitant subsistence. The guild is invisible, has no charter, yet exists in the distance, at the horizon.

Civil society initiatives and international politico-economic interventions tend toward ensuring that all members of a community become legally recognized subjects, protected by the state and considered equal in the eyes of the law. That is the standard definition of citizenship, which postcolonial studies of failing states and expanding megalopolises contrast with the pitiful skill of harnessing disorder to one's advantage (e.g., Daloz and Chabal 1999; Simone 2013). Africanist ethnographies teem with such imagery, locally created and evocative, about self-reliance, resilience, and coping with uncertainty (Whyte 1997; Waage 2006; Pype 2011). Categorized here together as "technicity," these capacities thrive in settings without a providing state. The settings prompt pity and charity, which at the same time signifies exclusion from the right as a citizen to livelihood, voting, education, and land. A European example of charity paired with exclusion is to have the administrative recognition of asylum seekers depend on arbitrary signs of need, such as illness or helplessness, hence on people's "bare life" (Ticktin 2006; Fassin 2007). The specter of surging neoliberalism, qualified by Agamben (1998a) as the desolate fate of *homo sacer*, has inspired a host of critical anthropological studies over the last two decades. The stresses of communication technology in the African urban context partake of the neoliberal specter. Its refractions in the form of new opportunities can be captured through the contrast between citizenship and technicity. The internet has extended the meaning of citizenship. As Bernal (2014) demonstrated for Eritrea, digital society expands the "imagined community" of the nation to comprise diasporas and their social media. The co-citizenship of the contemporary nascent street guild is another group formation and solidarity stratifying the network in city and campus so as to extrude some form of right and security.

DISTRUSTING THE STATE: TECHNOLOGY AS OPPORTUNITY

Could the state be perceived by its citizens as supporting them? What we argue next is that in a state of technicity the state becomes another player trying to make the most of it for itself. The state is distrusted for that reason, all the more because of its privileged access to the field of opportunities. This access means that the state's technicity does not collide with that of the other players in the field, for instance in the field of communication technology. The state in Tanzania is strangely enough the actor least likely to stimulate citizenship.

Think of M-Pesa, a Kenyan app invented to send money by phone. In Tanzania, the network providers such as Vodacom and Airtel make a profit by deducting a small percentage for every transaction (*miamala*). The deductions (*makato*) decrease proportionally if the sum transacted is higher. Opportunity knocked, we are told by a vendor. What emerged soon is a market of deductions (*soko ya makato*). The agent (*wakala*) with most clients can offer the better rates. Agents advertise their phone number wherever they can. They specialize in money that is not cash but "thrown" up in the air (*kurusha*), money that "floats." They are the lower middlemen, like the plot owners of artisanal mines inland making money out of the gold diggers but still depending on the dealers to get the gold sold and something returning after government taxes and the dealer's profit (Stroeken 2011).

We learn about the city's rules, the technicity, as we listen to stories of failure. The phone-network providers attempted to imitate the agents' success by emplacing their own agents with flashy booths on the best spots in the city. They failed because could not swap companies. They lacked flexibility, a key asset of technicity. Their freshly painted comfortable booths are usually empty or closed.

Now comes our point. The agents also inspired the government, which saw an opportunity in levying on the transactions. Going by comments online, newspaper articles, and informal conversations, the government intervention was seen as that of an additional party getting a piece of the pie.[2] The effort made by the minister of finance, Mwigulu Nchemba, to emphasize the common good that the levies (*tozo*) serve—"this country is yours"—is telling of the difficulty for state actors to introduce a logic of citizenship, at least an individualistic one of a citizen loyal and taxed in return for voting rights and public services. The affect the state's intervention in technology instills is distrust because the intervention has not emanated from technicities colliding in a playing field, as we described for markets and vendors in the previous section. After four weeks of levies on phone transactions, the minister calculated that the state had collected over two million euros "to implement various social development projects, including the construction of health centers, road infrastructure, and strengthening the education sector."[3] But he suspected the reaction would be only more distrust. His address to the general public about the levies sounded like a desperate call to transition from technicity to citizenship. The call was particularly ambivalent because of his confirmation that the government is a player with a stake: "My one request to Tanzanians who look at me is [to know] that this [money] is all ours and not the government's. This country is yours where you are, and the money is yours, and these things we were planning to do are yours, so all this is ours."[4]

A redistributive organization treating all citizens equally is indeed the condition required to speak of a state and citizenship. Yet the shift of perspective is not self-evident in a state of technicity. The facts actually contradict the idea that there would be a level playing ground and that the state would remain outside the network of competing actants. Further on, we will observe a similar challenge to Tanzanian universities for their top management and personnel to not appear as privileged players competing in the same field as students and predating on the latter's technical possibilities. It is through infrastructure that a government or a university can prove to be a provider, because of the affect attributed to materiality.

Paradoxically, the political figure most instrumental at some point in feeding suspicion of the government, undermining the role of the state as impersonal provider, was Tanzania's own president, John Magufuli. In his position as strong leader, he reproduced the image of a stateless field of competing technicities. In a speech a few months before his death, he called farmers the real *wasomi*, "the learned," because they came up with eco-friendly alternatives in electricity production, whereas his engineers of the parastatal TANESCO were lagging.[5] He had the confrontation televised between the two groups of players in the field.

Most notorious is Magufuli's fight against corruption, which drew attention to the personal benefits sought by civil servants as well as foreign governments and investors. Unlike democratic states presuming citizenship, here belief in the principle of government is not a given. Lying at the periphery of the cultural system, the belief will depend entirely on personal opinion, which fluctuates. To illustrate the volatility of the opinion, hence absence of the cultural principle of state and citizenship, a statistic may help.

More than 70 percent of a representative sample of the Tanzanian population agreed a year or two after Magufuli's election that corruption had

Table 7.1.

"In your opinion, over the past year, has the level of corruption in this country . . . ?"		
	% 2014/15	% 2016/18
Increased a lot	**39.0**	4.1
Increased somewhat	**27.6**	5.4
Stayed the same	14.7	8.8
Decreased somewhat	10.2	**51.1**
Decreased a lot	2.7	**21.4**
Refused to answer	—	0.1
Don't know	5.6	9.2
N	2,386	2,400

Source: Afrobarometer surveys R6 and R7.

decreased "somewhat or a lot" (see table 7.1). Just before his election, in the previous Afrobarometer survey, more than 75 percent said corruption had increased. How to explain this radical shift in only a couple of years? In a field dominated by technicity, the personal figure overshadows the office and political institution. Trust in a leader and his battle against corruption does not strengthen citizenship; rather it does the opposite. It stresses for everyone the necessity of technicity, of dealing with the shrewdness (*ujanja*) of the corrupt, as one had to before with witches through magical protection.

Magufuli's outspoken adherence to conservative Christian dogma about birth control, his Covid-19 denialism, and internationally anticonformist position also regarding LGBTQ rights were ever so many instances of refusal to submit to the secular power of a state and international body of states. On the continuum between technicity and citizenship, his views occupied the first pole. His battle against corruption, which could have laid the groundwork for a new state, was welcomed by the general public as an act of individual prowess, capturing the bad guys, firing or fining them. For all the rhetoric of his party about nation-building, he did not consider critical journalists as allies on the road toward a modern democracy of citizens (Cheeseman et al. 2021). They were opponents when showing better skills at captivating the audience, to be arrested on the accusation of false and inflammatory reporting (Paget 2021). On the continuum ranging between democracy and authoritarianism, his rule markedly belonged to the second pole, moreover in the Tanzanian postcolonial tradition (Becker 2021). But in his attitude to the Covid pandemic, he actually acted like many in the country: to distrust any type of national or supranational power; to not rely on imported vaccines and public health measures, whose workings one cannot verify and whose origins are a capitalist exploitative system reminiscent of colonial trauma; instead, to use herbal medicine. That is the pinnacle of technicity: Do not trust intrusive interventions in the body; rather, strengthen your immunity and have your daily infusion of ginger, lime, and lemongrass (*mchaichai*). The dominant perspective of the people and their leader remained oriented by technicity.

In Tanzania, it is accepted discourse to associate progress, *maendeleo*, with the fate of the nation (*taifa*) and government (Malipula 2014). The belief in organizing a nation in service of all, as stipulated by founding president Nyerere and the socialist party ruling until today, requires a cultural leap toward citizenship. It was preached as an ideology in political rallies and sung about in school (Askew 2002). But was it practiced? Not in the eyes of local hip-hop artists lamenting the necessity of "brains" (*bongo*) to survive in Tanzania (Stroeken 2005). The sector of education could offer that counterweight, displaying how the relation between civilian and state should be, in terms of rights and duties. In an ideal world represented by the relatively secluded space of a campus or classroom, students are to exert their right of information and freedom of speech. It is by thus preparing them for a life as citizens that they will be inculcated with the values of a level playing ground, a governing body, and the belief in its workings. These they will disseminate later as enlivened values. Besides knowledge, the students have access to technology as a pivot on the way to change in society.

The rest of the chapter explores whether the sector has met this challenge in Tanzania. Information and communications technology (ICT) for blended learning hands students the tools for a level playing ground. The teachers and university management support this "citizenship" of the student. Tanzanian civil servants have been trained to take their task of nation-building seriously. If not from the mind and soul of the educated elites, how else could the cultural basis for a state be built? The analysis of data is preceded by an introductory section on mobile learning in Africa.

MOBILE LEARNING AND ASSEMBLAGE

Over the past decades, smartphones have become ubiquitous in our lives due to their flexibility, portability, affordability, and easy-to-use multifunctionality. By the end of 2015 there were more than 557 million unique mobile subscribers in Africa alone; mobile penetration in Africa quickly topped that of electricity and safe and clean water (Fritschi and Wolf 2012). In a hands-on approach described by Mavhunga (2017b), Africans import and repair cheap or secondhand mobiles and reassemble the cases, parts, and applications to fit their needs of small-scale business, image-laden communication, and self-styling. The portability of smartphones permits entrepreneurial brico-lage, or "assemblage," by young investors with limited means (Afutu-Kotey and Gough 2019). Not coincidentally, smartphone apps are probably the first modern technology innovated by African youth. The kind of innovations concern task-related functions with broad accessibility, presuming a horizon-tal playing field of many users.

Besides the well-known invention of M-Pesa, the mobile money service, success stories across the continent include Ushahidi, meaning testimony, which was deployed to map reports of violence in Kenya after the elections in 2008. Others are the Eneza educational app, which offers SMS-based virtual tutor services; the Uganda-based Jumia/Kaymu/OLX app, offering online shopping possibilities to the registered retailers in East Africa; the Orin app from Nigeria, enabling fans of African music to share their favorite genre; the MoMath project at the University of Dodoma in Tanzania; the Moodle mobile research app at the University of Dar Es Salaam; and the MoLODUM at the University of Makerere (Muyinda et al. 2010). Knowledge is distributed across various and diverse networks and grows endogenously, unhampered by hegemony centers, thanks to the mobile materiality of the devices. Users skip the manual to let the software speak in response to their experimental trials. This "mutual causation" between user and thing, of which Mbembe (2016) discerned the precolonial roots in his Abiola lecture, has introduced a dimension of democratic access that modern technology was not used to. However, as argued by Mavhunga (2017a) as well as Odumosu (2017), African universities remain marginalized in science, technology, and innovation if their role is limited to the second-level design of reassembling modules to fit needs.

In Tanzania it is uncommon to find a university student or teacher with-out a mobile phone. The virtual spaces of WhatsApp, Facebook, Instagram, Linked-in, Messenger, and the like are connected and reconfigured to fit any variety of tasks. If well implemented, m-learning is an ideal alternative to overcrowded classrooms (Lehmann and Söllner 2014). Contingencies of mobile learning comprise, next to the digital literacy of students and teachers, the material connectivity and ability to pay for the internet as well as availability of content that reflects social needs. Mobility empowers and liberates if the infrastructure in itself is no issue and access to it is regulated. Otherwise the situation becomes one of hypermobility, a concept applied by Adams (2005) to transport systems that are congested and polluting.

The next section explores m-learning deployment on campuses in public universities in Tanzania. On top of annual periods of participant observation by both authors intensified since 2016, the second author conducted semi-structured interviews with open-ended questions among twenty-five lecturers, forty-eight students, and seven ICT experts from four universities in Tanzania: Mzumbe University, Open University of Tanzania, the University of Dodoma, and the University of Dar Es Salaam. These institutions were chosen based on their complementarities and diversity of characteristics, including number of students, level of experience, and the variety of study programs. Additionally, the second author explored policy documents to understand to what extent the management supports learning technologies.[6]

OBSTACLES TO CITIZENSHIP ON CAMPUS: A SMALL SURVEY

Mobility is key to m-learning: the learner should participate in the learning process without being constrained by time and space (Traxler and Kukulska 2016). Mobility depends on the connectedness of the learner's devices to public space (the internet) regardless of the location, on campus and off campus. In the African context and Tanzania in particular, two modes of connectivity for students exist: through the university infrastructure or through a mobile internet service provider. In our survey, mobiles ownership was 80 percent among students and 95 percent among lecturers. M-learning readiness among students was high. As described by a student from Open University Tanzania:

> I can say it is so helpful to us because regardless where you are, you can open the app and study. So I can say it helps us students regardless if we're on a *daladala* [commuting]. If someone sends you a question, you can refer to your notice and answer the question.

A bleak picture emerges, however, when probing general access. The four universities suffer from unreliable connectivity. Wi-Fi services are accessible in silos entailing low bandwidth (<80 Mbps) and networks overload. As described by a male MU student:

There is no internet at the hostels. When you want to use the internet, you have to go to a few classrooms. If you are late, you find classrooms are full. Then you will have to wait or come back at night.

In one of the universities the wireless hot spots are disconnected, whereas in the other three universities, if the hot spots are online, the quality of service verges on nonmobile. The universities count on students' and educators' owning quality devices and on their ability to pay for subscriptions to remain connected. This is where the promise of *universitas* is betrayed. Students' success depends on their technicity, making the most out of a situation without formal rules.

If the situation were the same for every student, one might discern a minimal level of equal rights. But this is not the case. Learners' abilities to own devices differ. At odds with the aforementioned enthusiasm about mobile phone ownership is the fact that few can afford the upkeep, with great variety in terms of connection speed and network access as well as data bundles. In Tanzania, students rely on insufficient government loans to buy devices; on as little as TSh 700,000 (USD 280) a semester to cover meals, accommodation, and stationery. It is out of necessity that students sacrifice meals and stationeries to buy cheap mobiles. Those not lucky enough to receive a loan may attempt to get a smartphone anyway yet be incapable of keeping the little machine operable at the level required for learning. How could they participate on equal terms in m-learning if to "bring your own device" (BYOD) is the model of participation? Without policy and effective intervention, mobiles divide the haves and have-nots instead of remedying the gap. For the majority of our respondents, m-learning is an ambivalent experience.

One would expect support from the teachers and management to safeguard the promise of citizenship for all. However, the infrastructural challenge is exacerbated by the variety in pedagogical engagement. To provide solutions to known educational problems or offer new possibilities that enhance the learning experience, educators have to be skilled and ready for the transition. Despite enthusiasm from the stakeholders, the absence of key expertise from multimedia instructional designers is what defines the studied universities. Tanzanian universities lag behind in ICT, which correlates with their stagnation in publication output and international rankings.[7] The majority of aforementioned apps come from the informal sector. Most university teachers in our sample lacked skills to design, develop, and conduct pedagogically sound mobile courses, to ensure quality delivery of courses as well as assessment and authentication, or to facilitate student engagement so as to reduce the transactional distance with the teacher, as advocated by (connectivist) theories of m-learning (see Siemens 2014). The decision to deploy m-learning seems shaped not by social need or by the will to subvert hegemonies or decolonize knowledge, but by technological buzz.

The confusing message of *preaching citizenship while expecting technicity* goes together with an antimobile discourse simmering among some lecturers, who pride themselves in banning use of phones during class sessions. The online space for student-teacher consultations remains empty. Clearly, digitization projects are not embraced by everyone at the universities. There is a generational resistance to change. Some lecturers still do not accept ideas obtained from e-sources. For all the democratic capacity incorporated in a device, when we look at use, the conditions are absent for a feedback loop to adapt the technology to the needs of a Tanzanian campus. Rather, the more the universities of our sample participate in the global digital field, the more the students and teachers perceive the widening gap with the rest of the world.

The institutional challenge and the role of top management cannot be omitted either. Most African countries have national ICT policies that embrace the integration of digital technologies in their education systems. Likewise, the universities and research institutions have policies aiming at enhancing teaching, learning, and research through the same technologies. Unfortunately, these policies are not coordinated at all levels of the government. (For example, the deployment of computers at pre-university levels in Tanzania does not take into account the basic fact of nonexistence of electricity in those schools.) Because of the policy gaps, universities and schools are forced to institutionalize their own rules and procedures, of which some, like the banning of mobiles on school premises, can be detrimental to bridging social gaps with the rest of the globe. On top of the policy gaps comes the lack of commitment to implementation. Despite exciting augurs concerning the deployment of the new computational tools, overreliance on traditional learning methods is what defines the universities in Tanzania.

HYPERMOBILITY ON CAMPUS: TECHNICITY AS RIPOSTE

A key concern for analysis of the data above is that universities count on students and educators to own mobile devices of high quality and carry the costs for their use. Part of the university's tasks and costs are thus transferred. An analogy can be drawn with our two cases of a network provider and a ministry reaping benefits from mobile transactions. Like them, the university then resembles a player in the field rather than a provider. The groundwork for a country of citizens is not laid when teachers expect the younger generation to cope through bricolage. The teachers did so in their time as juniors, surviving by combining jobs. Tanzanian civil servants have never had wages that could cover all costs of life, so they accumulated patronage relationships to obtain access, cultivated land in their spare time, built a guesthouse, or remodeled vans for transportation. In the same tradition do mobiles get entangled with learning while not being formally implemented by the university.

Mobiles offer the total package of access, mobility, and prestige. When respondents praise accessibility, flexibility, and personalization of learning, we have to keep in mind the sacrifices made, such as skipping lunches because mobiles compensate for the unfit infrastructure, including libraries. Social platforms such as Facebook and WhatsApp have become the main communication tool among students and teachers due to the lack of institution-based services. They are used to share class announcements, assignments, and lecture notices as well as to discuss concerns of the class projects. Students use WhatsApp to form multiple groups. These groups are often temporarily formed because task-related. The temporary groups rehash as well as bridge people's social networks. Users choose certain apps for particular tasks, and within the apps they structure groups or teaching modules according to their needs. The users are the nodes of the system co-designing the technology in practices stretching the manual's possibilities. The technology of apps is designed to permit adaptation and personal customization of functionalities.

On campus, however, what surfaces mainly is an immobilized environment. It has created a hypermobile learning network. The epithet "hyper" warns that this is an unsustainable, nervous riposte. Indicative is the ambiguous imbrication of private and public spheres that portable devices permit. Precisely what beguiles young mobile users sitting on the bus on their way home has unintended implications. As public services like schools count on their students' private means and time, the partitioning between private and public sphere of exchange is withering away. As we learned from the experiment of setting up a location-based social media app called mfunzi at Mzumbe University, students show little preoccupation with the risks of privacy infringements (Stroeken et al. 2015). The safely shielded institutional app mfunzi of the university community could not compete with the mentioned commercial social media blurring leisure and study. In fact, students expected an app to communicate across private and public spheres, for they then feel in charge as pluriversal users deciding on which groups to form.

The technicity deployed on campus is an informal remedy relying on the private sphere that comes with a cost: The reception of knowledge is mediated by the quality of one's device. Social inequality and the mechanism of the market driving consumer choices should not impact education. The groundwork for future citizenship withers under the frail imbrication of public and private spheres on and off campus. In the wider society, we pick up signs of criticism about social media conflating spheres. Whether Pentecostal Christians in Kinshasa (Pype 2017a) or Tanzanian *bongo fleva* artists in Dar es Salaam, the very groups that embrace and exploit the new opportunities lament the possible setbacks, as expressed in Jay Moo's "Nisaidie kushare" ("Help Me to Share") on pictures replacing rhymes. Such sharing is a sacrifice of privacy. The price for democratizing fame is a self turned into a public ID: "That's how powerful social media is." In the hip-hop song "Facebook Twitter" by Rose Mhando, which hit the national charts, the analogy is made with the former authority of the church. The lyrics urge people to manage the place of social media in their lives. Translated from Swahili: "Facebook Facebook Twitter, you the judge of today's church. Facebook Facebook Twitter, you the madness of the new generation." Wisdom is secondary to public persona: "Ooh God, see your church in bad shape. Pastors have lost the wisdom to solve problems. Who has bewitched them? Globalization. Students failing exams due to chatting. Drivers causing accidents due to chatting. Marriages broken due to chatting."

ENDOGENOUS CITIZENSHIP

The expected image of the university campus as safe haven amid a stressing urban environment should be revised on the basis of these data. Many students of Mzumbe University, for instance, would not choose to live on campus even if they could. They do not consider living in the town of Morogoro a disadvantage, despite the dangers after dark and the distance of about 50 kilometers in total to be covered daily to the campus. There, in town, *vinapatikana* ("things are available"), not only internet bundles and *fundi* but also part-time jobs and cheap food. A small fractal of town is reproduced in a makeshift commercial area at the periphery of the campus, behind a brick wall. What students also appreciate about urban settings is the network of solidarity. Indeed, out of the collision of technicities can grow endogenously, without external intervention, certain rights or terms of exchange and a belief in the total network—the town or city—honoring the terms. As in the metropoles described earlier, users can rely on institutions of solidarity and hierarchy that solidify into fairly well delimited sections of the social network.

We kept part of our survey data to the end of this chapter to collect these traces of endogenous citizenship, which point to means of obtaining rights other than through a democratic state. In response to the financial problem, respondents note the emergence of a new sociality, that of sharing a hot spot. A friend with enough data shows solidarity by sharing with the have-not. This response, of delegating, trading, or sharing one's hot spot with multiple others, is a sign of resilience. One might argue that such social a network arising on campus is a type of technicity, for it is merely coping. But then one forgets how this ICT solution fits within the redistributive tradition of better-off students sharing rooms and meals as a function of their fellows' capacity. The favor will be returned much later in their careers, after employment. Might that not be a sustainable solution after all? Users not only cross platforms as they please but also become temporary service providers. They build community within a nonsupportive, digitally immobile environment. Their temporary communality and their bricolage of secondhand material in smartphones continue an endogenous mode of technicity, which creates rights of its own.

Not all teachers are willing to invest their private means to be connected as students do. A couple of recalcitrant lecturers in our survey explained their apparent boycott as arising not from lack of digital skills. Inertia in the form of individual resistance to change is common during and after a system's deployment, but the explanations we registered set one thinking. In one encounter a lecturer questioned the justification for using personnel's own devices to accomplish a university-based task. An Open University of Tanzania lecturer exclaimed, referring to the cost of internet connectivity bundles: "Why should I use my own devices and bundle for the university work?" His claim contrasted sharply with the hypermobile remedies expected of students, but it also laid bare the teacher's unease with yet another institutionalization of informal measures to offset formal shortage, and to thus indirectly sustain the shortage. A parallel can be drawn with the informal deal famously described by Gluckman for the Zambian Copper Belt in the colonial era where farmer communities took the brunt in times of economic crisis by reserving land for migrants suffering seasonal layoffs in the colonizers' factories. Here we see the critique rehearsed that rights, whether state based or network based, as in this case, do not solve structural inequality by themselves.

CO-CITIZENSHIP

For all its ethical tenor, citizenship has as a disadvantage the trust it presumes in a state. The presumption is that the community of citizens can be politically organized and represented by a government acting in service of its subjects and respecting their rights irrespective of personal backgrounds. The trust is based on a belief, not a religious but civil one. Still, it is a belief. Cases of corruption and failed policies undermine the trust in a government or regime, but such empirical contraindications should not shake the belief in the principle itself of a state.

Our data indicate an infrastructural obstacle to the principle rooting itself in perhaps the most influential human resource of a state, the university. What hinders the required trust in the state is the traumatizing colonial as well as postcolonial reality of individual prowess being rewarded (Mbembe 2001). Do those at the top not have the technicity of knowing their rights best and where, when, or how to apply them? A better alternative seems access to collective rights via groups of technicity with a certain reach in the streets or on campus. This reach is also technical, producing connectivity and repairing parts of the smartphone that top-notch shops would not dare to open. Such harnessing of possibilities sedimented in solidarity networks is the upshot of what Pype (2017b) coined "smartness from below."

The ambiguity of professing citizenship while rewarding technicity characterizes neoliberal, late-capitalist settings. In sports, which celebrate the meritocracy of modern democracies, contenders caught doping will be expelled to safeguard the equality of rights at the start of the race: Formally each contender is treated as a citizen. The competition, however, has as a purpose to measure the contenders' technicity, a mental and physical quality of the individual. The school and university are meant to produce citizens, with an individualist orientation. The individual is formed and marked, evaluated against others. The acquired knowledge is assessed personally. Solidarity by peers should not interfere with measuring a person's intrinsic quality, a technicity reduced to talent and trained capacity. Friends helping each other during an exam is the pinnacle of transgression on campus. In society, your university degree, money, and innate intelligence will get you to the top. Therefore, streetwise hip-hop artists, and populist leaders, openly rejecting citizenship may come across as truer to reality than those designated as politically correct.

What we are questioning is the ethical opposition of citizenship and technicity. In settings of infrastructural uncertainty the state and democratic government fail to work. To speak with Graeber and Wengrow (2021), why has the centralized political system been our measure to assess social formations? An intermediate or third form is possible, which we encountered on campus and on the streets. It may be called co-citizenship. The analogy operates as follows. To avoid a technicity going out of bounds, where *homo homini lupus est*, a set of rights was established in the medieval city-state that all inhabitants would uphold. By observing those rights they pleaded allegiance to an abstract entity, "the city," consisting of people they had no relation with save through their belonging to the same place. Life in the city affords technicity because of its dynamic density. Whether for the survival of beggars in the street or for the wealth of notables, the city offers the practical possibility of reaching as many as possible at once, for communication, production, and consumption. This *technicity*, a place with technical and practical opportunities characteristic of population density, requires an adapted body of institutions.

Like the tight-knit technological communities of artisans, car mechanics, painters, and builders in the city, students develop solidarity in the face of campus disconnectivity. The rise on campus of a collective or cooperative citizenship, a "co-citizenship," may be compared to the membership in the guilds through which one inhabited a medieval city with rights. A locally salient comparison in Tanzanian and Kenya is the traditional initiation of peers supporting each other and signing off as a cohort. Co-citizenship is a socially adapted form of technicity that prevails on campus, as it does on the streets in Nairobi, Dar, and Morogoro. The emphasis on communicative technicity through smartphones and mobile money suggests the development in the South of an antidote against the individualist citizenship imported initially through education, bureaucracy, and information technology.

CONCLUSION

In Tanzania not only a city but also a university campus can create a setting where technicities collide. Does the collision exclude growth of citizenship? A campus should embody and emplace the values of science and critical debate, because a university draws its right of existence, as disseminator and evaluator of knowledge, from guaranteeing equal rights to all students. In brief, a university campus should create a place of maximum citizenship, reflected in its infrastructure, including ICT and connectivity. Our data show Tanzanian campuses that stimulate technicity instead. The infrastructural situation in the four universities strikes us as "immobile." In response to this immobile condition, learning with mobiles is a hypermobile strategy devised by students and teachers. Structural inequalities persist as they prompt hot-spot sharing, private sphere implosion, and task-related group formation on one's personal mobile.

Our interviews with teachers and students portray an ambivalent educational system, which bans the wayward smartphone in the formative primary and secondary levels yet counts on that very tool for students to accomplish their university studies. Available mobile networks are overloaded in such a way that students choose to wait until midnight to access them. The new forms of bricolage between technologies and life/work cycles, propagated as m-learning, in fact impede sustained power brokerage. A final observation is that this technicity seems of a certain kind because it engages the social network, calling on help of its members. In this co-citizenship we are witnessing an endogenous form of right that is not individualized or state led.

NOTES

1. Competing with this policy is the planned approach explored in the neighborhood of Mukuru in Nairobi (Muiruri 2021).

2. One thread of comments can be found following Msuya 2021.

3. "Kutekeleza miradi mbalimbali ya maendeleo ya kijamii ikiwepo ujenzi wa Vituo vya Afya, Miundombinu ya Barabara pamoja na kuimarisha Sekta ya Elimu." http://www.diramakini.co.tz/2021/08/live-serikali-ikitoa-ufafanuzi-mpya.html (accessed November 15, 2021).

4. "Ombi langu moja kwa Watanzania wanaonitazama kwamba jambo hili ni letu sote sio la serikali, nchi hii ni yako wewe hapo ulipo na pesa ni yako na haya mambo tuliyokuwa tunapangilia tuyafanye ni yako, hivyo haya yote ni yetu" (Malisa 2021).

5. https://www.youtube.com/watch?v=Y4xLi0uuP8o (accessed September 28, 2019).

6. The respondents were selected following the above theoretical sampling for grounded theory. During open coding, by the aid of Nvivo 10 software, the second author labeled data based on the emerging concepts. The concepts and labels were revised and compared with the rest of data so as to remain with the most relevant and acceptable concepts (148 in total) that define the actual situation.

7. A contribution by Jacob Mosenda in the journal *The Citizen*, https://www.thecitizen.co.tz/tanzania/news/why-tanzanian-universities-lag-behind-in-global-ranking-3581786 (accessed October 15, 2012).

CHAPTER 8

Digital Technology
and Urban Entrepreneurship

Gendered Tactics of Online Entrepreneurship
in and from Prewar Khartoum

GRIET STEEL

Technological innovation has been increasingly important in shaping urban landscapes across the globe. Since the mid-1990s, and with Graham and Marvin's (1996) publication on "telecommunications and the city," there has been an increased recognition of the role of new information and communication technologies (ICTs) in urban studies. These studies especially look how the internet and a plurality of digital media, theorized as "polymedia" by Madianou and Miller (2012), have shaped, transformed, and restructured urban lifeworlds all over the world. They, for instance, scrutinize the role of ICTs in creating sustainable urban environments and how "smart cities" can tackle some of the main problems of rapid urbanization (Angelidou 2014; Kitchin 2014; Datta 2019; Kummitah and Crutzen 2017; Slavova and Okwe-chime 2016; Luque-Ayala and Marvin 2015). These studies on the smart city generally focus on the interplay between digital technology and the urban environments in the Global North. They start from the premise that these "global cities" share the same characteristics, have a certain degree of uniformity, and equally aspire to become the new New York, London, or Tokyo of their respective countries.

Scholars focusing on African cities have criticized the idea of the smart city for its narrow technocratic and normative approach and finding its origins in Global North city dynamics and patterns of urban development in a digital age (Monstadt and Schramm 2017; Guma and Monstadt 2021; Pype 2017). As argued by the editors of this volume (Adunbi et al., this volume), more attention should be given to the post-global city, in which the particularities of urban developments in concrete urban contexts stand central, as well as the particularities in which these cities are lived and experienced differently according to gender, age, race, class, and so on. To gain a better understanding of the interplay between digital technologies and the African city, and the way this shapes social and economic practices, the authors in this volume therefore critically analyze the specific realities of urban populations and their day-to-day practices in a concrete urban context (see also Mavhunga et al. 2016).

Looking to African engagements and entanglements with digital technologies in more detail, several African scholars have employed a communication and sociality perspective to study the role of ICTs in civil engagement and political mobilization (Ali 2019; Bernal 2014; Hwang 2013; Root 2012), and digital payment systems (Rutten and Mwangi 2012; Kusimba 2018). They point to the fact that online engagements have created new opportunities to spatially expand people's connections (Archambault 2012; Burrell 2009; McIntosh 2010), to access alternative spaces for sociality (Archambault 2013; Pype 2016), and to protest and carry out civil disobedience (Akinbobola 2015; Root 2012). Most of these online interactions are entangled with on-the-ground social practices and interactions in and around the localities where they originate. Therefore, and as emphasized in this edited volume, the postcolonial city can be considered an excellent starting point to study the way digital technologies have shaped African lifeworlds in all their diversities.

To further scrutinize the interplay between digital technology and city life in Africa, this chapter zooms in on the concrete practices of digital entrepreneurship in prewar Khartoum, the capital of Sudan. All over the world, mobile phones and other digital communication technologies have triggered the rise of e-commerce, in which goods, products, services, and funds are bought and sold through the internet (Moriset 2020). In African studies, improved information and communication opportunities, access to markets and other supply chains, and low entry barriers have been emphasized as important advantages to create new entrepreneurial opportunities for bottom-up practices of e-commerce (Demiridirek et al., forthcoming; Mukolwe and Korir 2016; Steel 2017, 2021; Taura et al. 2019). These entrepreneurs work from home to exchange information, to market their merchandise, and to have access to a number of consumer goods that are not locally available.

However, as also emphasized by Graham (2019, 7), "ICTs do not necessarily shrink distance or bring a digitally shared space into being." When looking to the broader geographical embeddedness (and hereto-related geographical outreach) of locally based practices of digitality, it is therefore important to pay attention to place-specific dynamics and the local contexts in which these practices are shaped.

Building on the ethnographic narratives of female online entrepreneurs in prewar Khartoum,[1] this chapter analyzes the on- and offline practices of women using digital connection to buy and sell merchandise, including cosmetics, garments, fashion accessories, and perfumes. These online entrepreneurs live all over the city and come from different ethnic and socioeconomic backgrounds, but most of them are highly educated women who own a villa or apartment with their husband and children in what are designated by the government as "first class" neighborhoods of the city. These neighborhoods were the starting point of an ethnographic study on how Khartoum's online entrepreneurs have developed tactics to run their online business from home, to transgress gendered boundaries, and to build trust to connect with the Sudanese diaspora. By getting an in-depth insight on how female online entrepreneurs in Khartoum creatively use social media apps to make their business successful and the challenges and frictions they encounter in doing so, this chapter will contribute to broader debates on digital technology, African entrepreneurship, and urbanity.

The chapter builds on four months of ethnographic fieldwork in the city of Khartoum, in November and December 2014 and 2015, followed by online engagement. During fieldwork, on- and offline research methods were combined to maintain contact with almost fifty respondents, most of whom were recently married women and young mothers who used a smartphone to run a business from home. Together with my Arabic-speaking female research assistant, Wala, we visited our respondents at home to conduct interviews and participant observation.[2] We asked questions about the history and organization of their business, the networks and interactions with the Sudanese diaspora and the possibilities and challenges that their business has offered. To follow-up on these personal conversations, we extended participant observation through our respondents' online activities, "going digital" and becoming members of their Facebook pages and participating in other online vending platforms and WhatsApp conversations.

The chapter continues with a theoretical reflection on digital entrepreneurship by women living in African cities and is followed by some empirical sections. Before zooming in on the particular practices and tactics of the female online entrepreneurs to expand their business beyond urban, national, and continental borders, the empirical sections look at the digitalization of Khartoum and the role of women therein.

AFRICAN CITIES, FEMALE ENTREPRENEURSHIP, AND THE DIGITAL ECONOMY

Entrepreneurial practices are important aspects of African city life. Since Hart's (1973) study on informal activities of migrant workers from northern Ghana in Accra, several African scholars have analyzed the entrepreneurial activities of men and women who have developed a variety of economic practices, characterized by self-organization (Malefakis 2016), creativity (Adunbi 2022), and "globalization from below" (Lee 2014), to make a living in the city. These entrepreneurial practices are clear examples of what de Certeau (1988) describes as "the practice of everyday life," in which urban dwellers (re) appropriate everyday situations to subvert the rituals and representations that institutions and structures of power seek to impose upon them. These practices, or "tactics" to use the terminology of de Certeau, form an important aspect in structuring urban lifeworlds. As de Certeau (1988, 93) illustrates in the concrete act of walking, and as can be extrapolated to a variety of urban practices by all types of urban residents, these tactics turn its practitioners into active, but often invisible, city makers: people who "write" the city "without being able to read it."

Technology is an important aspect of turning African entrepreneurs into active city makers. In this edited volume, we find a variety of examples of African entrepreneurs, considered to be "experts" who develop, transform, and make use of technology to make a living in the city. Many of these experts are men, such as the engineers at the Inga dam (Carbon, this volume) or in the Menengai crater in Nakuru (Rahier, this volume), the *tradipraticiens* in Kikwit (Phippard, this volume), the welders in Port Harcourt and Yenagoa (Adunbi, this volume), and the bend-skin or moto-taxi drivers in Mbounda (Meli, this volume) and most of the tech entrepreneurs in Kinshasa (Pype, this volume). However, women are also important, "invisible everyday protagonists" that "innovatively and creatively experimenting, testing, trying out, and developing technologies" to make a living in the city (Adunbi et al., this volume). In contrast to men, women often give form to technology cultures in the rather "hidden" spaces of the urban landscape, such as in living rooms and in digital spaces (Steel 2017). In a subtle, and mostly invisible, way, they make use of technology to start a business from the more intimate spaces of African cities.

Digital technology and internet and social media in particular have become an important asset for women to participate in the urban economy (Mukolwe and Korir 2016; Steel 2017, 2021; Taura et al. 2019); though in a more invisible way than the more visible and more studied practices of market and trade women (e.g., Clark 1994; House-Midamba 1995; Prag 2013; Sylvanus 2013; Toulabor 2012). Especially for women who are marginalized in the city due to their legal status, or on the basis of conventional gender norms and religious grounds, the smartphone and digital media have opened new avenues for realizing their entrepreneurial ambitions. Demiridirek et al. (forthcoming), for example, scrutinize how social media have become of crucial importance in the entrepreneurial activities of Congolese refugees in Dar es Salam because they offer opportunities to get around permit requirements and to avoid exposure to discrimination. In the same vein, McAdam et al. (2020) have studied the emancipatory potential of female digital entrepreneurs in Saudi Arabia. They argue that in a city as Riyad, where women are constrained by male guardianship and legally enforced gender segregation, digital technology and social media in particular are a powerful asset for women to be able to accomplish their entrepreneurial ambitions.

At the same time, these few studies on digital or social media entrepreneurship in Africa warn against overstating the revolutionary potential of this type of online business. Through the creation of virtual spaces, traditional notions of spatiality and gender might be challenged. But as already argued by studies on digital entrepreneurship in a Western context (Daniels 2009; Dy et al. 2017; Dy et al. 2018), off-line inequalities are most likely to be reflected and/or replicated in the online environment. Digital engagements just come along with new challenges and go hand in hand with new dependencies and/or exclusions (see also Steel et al. 2017 for this argument). In certain cases, the online establishment of new connections can even lead to more exploitation (Easton-Calabria 2019). Therefore it remains of crucial importance to start studies on digital entrepreneurship from the concrete lived experiences of the entrepreneurs in specific socioeconomic contexts and to study the specific technological applications and innovations they generate. In the next sections I will do so by focusing on the case of female online entrepreneurs in prewar Khartoum.

WOMEN AND DIGITAL (DIS)CONNECTIONS IN THE POST-GLOBAL CITY OF KHARTOUM

Khartoum, the capital of Sudan, is a low-built city located at the confluence of the Blue and the White Nile. Urbanization trends started after independence in 1956 but accelerated by the desertification phenomenon of the 1970s. Also, civil wars in South Sudan (1953–1972 and 1983–2005) and the Darfur conflicts (since 2003) have provoked a huge wave of migration toward the capital, particularly of internally displaced people (IDPs). Apart from the impact of this massive influx of IDPs, especially on the periphery of the city, the urbanization process of Khartoum has also been triggered by the real estate investments by local and foreign investors (McGranahan et al. 2020). Due to the oil boom around the turn of the century (2000–2010), Khartoum has seen massive economic growth, with large development projects along the Nile, such as the Corinthia Hotel and the Greater Nile Petroleum Operating Company headquarters (Choplin and Franck 2010). These developments have sparked a building boom in the more affluent neighborhoods of the city, such as Kafoeri, Amarat, Riyadh, and Khartoum II, turning them into new investment frontiers of the city.

Although women are part and parcel of this urbanization process, they keep on holding an ambivalent position in Khartoum's urban landscape. Especially since the introduction of sharia, or Islamic law, in 1983, religion has become ever more important in shaping gender norms and defining the position of women in Sudanese society (Boddy 1989; Nageeb 2004; Willemse 2001).[3] The way Sudanese women should behave and dress in public is defined by the "public order" law, a guiding document on how women should self-represent in public, and what their domestic roles in marriage are supposed to be. For decades, the government has used this law "to police women's bodies" (Ali 2019, 112) and to "exclude women from public space" (Bahreldin 2020, 13). As a consequence, female informal workers (Nagi and Alkarib, n.d.), women's organizations (Ali 2015), and married women from high-income families (Miller 2021) have to continuously negotiate their urban presence.[4] Very little is known, however, about how ICT and social media in particular have further shaped these gender boundaries in Khartoum's cityscape.

The mobile phone has been part of Khartoum's communication landscape since 2000 (Brinkman et al. 2009). Almost simultaneously with the introduction of the mobile phone, the internet gained ground in Sudan and expanded in use over the past two decades. Although it is very hard to get detailed data on internet use in Sudan, the Internet Live Statistics (2020) websites estimates that the percentage of internet users in Sudan increased from 0.1 percent in 2001 to 26.4 percent in 2016. In January 2020, there were 13.38 million internet users, basically accessing the internet through mobile phones (62.3 percent), laptops and desktops (37.2 percent), or tablet computers (0.5 percent) (Kemp 2020). It is clear that the internet and digital platforms in particular have become an important medium through which to interact safely in a general climate of governance surveillance (Albaih 2015). However, what people can access through digital mediation has been very much censored during the thirty years of the authoritarian regime of El Bashir and afterward during revolution and wartime. In combination with trade sanctions and an American prohibition on the importation of many software programs, there are many obstacles to accessing the internet freely (Freedom House 2017). In addition, because of increased access costs due to an inflation rate that reached more than 200 percent in 2020 (Schipani 2021), a growing intensity and frequency of electricity cuts, and other urban infrastructure breakdowns, the digital connectivity of Khartoum's inhabitants is hampered on a daily basis. In the case of social media and internet use in Kinshasa, Pype (2019, 13) discusses these day-to-day internet disruptions as "experiences of involuntary 'cutting off.'"

Despite these general disruptions, women in Khartoum are important internet and social media users (Ali 2019; Kadoda and Hale 2015). Although initially Facebook was the most used digital platform for these digital engagements, over the years WhatsApp has replaced the popularity of Facebook. As one of the Sudanese women, running a food business from her home in Khartoum north (Bahri) stated, "There are so many housewives [who] know how to use WhatsApp even more than how to use the smartphone itself. . . . In our community even the well-educated women, the women who are woooow, they know only WhatsApp" (interview, Manal, November 16, 2015). In this sense the internet and social media have become part and parcel of the everyday lives of Sudanese women who have a smartphone and can afford an internet connection.

Especially for housewives, the digital or virtual world has become an important space to engage in socio-political activities from which they feel excluded in the offline world. For instance, many women confined to the house due to family responsibilities and conventual gender and class norms consider the smartphone an important alternative to physically moving through space. As Wala, a housewife in her fifties who recently started to access social media platforms through the iPad of her ten-year-old daughter, reflects, "With WhatsApp and Facebook you find all what you want on the [inter]net and there is no need any more to rush from here to there" (interview, December 13, 2014). The internet offers an important medium for women to access new styles and fashions that are not available on the Sudanese domestic market and to replace physical shopping in male-dominated public markets that they prefer to avoid due to traffic congestion, hot weather, and the risk of being criticized by their husbands and other male relatives for their public appearance.

In the following paragraphs I will further analyze how these women fall back on digital mediation to circumvent mobility restrictions, connectivity disruptions, and other urban challenges by establishing online businesses in female fashion and other luxury goods such as kitchen equipment, jewelry, and cosmetics.

MASTERING ON- AND OFFLINE DYNAMICS AND OTHER TACTICS OF FEMALE ONLINE ENTREPRENEURSHIP IN PREWAR KHARTOUM

Jina is a Sudanese woman living in one of the affluent neighborhoods of Khartoum north, Bahri. After graduation, she worked for the United Nations, but when she got married she was heavily criticized by her in-laws for working outdoors. They forced her to stay home, and she looked for other opportunities to "keep being busy from the home" because, as she recalls, "I missed going out and feeling free. At home I feel tight, I feel in a shell, and if I want to go out I need permission [from my husband] to go out." Subsequently Jina started an online business in natural, homemade cosmetics and herbal extracts. One of her popular products, in high demand from Sudanese clients in Sudan, elsewhere in the Arab world, and Europe, is what she calls "magic potion," a product that is supposed to clean and to shrink the vagina. Jina advertises this product "for happy marriage" under her business pseudonym in online platforms and WhatsApp groups for women only.[5] She says that this means of commercializing her products is the only way to sell them because, especially for the "magic potion," women are generally too shy to ask about such products in offline female spaces such as beauty salons and female bazaars or markets. Selling online makes it easy to anonymize herself as a vendor, to hide her economic activities for her family in law, and to fulfill her husband's expectation that she will stay at home to take care of it, the children, and him (interview, December 8, 2014).

Jina's narrative exemplifies the business trajectories of many of the online entrepreneurs I met in Khartoum. They are mostly highly educated women who had jobs at universities and international organizations from which they resigned as soon as they got married or gave birth to their first child. Through the mediation of the smartphone and tablets, they sell consumer goods such as Sudanese cosmetics, perfumes, and dresses as well as Western female fashions, kitchen equipment, and bed linens. They post pictures of these items on digital platforms such as Facebook and in WhatsApp groups. Potential clients can take contact with them through digital mediation. Subsequently, they can make their order online or come to the home of the entrepreneur to personally assess the quality, style, and state of the consumer goods. The online merchandise might be purchased on location or, when no in-person meeting between client and vendor takes place, by the support of delivery boys or taxi drivers. These face-to-face encounters are inevitable even with online purchases because, in contrast to many other African countries (e.g., Kusimba 2018), Sudan does not yet have digital payment systems. There are only few women who accept credit payments on their mobile phone, which they can convert to cash at local supermarkets for a 10 percent fee. In all the cases, however, female online entrepreneurship remains engendered in the capital's urban infrastructure—such as internet connections, (public) transport, road and air connections, shops, banks, and markets, but also social connections and support networks of husbands, delivery boys (and girls), and other female vendors and buyers. As vending is only partially materialized in Khartoum's digital spaces, a continuous juggling of online and offline interactions shapes the success of these women's sales activities.

The digital connections are clearly important for women to operate with a degree of discretion, being selective in what they sell, and deciding to whom they reveal their activities and goods. In her article on cell phone use among young people in Inhambane, Mozambique, Archambault (2013) conceptualizes (in)visibility dynamics as "the politics of display and disguise." The anthropological notion of secrecy (Barnes 1994; Simmel 1950; Taussig 1999) is imperative in research on mobile phone use because, in their digital practices, Inhambane's youngsters constantly seek a balance "between displaying enough without revealing too much, between accessing social status and deflecting envy, and between having a good time and preserving respectability, while embellishing reality, often through concealment" (Archambault 2013, 88).

With the introduction of the smartphone, the dynamics between display and disguise add another layer. The smartphone not only permits discretion in individual communication but, with all its extra online applications, also offers opportunities to create what in the literature has been mentioned as "safe spaces" (Daniels 2009; Demiridirek et al., forthcoming; Nouraie-Simone 2005) that restrict group communication to a particular kind of participant. It offers a special opportunity for opening up new urban spaces in which women can interact outside the male gaze. As exemplified by the case of Jina, one of the main benefits of the relatively easy access to digital media is that smartphones offer opportunities for women to be commercially active outside male surveillance and supervision by operating in women's groups only. And although these operations are not without risks, sometimes resulting in abuse by men who enter Facebook and WhatsApp groups by pretending to be a woman, they allow women to be socioeconomically active outside the male gaze and to challenge the gender barriers they encounter in their day-to-day, offline lives (McAdam et al. 2020).

Digital technology also offers the ability to avoid the American software ban, without revealing that online activities are managed and structured somewhere else, and to disguise the support of men in interacting with the outside world of clients and other female entrepreneurs. Hala, for instance, is a Syrian refugee with an online business selling Syrian cotton in Khartoum. She gets lots of support of her brother, Saeed, who flew with his family from Syria to Saudi Arabia. The brother explains: "In Saudi we have very good access to the internet, so I established a Facebook account for Hala [from Saudi] and started to put the pictures of the products on the Facebook page. I constructed the account with a Sudanese address (in Khartoum) to make sure that I would reach the Sudanese clients. So I drive the page from Saudi but have put the name of my sister on the account, so it is a page only for women." Women in Sudan consulting the page don't know that it was developed in another country by a man. Saeed continues: "Honestly, it is a funny thing to run a Facebook page for women as a man. . . . The women chat with me and think that I am a woman, and sometimes I feel seriously embarrassed when the female clients start to ask details or start to talk about private things. If you go to a shop and you see it is a man that is behind the counter, you can react to the situation, because you know whom you are negotiating with. But online it is more complicated" (interview, December 6, 2014). In these awkward situations, about which vendors and clients tell lively anecdotes, Saeed decided to identify himself to avoid further confusion. Even as the female online entrepreneurs do, he refers potential customers to the WhatsApp account of, in this case, his sister for more personal conversations and product and sales details.

Switching from one digital medium to another or from an online to an offline space is thus a fundamental tactic to let the business run. With broad outreach via Facebook, entrepreneurs try to expand the potential pool of clients in and beyond their direct network of friends and relatives, then strengthen the relation and be in direct contact with the clients via WhatsApp or mobile phone services for chatting and calling. More private message exchange services seem to be preferred for concrete economic transactions, in which asking for the telephone number of the client is a way of personalizing the connection established online. In addition, clients often insist on a visit to the vendors' home to personalize the interaction and build trust.

Nabila, living in an apartment with her husband and her two-year-old child in Mamoura, Khartoum, is a frequent internet shopper for fashion, underwear, gold, and cosmetics. She is especially happy to have found an alternative to buying items of underwear from public markets in Khartoum because, as she indicates, "I was embarrassed to buy them from markets, as most of the vendors are men" and it is difficult to find good quality. Even with cosmetics, the better and well-known brands are only offered online. Especially the first time she buys from a specific entrepreneur, she goes for an in-person visit to develop "a good relation with the vendor" and to be sure of the products' quality, because there is a lot of cheating about their origin. "If I want to order a next time, I could ask for delivery, but I never deal with Facebook vendors who do not welcome their customers in their houses or stores. I do not trust them" (interview, December 9, 2014).

So especially for a first purchase, the vendor-client connection established in the digital space is not considered reliable enough. In this sense, Nabila's case brings us back to the argument that the online and the offline are not mutually exclusive. Offline networks, interactions, and practices remain an intrinsic feature of the mundane practices of e-commerce that we see growing in popularity in Khartoum. Entrepreneurs and their clients welcome the digital spaces in which their online practices are entangled but still consider them "too public" and "too unpredictable" platforms to fully trust virtually performed identities and displayed products, and digitally established connections and commitments. The partial invisibility of the virtual city offers opportunities as well as risks and challenges. In this sense, as already emphasized in the literature discussed in the first sections of this chapter, online interactions do not fully transgress the offline disruptions of economic decline, bad connectivity, poor access to markets and software, and the limitations of gendered conducts of social interactions. Digital technology just creates social webs to connect the post-global city in a more invisible way than the highly mobile, male moto-taxi drivers in Mbounda (described by Meli, this volume). In the next section, I will show that these tactics of connecting extend far beyond the concrete city boundaries of Khartoum.

THE SMARTPHONE AS AN "EXIT TO THE WORLD": EXPANDING BUSINESS BEYOND KHARTOUM

In principle, online advertisement has no geographical restrictions. Although most clients of Khartoum's online entrepreneurs are urban women living and residing in Khartoum, ever more women outside the city have caught a glimpse of their pictures and have become promising clients. The strong digital connections between Sudanese women living in Khartoum and those living in the diaspora have also offered shopping and selling opportunities to Sudanese women living abroad. Nabila, the frequent internet shopper introduced in the former section, was waiting for an order from Dubai when we interviewed her. Scrolling through different Facebook posts, she discovered that one of her favorite *toob*[6] designs was offered by a Sudanese woman living in Dubai. When she saw that for payment and pickup of the order she could fall back on the sister of the designer, living in Khartoum, she had the full confidence in an online order. In other cases, the back-and-forth movements of migrants are intermingled in the business designs of the online entrepreneurs in Khartoum (Steel 2021). Even as with Kinshasa's tech entrepreneurs, described by Pype (this volume), connections with the diaspora are manifold.

Fadilah, for instance, is a Sudanese ICT specialist who lives with her two children and her husband in Khartoum north, Bahri. She entered the world of online entrepreneurship through one of her Sudanese friends in the United States who asked her to sell creatine and other US hair products online in Khartoum. She just supported her friend in this business but did not make money out of it. Building on this experience, she decided to start her own online business in bedsheets that she imported from Dubai. She started to work as a suitcase trader with the support of her husband and some Sudanese relatives living in Dubai. Every two months her husband travels to Dubai for work and comes back with luggage filled with bedsheets that Fadilah's uncles bought in Dubai at her request. Over the last few years, her suitcase trade has expanded toward a transnational business in which Fadilah imports fabrics from Dubai to Sudan by post, employs a tailor in Khartoum, and sells tailor-made bedsheets to women who make their orders online. Fadilah explains that "all my selling is organized through WhatsApp and Facebook. My computer background has helped me to make a Facebook page and to play with the colors of the pictures that I post on Facebook and WhatsApp. I give every bedsheet a code to which my clients can refer if they make an order online." In this way Fadilah sells thousands of bedsheets a month and works with sales representatives in cities outside Khartoum. Most of Fadilah's clients are based and raised in Khartoum, but she has a growing number of requests from Sudanese women living in other parts of Sudan, Kuwait, Dubai, Saudi Arabia, Germany, and Canada. She even has orders from the Emirates, which she finds paradoxical because she buys her fabrics from there. She only processes the bedsheets in a workshop in Omdurman and then send them back to where they are imported from (interview, November 27, 2014).

The transnational connections with Sudanese friends in the United States, family in Dubai, a husband traveling between Dubai and Khartoum, tailors in Dubai, and Sudanese clients in the diaspora are the backbone of Fadilah's business. Like many other online entrepreneurs in Khartoum, she relies on connections with Sudanese women and men living in the diaspora for the smooth running of her online business. They, for instance, import beauty and hair products through Sudanese friends living in the United States, let their family in Saudi Arabia and the Gulf travel with kitchen equipment, bedsheets, and other fabrics to sell online in Khartoum, or rely on Sudanese friends in Europe, the United States, and Asia to physically stroll through markets or search for cheap and fancy products on international e-commerce platforms such as eBay, Alibaba, and Amazon.

We do not observe the same pride and effort to promote locally made things among the online entrepreneurs in Khartoum, as with the promising "Made in DRC" label applied by tech entrepreneurs in Kinshasa (Pype, this volume). However, the fact that their commodities are imported from foreign countries seems to offer a guarantee of the quality of their products. Eiliyah, an online entrepreneur who started as an old fashion *delalia*, or suitcase trader, going door to door to sell female consumer goods that she brought back from trips to Dubai,[7] told us, "People are getting crazy when something comes from Dubai. They even do not need an extra description of the product. The fact that it is from Dubai exceeds their imagination" (interview, November 9, 2014). Indeed, as indicated by Pype (this volume), it is no longer the quality of products imported only from the United States or Europe that is taken for granted; Dubai and other Asian cities have become important "spaces of desire."

Dependence on technology and diaspora networks to access these shopping spaces, however, enlarges the risk of losing control over one's practices. Sarah, for instance, relies on the cooperation of Sudanese migrants traveling between Khartoum and Madrid to bring back merchandise that her female friend living in Spain buys at stock sales in Madrid. At a certain moment she lost contact with this friend and a possible transporter. As a result, she temporarily lost access to her investment because she could not transport handbags from Madrid to Khartoum. Reliance on diaspora networks and back-and-forth movements of migrants, in particular, has turned her online business into a nerve-racking and time-consuming practice (interview, December 24, 2015). As I also observed in other cases, Khartoum's online entrepreneurs run a permanent risk of losing profits through products that might arrive too late or through unexpected changes in taxes or foreign exchange rates. When the entrepreneurs in Khartoum rely on connections with traveling migrant to compensate for the lack of low-cost international shipping carriers or on the foreign bank accounts of relatives living abroad, they run the risk of losing control over the rhythm, flow, and speed of their practices. Even as with other urban infrastructures, this limitation "demarcates both literally and figuratively which points in urban contexts can and should be connected, and which should not, the kinds of people and goods that can and should circulate easily, and which should stay put, and who can and should be integrated within the city, and who should be left outside of it" (Rodgers and O'Neill 2012, 402). In this sense, it is again clear that digital connectivity does not necessarily overcome all offline infrastructural challenges and gender restrictions on doing business in Khartoum; it just adds an extra layer of opportunities and constraints.

CONCLUSION

In keeping with the general theme of this volume, this chapter has contributed to the decolonization of technology studies in Africa (Adunbi et al., this volume) by starting from the lived experiences of female online entrepreneurs in prewar Khartoum. I have shown that they creatively develop a variety of tactics to turn their living rooms into tech hubs from which they can be digitally connected with Sudanese women in Khartoum and far beyond. However, the practices of female online entrepreneurs cannot be understood in separation from the specific context in which they occur. In Khartoum, it is an urban context in which the challenges of setting up a female business, be it online or offline, are manifold. As illustrated in the chapter, women, especially the ones who can afford to stay at home, are discouraged by their husbands and other family members from working outdoors or going to Khartoum's' public markets to buy and sell commodities. Apart from these gender limitations, more general infrastructure constraints also challenge the success of female online entrepreneurs. Due to the American ban, international software and computer programs are still blocked from Sudan, and online connections are far from stable. In combination with a lack of a mobile money service in Sudan, these factors make it impossible to fully conduct vending in an online space.

Furthermore, the urban context in which the women under study try to establish their businesses is in constant flux. As indicated in the introduction, fieldwork for this chapter took place in 2014–2015, when President Omar Al Bashir was still in power. The entrepreneurial practices analyzed in this chapter have been challenged by the civil war that broke out in April 2023 and almost completely flattened the city of Khartoum. Due to this violent conflict between the army and the militias, most of the online entrepreneurs central to this chapter fled the country, as they belong to the more affluent urbanites who have the money and the transnational networks to do so. There are only few online entrepreneurs who still struggle to survive on the overcrowded outskirts of the city or with relatives in the countryside. If they are still in Sudan, they have put their business on hold, as internet has become even more unreliable. It has been internationally reported that internet disruptions are used as a weapon of war in Sudan to silence the population and avoid foreign interference in the conflict. Some of the entrepreneurs who have fled to neighboring countries keep on posting their merchandise and continue their business from their life in exile, but many others lost their drive due to the trauma of fleeing the country and worries about the survival of family members either with them or left behind. Although I can to some extent follow their hustle and bustle online, there are also many women of whom I have lost track.

In this sense, we have seen that the potential of female online entrepreneurship shouldn't be overrated. The ability to virtually interact with Chinese merchants, Sudanese clients in Europe, or website developers in the Gulf does not yet mean that female online entrepreneurs are able to do business from any kind of place across the globe. Their activities are locally embedded, and as soon as this local context changes, their modalities of doing business or making a living will change as well. At the same time, the chapter has clearly illustrated that although digital technology facilitate married women's participation in the urban economy of Khartoum, these new economic opportunities have to fit within Khartoum's practice of doing business.

It are especially these place-specific dynamics that deserve more attention in future research on digital entrepreneurship, because they dispute the narratives of technologic utopianism in which economic activities are considered no longer being confined to place. They counter the global city narrative that all cities are developing in the same direction and experience the digital era and other inputs from globalization in the same manner. At the same time, they nuance the more optimistic account of cyber feminism that considers female online entrepreneurship a way to transgress all gender constraints (Brophy 2010). The virtual world and the post-global city are both gendered spaces that, on the one hand, create exclusive opportunities and transformation for women but, on the other hand, enforce and reproduce certain gender norms and restrictions.

NOTES

1. The geopolitical climate of Sudan is in constant flux and has been at a critical point of transformation since the fall of President Omar Al Bashir on April 11, 2019, the outbreak of the Covid-19 pandemic in 2020, and the armed conflict between the national army and the Rapid Support Forces that started in April 2023. These national and global events took place after the main fieldwork of this chapter was finalized. Although they further shape the dynamics, rhythm, and directions of the kind of entrepreneurship I analyze in this chapter, they are not yet reflected upon in this chapter.

2. Apart from the name of my research assistant, all respondent names have been changed to pseudonyms to preserve confidentiality.

3. After independence in 1956, Arabic became the official language of Sudan and Islam the overall religion of the state (Sharkey 2008). However, especially after sharia was proclaimed the law of the country by Numayri in 1983, religion has become an important factor framing the position of women in Sudanese society.

4. These gender restrictions were highly contested during the Sudanese revolution in 2019, in which women had a prominent position, but as the main research on which this chapter is based took place before the revolution, this is a discussion outside its scope.

5. Jina is a pseudonym of her own business pseudonym, adopted so that her relatives cannot trace her business or see that she is selling these products online.

6. This is a typical Sudanese dress for women and comprises a long bolt of fabric that is wrapped around the body and head.

7. In the interviews most suitcase traders referred to their trade connections with Dubai, although different studies refer to trade connections between Sudan, Dubai and China for the import of low-cost, Chinese-manufactured goods, especially after the liberalization of the Sudanese markets in the 1990s (Chevrillon-Guibert 2013).

CHAPTER 9

The Oil Cities

Urbanity, Engineers, and Innovators in the Construction of Refineries in Nigeria

OMOLADE ADUNBI

Isaac Adaka Boro Park in the city of Port Harcourt is unique in many ways. The park is named after an Ijaw icon credited with starting the first insurgency against the Nigerian state in the 1960s. Boro, an undergraduate at the University of Nigeria, Nsukka, had left college to start the Niger Delta Volunteer Force, NDVF, demanding control and equitable distribution of the region's oil wealth (Adunbi 2015; Oriola 2016). As I disembark from a taxi at the roundabout in Boro Park in the summer of 2018 to meet with Jude for an appointment, the iconic figure of Boro among Niger Delta activists and youths reverberates in my mind. Boro Park is ever busy and bustling, and it is the web that connects the entire city of Port Harcourt. From Boro Park, you can get a taxi to any part of the city. The park is also a stone's throw from the state's Government House, the seat of power. Standing around in Boro Park evokes power, memory, martyrdom, connections, and the idea of the center of an oil city. The memory of Adaka Boro and his historic struggles against marginalization evokes his martyrdom among Ijaw dwellers in the oil city. The proximity of the Government House evokes power in the management of the oil city, while connecting taxis and buses to different parts of the city shape how people think about Port Harcourt as a garden city that has undergone what I call a "shift from a garden city to an oil city." My use of "oil city" stems from the fact that Port Harcourt is one of the most prominent Niger Delta cities with the presence of oil infrastructures in Nigeria. I describe an oil city as a space that is awash with oil money because of the extraction of oil in creeks adjoining the city as well as the presence of oil expatriates, infra-structures of oil, and multinational oil corporations.

Boro Park serves as a memorial ground during the annual Armed Forces Remembrance Day, workers' day, and other memorable events. While Boro was considered an outcast who took up arms against the Nigerian state during his lifetime, he has today become an iconic figure who is celebrated by states of the Niger Delta such as Rivers and Bayelsa as well as by many Ijaws—a major ethnic group in the region. As I waited for Jude at the park that summer of 2018, I observed the hustle and bustle that the area is noted for. Traders, street hawkers, professionals on their way to work or back, and others were freely mingling and transacting businesses. Taxis, buses, cars, and bikes were making their way to and from the different intersections at the roundabout that connects about five streets to the park and the old Government Reserva-tion Area, where the Government House is located. As I continued to observe these movements, Jude[1] alighted from a bike and we exchanged pleasantries.

Jude is forty years old. He was born in Yenagoa, Bayelsa state, but has lived most of his life in Port Harcourt.[2] Jude has five children, with three of them teenagers. Although Jude trained as a welder, having served as an apprentice[3] for close to seven years before gaining independence, he constantly refers to himself as an "engineer." Jude is one of the welders (engineers) who special-izes in turning iron rods and sheets into what he calls a "masterpiece." Jude helps construct iron gates for houses within and outside of gated communi-ties in the city of Port Harcourt.

Gated communities are residential areas for the mostly middle to upper class who want a serene atmosphere within an urban space, devoid of the hustle and bustle of the city. Most gated communities rely on the expertise of welders to cast iron for the construction of gates to such a community. Hence, gated communities within an urban space have resonance with what Murray (2017, 145) calls "cities within cities" in an urban space. Jude's day job is to construct gates and other materials needed in a typical house within gated communities and outside of it in an urban space such as Port Harcourt, but, in the last few years, he has also been involved in making artisanal refineries in many creeks of the Delta. Today he combines his day job of catering to the needs of urban dwellers who need gates for their houses with creating and constructing materials for artisanal refineries. Thus, our meeting during this summer of 2018 is the beginning of my journey to the lifeworld of former apprentices and other artisans who specialize in engineering a new form of oil-extractive practices in the Niger Delta creeks. Jude is not alone in this practice, as I reveal in this chapter.

This chapter investigates how local technologies shape extractive practices in the Niger Delta region. The state and young men in the Niger Delta are engaged in a process that is reshaping extractive practices in Nigeria. Drawing on over four years of ethnographic fieldwork conducted in the cities of Port Harcourt and Yenagoa—two oil cities of the Niger Delta—this chapter shows how local technologies have become important in the establishment of artisanal refineries in Nigeria. Artisanal refineries are small oil-processing facilities constructed with the use of local materials by largely disenfranchised youth in the Niger Delta. The refineries are organized into an effective oil distribution network that meets local demands in many areas of the Niger Delta and other parts of Nigeria. The chapter further shows that creativity and artisanal ingenuity help in mimicking a form of technology often seen as the exclusive preserve of multinational oil corporations. Thus, my ethnographic analysis reveals complex, integrated, and innovative forms of extractive practices engaged in by youth groups within many Niger Delta communities.

My interest is to interrogate the ways in which local artisans who went through different layers of apprenticeship deploy their knowledge in producing complex and integrative technologies outside of the purview of their training in producing innovative technologies used in extracting and distributing crude and refined oil. In my analysis, I take a historical look at the uses of apprenticeship—especially among welders, masons, iron casters, etc.—in the Niger Delta to provide a window through which to understand the important role the artisans play in deploying new technologies of extraction. These artisans, using local knowledge, are redefining extractive practices in ways that are reshaping notions of energy consumption, distribution, and production in the Niger Delta region of Nigeria. The chapter asks, for example: How do artisanal processes and structures of extraction reflect innovation and creativity among artisanal practitioners? How might local technologies of iron casting and construction help understand today's energy practices in the oil enclave of the delta? The chapter argues that a cursory look at the creativity of welders, iron casters, and masons provides a useful lens with which to see how technologies of extraction are reshaping livelihood practices, community relations, and governance in two oil cities in Nigeria.

The chapter is organized in four key sections. The first looks closely at the relationship between the city and the creeks. By looking at the city and the creeks, I examine the ways in which technologies travel across time and space. Technologies fabricated in the cities—Yenagoa and Port Harcourt—make their way to the creeks where artisanal refineries are situated. The central question for this section is how concealment helps in shaping technologies in the cities by creating spaces in which those technologies travel in order to participate in the production and distribution of crude and refined oil. This section ethnographically maps the lifeworld of three individuals who engage in producing technologies of refining in the cities. These technologies are then used in the creeks to produce refined oil that is in turn networked into energy practice across the Niger Delta and other parts of Nigeria.

The second section examines the impact of what I call disruptive technology use on communities and the environment. The section specifically analyzes the effects of the deployment of these technologies in the creeks of the Niger Delta, particularly the ways in which such technologies are creating certain environmental effects that may have lasting consequences for the lives of their operators as well as for community members. I use "disruptive" to denote practices that create leakages in the oil revenue stream of the state, resulting in catastrophe for the communities of extraction and for corporate energy practices.

The third section shows how two cities—Port Harcourt and Yenagoa—serve as centers for the incubation of these technologies that are deployed in the creeks for the purposes of oil refining and production. This section specifically looks at the ways in which artisans organize incubating meetings where design ideas are discussed, debated, and agreed upon. Here I show how artisans engage in strategies of circumventing state practices through the production of ideas of machine designs.

The final section interrogates the connection between cities and technology. Here I speculate about the rightful place of urban centers' attraction to technology as an object of desire. My use of "object of desire" is a way of showing how technology in the city lends itself to the various appurtenances of practice. The specific importance of Yenagoa and Port Harcourt—two interconnected oil cities at the heart of Nigeria's oil economy—to the network of producing, constructing, and distributing what I call "local technologies of oil" becomes an analytical tool for understanding artisanal technological practice in the world of oil. Seeing technology and its connection to the city this way reveals a process that shows a desire to innovate and to conceal what is innovated.

Thus, the Niger Delta, I suggest, represents an example of a form of use of technologies of oil and techniques of power that is illustrative of energy practices in oil creeks. In the cities of Port Harcourt and Yenagoa, cosmopolitan as they maybe, artisans who make technologies of affect are engaged in practices that are reshaping new meanings and the deployment, distribution, and production of technology and energy practices in the Niger Delta in particular and Nigeria in general. The stories told in this chapter are emblematic of these practices.

TECHNOLOGIZING FOR OIL: ARTISANS AS CREATIVE ENGINEERS IN THE CREEKS

Port Harcourt is a major industrial and urban center in Nigeria, operating as the region's headquarters for the oil industry. Besides oil, which is the dominant industry in the city/region, a myriad of other activities take place in the city, including sawmilling, food canning, and the production of rubber (though rubber production ceased with the exit of Michelin from Nigeria), glass, metal, and paper products. With increased oil production in the surrounding creeks and onshore areas, the city has also witnessed an explosion in what are classified as small-scale industries. One such industry is welding, which has played an integral part in meeting the construction needs of the inhabitants of this city. Jude, Raphael, and Beku all play an important role in meeting some of these construction needs. Jude trained as a welder, Raphael is a metal fabricator, while Beku is a mason. These men—Raphael, Beku and Jude—all started their journey into the construction and fabrication of metals as apprentices. As Jude told me, "I was twelve years old when my parents told me to go and learn a trade. I had just finished primary school in the village. They took me to my master's place along Ogbunabali in Port Harcourt. I trained there for a few years before becoming independent and starting my own small business."[4] Learning a trade means becoming an apprentice to a "master" who already has his own workshop, and this was exactly what Jude did when he started learning welding in the city of Port Harcourt as well as other cities in the Niger Delta and Nigeria. As Weman (2003) notes, welding (joining) and fabrication play an important role in society and are involved in nearly 98 percent of manufacturing industry activities. Welding is used in activities like the construction of nuclear and chemical-engineering plants, buildings, bridges, offshore installations, pipelines, shipbuilding, aviation, automobiles, military hardware, agriculture, and domestic appliances. Despite its importance in industrial activities, welding has historically been perceived as "dirty, dusty, and dangerous" work (Dehelean 2009, 957). For those who train as apprentices, especially in places like Nigeria, welding is considered a vocation for school dropouts, and such is the case with Jude,

Figure 9.1. Tanks at an artisanal refinery, connected to a cooking pot where kerosene, gasoline, and diesel are refined. Photo by Omolade Adunbi.

who feels that his parents pushed him into the trade because they did not have the means to pay the fees required for his secondary education.

Welding, a dirty, dangerous, and dusty job, is what Jude and others now practice as a vocation that enables them to build artisanal refineries in the creeks of the Niger Delta. This is exactly why Raphael calls himself "an engineer who engages in the practice of construction." When asked why he refers to himself as an engineer when he has no formal education, Raphael responds thus: "Why shouldn't I call myself an engineer? What do engineers do, my brother? I have seen a few of them who work for Shell and Chevron. They put on a hard hat, and I do the same here too. Importantly, they fabricate iron metals into pipes used in oil operation, and that is what I also do for my guys in the creek who operate artisanal refineries."[5] Raphael draws an equivalency between the work of a Shell or Chevron engineer and the work he does in helping construct artisanal refineries. In making this equivalency, Raphael sees no distinction between the sophistication of oil extraction by the multinational corporations (MNCs) and the ways in which artisanal refiners extract oil for refining in the creeks. Raphael is not alone in drawing this equivalency. Many operators of artisanal refineries and those who help build them draw on their production and distribution network in speculating about the efficacy of their practice. The efficacy of their practice is embedded in the notion that disruptive technologies can compete for a space where sophisticated technologies compete, in this case the urban space as well as the creeks. To the engineers, by helping build technologies of extraction, they are engaging in activities that help disrupt the revenue stream of the Nigerian state, especially when oil tapped from multinational oil corporations' pipelines accounts for much of the crude they use in the artisanal refineries. The urban space, where Shell and Chevron expatriate workers dwell within their gated communities, is the same urban space that provides the opportunity for Beku and others to hone their trade and perfect new technologies that are deployed in the creeks. Beku also considers himself a construction engineer because his specialization is building platforms that tanks constructed by Raphael and Jude sit on. The three men got into the business of building refineries by accident, and as one of them told me, it is their creativity that led them into the business, which has become lucrative for them.

Today, Jude, Beku and Raphael practice their trade at their Port Harcourt workshops where they attend to customers interested in constructing iron gates for their houses, building houses, and other construction work. While these jobs can be said to be their day job, these men also have other jobs that are more lucrative than just attending to customers during the day: helping build refineries for artisans who turn crude oil into refined oil for local consumption. This takes Jude, Raphael, and Beku away from their workshops to the creeks where the refineries are located. As Beku told me, "We use canoes and move some of our materials to the creeks, and it is in the creeks that we construct the refineries for our customers."[6] No one taught these men how to turn corrugated iron and other metals into refineries, but what they all learned from their apprenticeship has become an important tool that they now deploy in the construction of refineries. Apprenticeship is not new in Nigeria. The art of learning a trade is something that has been with many Nigerian communities for a very long time, and Jude, Beku, and Raphael are not exceptions. It is typical for many families who cannot afford the prohibitive cost of education to send their wards to places where they can learn a trade.

APPRENTICESHIP AND THE CONSTRUCTION OF AN OIL TECHNOLOGY

Anthropologists studying traditional apprenticeship in West Africa have described it as a learning system in which training is immersed in a learning environment that both facilitates technical learning and also passes on the practitioners' social knowledge, worldviews, and moral principles that mark membership and status in the trade (Marchand 2008). Argenti (2002) goes on to argue that apprenticeships pass along both technical knowledge and cultural values, with practitioners shaping the normative expectations of the trade. In Nigeria, as in many other Sub-Saharan countries, traditional apprenticeship emerged from the family apprenticeship system of the pre-colonial era, developed to transmit dominant lineage occupations to the next generation (Liadi and Olutayo 2017). Olutayo (2010) argues that these familial arrangements were a process by which knowledge of survival in an environment was passed through the family with the head of household serving as the "expert" who showed his "apprentices" (children) how to do tasks. Thus, to a large extent, labor mobilization for economic purposes was created in the family, making it unsurprising that acquisition of the essential skills required to participate in the trade occurred through the family. These traditional apprenticeship arrangements form a central part of most African societies. Despite this, apprenticeship remains outside the purview of formal education policies in many African nations. As Liada and Olutayo (2017) argue, in Nigeria, traditional apprenticeship receives little or no government attention and patronage. Instead, it is largely self-regulating and self-financing and is structured around "kinship, friendship and philanthropy" (Johanson and Adams 2004). In the absence of formal rules and regulations, apprentices are often not aware of what is expected, resulting in the social context of learning and the structure of relations being based on experiential reality. It is exactly the flexibility of experiential learning that has given Jude, Raphael, and Beku the opportunity to experiment with various refinery designs that they now help install in many creeks of the Niger Delta. To these men, apprenticeship serves its purpose, which is to help them develop skills that can be experimented with in a variety of ways. As my interlocutors told me, when they first started thinking about designing refineries, they experimented with small and medium drums to test drive their designs. When this was done, many of these resulted in accidents, hence the need to do more research and build something much more durable. For example, small drums were found not to have the capacity to withstand the kind of heat required for refining oil, whereas tanks perform better in such circumstances.

While apprenticeship might be seen as experiential learning that enables apprentices to learn new trades, I am more interested in the application of the new trade to the formation of new social structures in communities rich in oil. Social structures around kinship and friendship (Johanson and Adam 2004) help patterns of social relations that exist between and among practitioners in apprentice-based trades because "expert masons and their apprentices engage one another based on established practices structured by and rooted in age-long masons' customs . . . Much of what a new apprentice learns come from those before him on the job which suggests he/she is made to go through some sort of initiation into the job by understanding his/her place/role in the entire apprenticeship structure" (LIada and Olutayo 2017:209). Apprenticeship therefore provides a new way of forming kinship networks in making new technologies for extractive purposes. Apprenticeship molds "engineers" such as Beku, Raphael, and Jude in becoming extractive experts through learning by doing. in this way, technology can be said to be a process that is embedded in practices that become a routine. Routinization of these forms of technological practices creates what I call an "artisanal perfection of extractive technologies of practice." It is these extractive technologies of practice that are helping shape new forms of extractive practices in the creeks of the Niger Delta. How then are these technological practices routinized and deployed in the extraction and refining of oil? How is the technology constructed and used? Creeks awash with oil to be refined provide a clear answer to how these technologies are made and remade in the Niger Delta region of Nigeria.

CREEKS AWASH WITH OIL: REFINERIES AS EPITOME OF TECHNOLOGY USE

Niger Delta creeks serve as freshwater for many communities in the region. At the same time, the creeks also serve as conduits for pipelines and other oil infrastructures installed by multinational oil corporations. In recent times, many of these pipelines have become conduits for artisanal refining activities in the region (Adunbi 2022). Artisanal refinery operators, with good knowledge of the terrain, now tap oil from the pipelines for use in their refineries. As has been documented (Adunbi 2022) over two thousand artisanal refineries litter the creeks of the Niger Delta, and many of these refineries feed from the oil infrastructure built by multinational oil corporations through tapping. This process of tapping is most often facilitated by engineers and designers such as Beku, Raphael, and Jude.

It is another good morning when they come to my small hotel room in Yenagoa. We had agreed to meet in the morning for breakfast before proceeding to the creeks, where they have a project to complete. As always, Jude is the first to arrive, right on time, and he quickly reminds me that he doesn't believe in "Nigerian time"—a term snipingly used to describe being late at events. Jude quickly tells me that in his world, fast is business, and that he doesn't like to waste time at all when it comes to business, especially the business of building refineries. As we settle down at the breakfast table, Raphael and Beku arrive, and we all have breakfast before taking a "Keke"[7] to the waterfront, where we are to board a canoe to the creeks. At the waterfront, there are five other guys waiting for us all dressed in their work gear. The men look more like teenagers, and they are quickly introduced to me by Jude as their apprentices. We all board a canoe, and the journey takes about twenty minutes. On arrival, we are quickly ushered into the site where they have their equipment. I am there to see how they couple some of the tanks and pipes used in making the refineries.

The engineers' days usually start with the apprentices and other workers assembling the irons and sheets into place. This process is followed by measurement to determine the appropriate amount of iron that is needed to connect pipes and build tanks and gas flaring pipes, and the number of concrete blocks needed to seat the tanks. Beku and his men mix cement and sand with water and dig a hole around the space where the tanks will be placed to build a solid foundation for them. For Beku, "A solid foundation is required in order for the tanks and the pipes to be comfortable in their spaces."[8] The most complicated part of Beku's work is constructing the space where the crude is deposited for refining. In refining oil at these artisanal spaces, four to five tanks are interconnected, with one tank placed at a distance of over 300 meters from the four others (Adunbi 2020). The tank where the crude is deposited is built in such a way that there is a fireplace underneath it. Beku makes sure that the fireplace is well constructed to withstand the menacing fire that is required for "cooking" the crude before it turns into refined oil. Beku's experience as the son of a blacksmith becomes useful here. Beku's apprenticeship actually started with his father while he was a kid in his village. His father is a blacksmith, and he would follow his father every day to the back of the house where his father practices his smithing. By the time he decided to become a mason who also works in building refineries, his experience working with his father became useful. Beku can here be seen as an epitome of the learning by doing that makes the engineering of technology an everyday practice. Once a fireplace is constructed, Beku builds a rotund platform on top of the fireplace where a huge tank will be placed. The tank will then be supported by concrete to make it sit comfortably. The construction of the "cooking pot" could take two to three days depending on the availability of materials and time at the creeks. The Nigerian state still considers artisanal refineries illegal; hence, most of the work is done at odd hours (Adunbi 2020; Ugor 2013).

Welding and joining pipes and tanks together requires electricity, so Raphael and Jude have a standby generator that they travel with to their work sites. A hard hat, welding goggles, and thick gloves are among the materials that Raphael, Jude, and their apprentices and other workmen use in building tanks and pipes for the refineries. Iron sheets are used in making tanks, with smaller pieces of iron welded into place to allow them to stand on a platform. Once the tanks are put together, four long pipes are then connected to the first tank that sits on the fireplace. These pipes are about 200 to 300 meters long. The pipes are connected from the cooking pot to the four other tanks. The four other tanks process gasoline, diesel, and kerosene, with the fourth tank being used as a waste disposal tank. The four tanks are placed in proximity to each other and smaller pipes that connect all the four together. The final job of the engineering crew is building a gas flaring pipe for the refinery. The gas flaring pipe can sometimes stand up to 500 meters or more tall and sits atop the cooking pot. The gas flaring pipes are important because they help flare the associated gas into the atmosphere. The construction of the gas flaring pipes is the most delicate because if it is not properly done it can trigger a fire that could be fatal. Raphael considers himself the most "knowledgeable refinery engineer" in constructing gas flaring pipes. Raphael's knowledge is derived from having previously worked as a contract staff member for one of the multinational oil corporations. After Raphael completed his apprenticeship as a welder a few years ago, one of the MNCs was looking for welders, and Raphael was one of the lucky few that got the job. Although he was only there for about two years, he strongly believes that those two years gave him a learning curve that puts him head and shoulders above those who are in the business of building refineries in the oil creeks of the delta. He never shies away from bragging about his special knowledge. While the construction takes place in the creeks, ideas are incubated in the cities.

INCUBATING TECHNOLOGY IN THE URBAN SPACE: YENAGOA AND PORT HARCOURT AS CITIES OF ENGINES OF OIL

The cities of Port Harcourt and Yenagoa have several things in common. Both are capitals of oil-rich states, of Rivers and Bayelsa, respectively. They were part of the same state until the military administration of General Sani Abacha created Bayelsa out of Rivers state in 1996. The states are in proximity to each other, and kinship ties are still strong across the boundary of these two states and their capitals. One other major similarity is that both states boast over one thousand artisanal refineries scattered all over the creeks of the region (Adunbi 2020; Ugor 2013). These refineries are constructed by artisans who have undergone different stages of apprenticeship in masonry and welding. One of the defining characteristics of both cities is the preponderance of welders, masons, and other artisans who practice their trades on major street corners in the cities where they weld gates. While not all masons and welders in the two cities engage in constructing artisanal refineries, the few who do use the cities as incubation centers for their ideas, which are helping transform the creeks into sites of artisanal extractive practices. As Mutagwaba et al. (1998) show, technology can be seen as the "aggregate of mental and physical capabilities designed to address a certain issue . . . it involves the application of both human potential (skills, knowledge, information) and physical or material aspects (equipment, tools, and artifacts)" (10). Similarly, Nguluma (1990) reminds us that technology not only entails mechanistic aspects but also embodies social aspects related to the organization of production, distribution, and consumption. Hence, technology does not operate in a social and political vacuum because a "technology climate" determines the exact nature of the technology and its use, its effectiveness, and its social and economic implications (Chungu and Mandara 1994). The climate of Port Harcourt and Yenagoa as oil cities creates possibilities for the "engineers" to incubate and develop technologies that help in refining oil for local consumption.

Raphael's, Jude's, and Beku's expertise in designing refineries is incubated in the cities during meetings with other colleagues. As I was made to understand, these meetings are sometimes nocturnal, but the anonymity of city life makes congregating for design meetings possible. Such meetings are called to discuss processes of designing, gathering materials, and assembling the materials to make refineries. It should be noted that Beku, Raphael, and Jude are not alone in the business of making refineries, but they exemplify how the practice is prominent in city life. Many of the welders who have their workshops in the cities, when asked if they partake in this business, initially respond with a categorical no. When introduced by someone who is well known within the "business community," the answer becomes much more interesting, and practitioners might be willing to share their experiences. As I discovered in my interactions with many operators, one skill that has become important is something many learned while in secondary school. Many of them—Beku and Raphael included—had taken technical drawing, which allows them to express their skills by drawing things. Technical drawing skills help shape the ways in which they see how refineries should operate. It is these skills, combined with many years of apprenticeship, that have helped the process of design and development of artisanal refineries. Thus the routinization of technology as practice takes root in cities such as Port Harcourt and Yenagoa.

This form of routinization is embedded in a practice that combines a particular knowledge of certain design methods with regular construction to end in the perfection of a technology that helps refine oil. As Raphael told me, "When we started designing and constructing refineries, my mother's *ogogoro* business was the model for us."[9] Raphael and his fellow "engineers" studied the process of *ogogoro* refining and applied that to making a refinery because liquor refining is similar in practice to oil refining. What is different in this case is that Raphael's mother's small business of *ogogoro* refining in the city of Yenagoa provides the space within which they studied how the process works. The technical drawing skills they acquired in secondary school were deployed in designing the refineries based on the *ogogoro* model. Thus, before reaching "perfection," they tried many times on a smaller scale before scaling the process up to produce what they have today. For example, at their meetings, members are asked to come with designs for discussion. Each member who comes with designs will make oral presentations on the utility of their designs and how they will be able to weather the storm of heat generated by crude refining. As mentioned earlier, the use of small and medium drums

Figure 9.2. Cooking pot in an artisanal refinery. Crude oil is poured into the pot that sits on top of a molded platform with fire underneath the platform. The pots are connected to different tanks within a radius where gasoline, diesel, and kerosene are refined. Photo by Omolade Adunbi.

was found not to be suitable; hence, they returned to the drawing board to perfect their designs. The drawing board here is the several meetings that take place at which engineers make oral presentation about new designs.

The city space that provides cover for the nocturnal practice of designing also helps in shaping ideas of constructing in the creeks. Many of the materials used in constructing refineries are sourced from the cities. Corrugated iron sheets, pipes, aluminum, cement, and so are sourced from the cities and transported to the bank of the river, where canoes are used to move them to the creeks. The importance of the city in the design and construction of artisanal refineries shows clearly how cities help incubate ideas in a variety of ways. Ideas incubated in cities are then transposed to the creeks for the purposes of producing technologies that shape refining practices, created by many youths of the Niger Delta.

THEORIZING TECHNOLOGY: THE SOCIAL CONSTRUCTION OF TECHNOLOGY IN AN URBAN SPACE

Technology use, effective in creating an atmosphere of belonging in society (Adunbi 2017; Murray 2017; Pype 2016), can also bring some complications in its applications. As Marx reminds us, the study of technology is critical, as it "discloses man's modes of dealing with nature, the process by which he sustains his life" (1938, 197); technology use has always been one of the defining moments of humankind. In Pfaffenberger (1998), the argument is made that technology was rarely seen within anthropology as a subject of interest, as it was frequently equated with material culture or conceptualized as a force to which communities and beliefs were obliged to adapt. But in the last two decades, social theorists—anthropologists and scholars in other disciplines included—have been theorizing technology and its use through the lens of social media (Adunbi 2017; Pype 2016), infrastructure and its appurtenances (Anand 2018; Chalfin 2017; Doughty 2018), technology as a tool for the creation and maintenance of an urban space (Anand 2017; Murray 2017), and oil and its infrastructures (Adunbi 2015; Apter 2005, Sawyer 2004; Shever 2014). In thinking through the importance of technological infrastructure to the social construction of urban spaces, Anand (2017) reminds us of the nexus between the use of technologies and power. In what Anand calls the "hydraulic city," he reconsiders Wittfogel's framing of the "hydraulic system" as "a centralized formation of power and knowledge" by suggesting that we rethink the ways in which technologies and the city interact as a decentralized network that relies on both human and nonhuman actors (Anand 2017, 12; Wittfogel 1957).

This decentralized system combines two elements: policies and infrastructures. Anand describes these two elements as the "technologies of politics" and the "politics of technologies," respectively (2017, 10). These elements, Anand contends, jointly govern "hydraulic citizenship—the ability of residents to be recognized by city agencies through legitimate water services" (2017, 10). Anand explicates the ways in which water policies and infrastructures jointly govern experiences of citizens in urban spaces within the state. Anand's idea of water governance as a decentralized network draws on Latour's conceptualization of relations between human and nonhuman forces in politics more broadly—a concept Latour refers to as "object-oriented democracy"

(Anand 2017; Latour and Weibel 2005). Latour's epistemological framing of politics is useful here to the extent that it defines humans and nonhumans as equally relevant actors in effecting sociopolitical phenomena (Anand 2017, 258), a framing that defines how many of my interlocutors who live in urban spaces of the Niger Delta interact with technologies in constructing refineries located in the creeks. The "technologies of politics" idea constitutes the "human" aspect of the establishment of a network of artisans who use their knowledge of the urban spaces of Port Harcourt and Yenagoa and their experience of technology use in these urban spaces in developing the technologies to achieve a set goal of producing locally made refined crude oil. The "politics of technologies" notion frames infrastructure as a nonhuman actor in politics—an idea complemented by that of Plummer in her study of Chinese infrastructural development in Kenya (Plummer 2019). In asking for whom infrastructure exists and by whom it is developed, Plummer frames infrastructure delivery and development as a political process. Plummer's analysis follows that of Mitchell (2009, 2014), who conceptualized infrastructure as "a politics of nature" that renders resources governable (Meehan 2014; Mitchell 2009, 2014; also see Rodina and Harris 2016). I invoke these ideas in my discussion of how oil infrastructures are constituted in urban spaces, then constructed and deployed in the creeks for the purposes of producing refined oil. As I show, this is a clear indication of how urban spaces interact with oil creeks of the Niger Delta. It is a form of interaction that makes technologies of the urban spaces accessible in the creeks of oil.

While technology remains a means through which human creativity is embedded in control and management of nature and natural resources (Apter 2004; Schon 1967; Shever 2014; White 1967), technology can also be disruptive to established norms, especially in the governance of natural resources such as oil. The disruption of technologies of extracting oil in Nigeria follows two interrelated tropes: the reimagining of an oil city and the redefinition of extractive practices. Oil cities are known to be centers of oil capitalism. As Ferguson (2006) shows, oil sites serve the production of what makes gargantuan profit for the oil city. Using the example of Angola, Ferguson demonstrates how the profit made from oil in the enclaves where it is produced in Cabinda can hop all the way to places as far away as San Francisco, where the headquarters of Chevron is situated (Adunbi 2015; Ferguson 2006; Watts 2004). While profits from sites of extraction do find their way to metropoles such as San Francisco, Amsterdam, London, Austin, and so on, enclaves of oil also boast of cities such as Port Harcourt that serve as local headquarters of different oil corporations. These local headquarters serves as markers and sometimes transit points for foreign oil workers, as we see in the case of different gated communities in different parts of the city of Port Harcourt—for example, Agip Camp, Shell Camp—where oil expatriates and the upper-level Nigerian staff live (Adunbi 2015).

In reimagining an oil city, what we see is the shaping of a new narrative where those like Jude, Beku, Raphael, and others who produce their own technologies of extraction are using urban spaces to construct a new narrative of an oil city. To this group of artisans, an oil city is no longer a city that is dominated by the MNCs but an urban space that is shaping up for new innovations of technological development and that also engages in extractive practices that mimic MNCs. As Winner (1986) reminds us, when technologies are developed and used, "They bring about significant alterations in patterns of human activity and human institutions" (6). In particular, he writes, "Individuals are actively involved in the daily creation and recreation, production and reproduction, of the world in which they live. Thus, as they employ tools and techniques, work in social labor arrangements, make and consume products, and adapt their behavior to the material conditions they encounter in their natural and artificial environment, individuals realize possibilities for human existence" (6). Winner (1986) goes on to show that technological somnambulism leads us to ignore the choices that exist in the process of technological development and subsequent societal impact, leading us to accept whatever form of technology those in power choose. In other words, the human choices and decisions behind technology development and use are hidden, resulting in technology seeming to operate outside of and beyond human control as an embodiment of an inevitable process. Thus, technology becomes a powerful agent that shapes the patterns of human social and cultural life and helps reimagine, in the case of Port Harcourt and Yenagoa, a new oil city. In constructing this new narrative of an oil city, technology, as Pinch and Bijker (1984) suggest, is socially constructed because social construction of technology occurs when one set of meanings for an artifact gains dominance over others and so wins expression in the technical content of said artifact. The new reimagination of an oil city where artisans design and construct new technologies for oil refining in an urban space should therefore be seen as a system, not just of tools, but of social behaviors and techniques (Ferguson 1977) that allows for the shaping of new narratives about extractive practices in a changing meaning of an oil city in a nation-state such as Nigeria. As Pfaffenberger (1988) argues, "Technology can indeed be defined as a set of operationally replicable social behaviors: no technology can be said to exist unless the people who use it can use it over and over again . . . technology, then, is essentially social, not 'technical'" (241). In the deterministic view, technology is seen as the "independent variable to which the forms of social relations and politics stand as dependent variables" (Pfaffenberger 1988, 242). Conceptualizing technology this way would suggest that it is emptied of social relations, to exist in what Marx terms a "fetishized" form (Pfaffenberger 1988). Hence, Pfaffenberger would suggest that anthropologists must work to view technology as humanized nature, "to insist that it is a fundamentally social phenomenon: it is a social construction of the nature around us and within us, and once achieved, it expresses an embedded social vision, and it engages us in what Marx would call a form of life" (1982, 244).

In rethinking extractive practices in an urban space, my use of disruptive technologies of extraction resonates with what Pinch and Bijker (1984) call the "social construction of technology framework" (SCOT), defined as how technology design is a fluid process that can produce different outcomes dependent on the social circumstances of its development. Pinch and Bijker's (1984) four key components that make up the process of SCOT are exemplified in many ways by my interlocutors, who daily design technology for extractive purposes in the Niger Delta. The first of the four elements is the notion of flexibility, which reveals how technologies are the product of intergroup negotiations and are sufficiently open-ended in design to allow for multiple possibilities. The second concept is that of relevant social groups. This component highlights that technology development is a process in which many groups, each representative of an understanding of an artifact, see and construct objects differently. From this we can see that design of a technology does not cease because it "works" but because the set of relevant social groups accepts that it works. So is the case with the youths who design and produce the technologies used for artisanal refineries in the Niger Delta. The third component is that of closure and stabilization. Different groups may have conflicting interpretations of an artifact and its use. Design of said artifact continues until such conflicts are resolved and the artifact no longer poses a problem to the social group—the process reaches closure, and the artifact stabilizes in its final form. Designing a tank that connects to three other tanks in order to process crude oil into a refined oil becomes a way of stabilizing a technological process that defines closure for operators of the new technologies of affect in the delta. Closure here is interpreted to mean the ways in which technologies are designed to create a path for the successful processing of crude oil, a process traditionally considered to be exclusive to those who have mastered and become experts in the technology—the MNCs. The fourth and final component is the wider context. Pinch and Bijker (1984) argue that the wider sociocultural and political milieu in which a technology is developed is a critical component in understanding the nature of the technology. The wider connection in this sense is how marginalized youths are designing technologies that are meant to help capture a form of energy they consider to be theirs (Adunbi 2020; Watts 2007). Critics of the SCOT framework argue that it overstates agency and neglects the involvement of structure (Klein and Kleinman 2002), but if we move away from this criticism for a moment, we may see a reason why such a SCOT framework can be applied to the emergent design and application of technologies of affect in the oil creeks of the Niger Delta.

Although the meaning and use of technology continues to engage the interest of scholars, most especially anthropologists, recent scholarship on the governance of extraction in the postcolonial state focuses on the effects of resource extraction on power circulation both in and beyond the nation-state, how and what constitutes postcolonial imaginaries, and the interrogation of development or the production of modern subjects (Adunbi 2015; Askew 2002; Bayart 1998; Chalfin 2010; Ferguson 2006; Hicks 2015; Mamdani 1998; Mbembe 2001; Mitchell 2002, 2009; Shever 2012; Watts 2004). While such scholarship remains valuable in informing our understanding of the politics of extraction in postcolonial states, I expand scholarship on the postcolonial state by moving away from the emphasis on the effects of resource extraction and paying attention to the processes through which disruptive technology use can be adapted by various actors in producing an extractive practice outside of known norms of technological production. By "known norms of technological production," I refer to a process that produces sophisticated technologies known to a particular form of science—the science of engineering technology for public use. The production of sophisticated technology and the engineering of extraction in oil creeks are today being disrupted by a new form of technology that is local and produced by artisans. As I have shown, this form of technology is crafted in an urban space such as Port Harcourt and Yenagoa but deployed in rural creeks of oil. It is this particular practice that shapes how technologies of extraction interact with urban spaces. The articulation of the creativity of artisans who proclaim membership in the production of technologies of extraction in the creeks of oil makes the spaces of energy practices accessible.

CONCLUSION

Technologies and the city sometimes operate like Siamese twins. Technologies make urban spaces a site to behold for their inhabitants. They shape behavioral patterns among urban dwellers, but as I have shown in this chapter, technologies can also be disruptive through a process that constructs alternative narratives about urban spaces. While oil extraction has always relied on sophisticated technology in its extractive process, many youths in the Niger Delta are creating new technologies that are been used to extract oil. These new technologies, as I have shown, rely on urban spaces for their creation but have found spaces in creeks rich in oil for their application.

The crafting and deployment of technologies made by artisans for the purposes of extracting oil in the creeks is also reimagining the ways in which we visualize an oil city. Oil cities have always been seen as spaces dominated by multinational oil corporations and their expatriate workers. While Port Harcourt and Yenagoa have all the appurtenances of an oil city, both cities are also becoming sites where the narrative of what constitutes an oil city is changing. The two cities are today home to many artisans who plan, innovate, and create technologies that are daily being deployed for the sole purpose of extracting oil for refining purposes in the creeks of the delta. The oil city has become a space that is not dominated by the MNCs but one where artisans compete for a reimagined notion of what constitutes an oil city.

Creeks awash with oil are sites where technologies developed in the city space gain their own meaning. This meaning includes the insertion of the creeks into an economy that is no longer being dominated by the MNCs. Youths who have gained experiential knowledge based on many years of apprenticeship are today using that acquired knowledge to transform the creeks into sites for the practice of artisanal refineries. Knowledge of iron casting, masonry, and other design endeavors used in building gated and ungated communities for the elite who live in them is also being used to design technologies that circumvent the same elite who dominate the oil industry.

NOTES

1. To protect the identity of my informants, I will be using pseudonyms to represent all of them. The only exception would be if the informants are public figures and would want their names in print.

2. Bayelsa state was created from Rivers state with Yenagoa as the capital. Many

people still shuttle between the two states because of their ethnic and geographic proximity to each other.

3. Apprenticeship is common among artisans in Nigeria. Usually, people become apprentices at an early age, and once they are certified by their boss as good enough to be independent, a "freedom" ceremony is organized where the boss will pray for the apprentices and certify them as good enough to begin their own trade. At this stage, the former apprentices set up their own businesses and take on those who might also want to learn from them.

4. Interview conducted in Port Harcourt, July 2018.

5. Interview conducted in Port Hacourt, June 2018.

6. Interview conducted in Port Harcourt, July 17, 2018.

7. *Keke* is what tricycles used as taxis are called.

8. Interview conducted in one of the creeks of the Niger Delta, July 25, 2018.

9. *Ogogoro* is a local gin. I have written elsewhere about the connection between technologies of *ogogoro* extraction and artisanal refineries. See, for example, Adunbi 2015, 2019.

BIBLIOGRAPHY

Adams, J. 2005. "Hypermobility: A Challenge to Governance." In C. Lyall and J. Tait, eds., *New Modes of Governance: Developing an Integrated Policy Approach to Science, Technology, Risk and the Environment*, 123–39. Aldershot: Ashgate.

Adamu, J. K., E. W. Dzasu, A. Haruna, and K. S. Balla. 2011. "Labour Productivity Constraints in Nigeria Construction Industry." *Continental Journal of Environment Design and Management* 1.2: 9–13.

Adesina, K. A. 2008. "Indigenous Building Artisans' Roles in Pro-Poor Housing Development in Peri-Urban Communities in Ibadan." Sc. Project, Department of Urban and Regional Planning, University of Ibadan.

Adunbi, O. 2015. *Oil Wealth and Insurgency in Nigeria*. Bloomington: Indiana University Press.

Adunbi, O. 2017. "The Facebook President: Oil, Citizenship, and the Social Mediation of Politics in Nigeria." *PoLAR: Political and Legal Anthropology Review* 40.2: 226–44.

Adunbi, O. 2020a. "Crafting Spaces of Value." *Cambridge Journal of Anthropology* 382: 38–52.

Adunbi, O. 2020b. "Extractive Practices, Oil Corporations and Contested Spaces in Nigeria." *Extractive Industries and Society* 7.3: 804–11.

Adunbi, O. 2022. *Enclaves of Exception: Special Economic Zones and Extractive Practices in Nigeria*. Bloomington: Indiana University Press.

Afutu-Kotey, R. L., and K. V. Gough. 2019. "Bricolage and Informal Businesses: Young Entrepreneurs in the Mobile Telephony Sector in Accra, Ghana." *Futures* 135: 102487.

Agamben, G. 1998a. *Homo Sacer: Sovereign Power and Bare Life*. Translated by Daniel Heller-Roazen. Stanford, CA: Stanford University Press.

Agamben, G. 1998b. *Stanze: Parole et fantasme dans la culture occidentale*. Translated by Yves Hersant. Paris: Editions Payot & Rivages.

Agier, M. 1999. *L'invention de la ville: Banlieues, townships, invasions et favelas*. Amsterdam: Archives contemporaines.

Aker, J. C., and I. M. Mbiti. 2010. "Mobile Phones and Economic Development in Africa." *Journal of Economic Perspectives* 24.3: 207–32.

Akinbobola, Y. 2015. "Theorising the African Digital Public Sphere: A West African Odyssey." *African Journalism Studies* 36.4: 47–65.

Akmel Meless, S. 2017. "Impact socioéconomique des 'mototaxis' sur les populations de Bouaké (Côte d'Ivoire)." *International Journal of Multidisciplinary and Current Research* 5: 690–98.

Akpan, A. C. 2003. "The Quality of Training Received in Electricity and Electronics Programme by Technical College Graduates in Akwa Ibom State." Master's thesis, Department of Vocational Teacher Education, University of Nigeria, Nsukka.

Akrich, M. 1989. "La construction d'un système socio-technique: Esquisse pour une anthropologie des techniques." *Anthropologie et Sociétés* 13.2: 31–34. https://doi.org/10.7202/015076ar

Albaih, K. 2015. "How WhatsApp Is Fueling a 'Sharing Revolution' in Sudan." *The Guardian*, October 15. https://www.theguardian.com/world/2015/oct/15/sudan-whatsapp-sharing-revolution (accessed May 6, 2021).

Ali, N. M. 2019. "Sudanese Women's Groups on Facebook and #civil_disobedience: Nairat or Thairat? (Radiant or Revolutionary?)." *African Studies Review* 62.2: 103–26.

Amin, A., and M. Lancione, eds. 2022. *Grammars of the Urban Ground*. Durham, NC: Duke University Press.

Amin, B. 2012. "Youth, Ojeg and Urban Space in Ternate." *Asia Pacific Journal of Anthropology* 131: 36–48.

Anand, N. 2017. *Hydraulic City Water and the Infrastructures of Citizenship in Mumbai*. Durham, NC: Duke University Press.

Anand, N., A. Gupta, and H. Appel. 2018. *The Promise of Infrastructure*. Durham, NC: Duke University Press.

Angelidou, M. 2014. "Smart City Policies: A Spatial Approach." *Cities* 41: S3–S11.

Appadurai, A., ed. 1986. *The Social Lives of Things*. Cambridge: Cambridge University Press.

Appadurai, A. 1996. *Modernity at Large: Cultural Dimensions of Globalization*. Minneapolis: University of Minnesota Press.

Apter, A. 2005. *The Pan African Nation: Oil and the Spectacle of Culture in Nigeria*. Chicago: University of Chicago Press.

Archambault, J. S. 2012. "'Travelling While Sitting Down': Mobile Phones, Mobility and the Communication Landscape in Inhambane, Mozambique." *Africa: Journal of the International African Institute* 82.3: 393–412.

Archambault, J. S. 2013. "Cruising Through Uncertainty: Cell Phones and the Politics of Display and Disguise in Inhambane, Mozambique." *American Ethnologist* 40.1: 88–101.

Arènes, A., B. Latour, and J. Gaillardet. 2018. "Giving Depth to the Surface: An Exercise in the Gaia-graphy of Critical Zones." *Anthropocene Review* 5.2: 120–35.

Argenti, N. 2002. "People of the Chisel: Apprenticeship, Youth, and Elites in Oku (Cameroon)." *American Ethnologist* 29.3: 497–533.

Ash, J. 2015. "Technology and Affect: Towards a Theory of Inorganically Organised Objects." *Emotion, Space and Society* 14: 84–90.

Askew, K. 2002. *Performing the Nation: Swahili Music and Cultural Politics in Tanzania.* Chicago: University of Chicago Press.

Au, S. 2017. "Cutting the Flesh: Surgery, Autopsy and Cannibalism in the Belgian Congo." *Medical History* 61.2: 295–312.

Bahreldin, I. Z. 2020. "Beyond the Sit-In: Public Space Production and Appropriation in Sudan's December Revolution, 2018." *Sustainability* 12.12: 51–94.

Balandier, G. 1951. "La situation coloniale: Approche théorique." *Cahiers Internationaux de Sociologie* 11: 44–79.

Banégas, R., and J.-P. Warnier. 2001. "Nouvelles figures de la réussite et du pouvoir." *Politique Africaine* 822: 5–23.

Barnes, J. A. 1994. *A Pack of Lies: Towards a Sociology of Lying.* Cambridge: Cambridge University Press.

Bastide, R. 2003. *Le rêve, la transe et la folie.* Paris: Seuil.

Bayart, J.-F. 2000. "Africa in the World: A History of Extraversion." *African Affairs* 99.395: 217–67.

Bayart, J.-F., et al. 1992. *Le politique par le bas en Afrique Noire: Contribution à une problématique de la démocratie.* Paris: Karthala.

Beck, K. 2013. "Roadside Comforts: Truck Stops on the Forty Days Road in Western Sudan." *Africa: Journal of the International African Institute* 83.3: 426–45. https://doi .org/10.1017/S0001972013000259

Beck, K., G. Klaeger, and M. Stasik, eds. 2017. *The Making of the African Road.* Leiden: Brill.

Becker, F. 2021. "Tanzania's Authoritarian Turn: Less Sudden Than It Seems." *Current History* 120.826: 189–95.

Bedi, T. 2016. "Taxi Drivers, Infrastructures and Urban Change in Globalizing Mumbai." *City and Society* 28.3: 387–410.

Bekaert, S. 2000. *System and Repertoire in Sakata Medicine, Democratic Republic of Congo.* Uppsala: Acta Universitatis Uppsaliensis.

Bell, D., and M. Jayne. 2006. "Conceptualizing Small Cities." In D. Bell and M. Jayne, eds., *Small Cities: Urban Experience Beyond the Metropolis,* 1–19. New York: Routledge.

Bennett, J. 2001. *The Enchantment of Modern Life.* Princeton, NJ: Princeton University Press.

Bernal, V. 2014. *Nation as Network: Diaspora, Cyberspace, and Citizenship.* Chicago: University of Chicago Press.

Bernal, V., K. Pype, and R. Daivi-Taylor, eds. 2023. *Cryptopolitics: Digital Media, Concealment, and Exposure in Africa.* New York: Berghahn Books.

Bleecker, J. 2009. "Design Fiction: A Short Essay on Design, Science, Fact and Fiction." In S. Carta, ed., *Machine Learning and the City: Applications in Architecture and Urban Design,* 561–78. Hoboken, NJ: John Wiley and Sons.

Boddy, J. 1989. *Wombs and Alien Spirits: Women, Men and the Zar Cult in Northern Sudan.* Madison: University of Wisconsin Press.

Bradbury, R. 1955. *Fahrenheit 451.* Translated by A. Audiberti. Paris: Denoël.

Braun, L. N. 2015. "Cyber Siren: What Mami Wata Reveals About the Internet and Chinese Presence in Kinshasa." *Canadian Journal of African Studies* 492: 301–18.

Braun, L. N. 2019. "Wandering Women: The Work of Congolese Transnational Traders." *Africa: Journal of the International Africa Institute* 892: 378–96.

Bridge, G., G. Özkaynak, and E. Turhan. 2018. "Energy Infrastructure and the Fate of the Nation: Introduction to Special Issue." *Energy Research & Social Science* 41: 1–11. https://doi.org/10.1016/j.erss.2018.04.029

Brinkman, I., M. Bruijn, and H. Bilal. 2009. "The Mobile Phone, 'Modernity' and Change in Khartoum, Sudan." In M. de Bruijn, F. B. Nyamnjoh, and I. Brinkman, eds., *Mobile Phones: The New Talking Drums of Everyday Africa*, 69–91. Leiden: Brill.

Brophy, J. 2010. "Developing a Corporeal Cyberfeminism: Beyond Cyberutopia." *New Media & Society* 12.6: 929–45.

Brown, M. G. 2015. "Fashioning Their Place: Dress and Global Imagination in Imperial Sudan." *Gender and History* 26.3: 115–31.

Brown, R. 1990. "Sudan's Other Economy: Migrants' Remittances, Capital Flight, and Their Policy Implications." Money, Finance and Development Working Paper no. 31, Institute of Social Sciences. https://ideas.repec.org/p/iss/mfdwpr/31.html

Bruijn, M. E. de. 2019. *Digitalization and the Field of African Studies.* Basel: Basler Afrika bibliographien.

Bruijn, M. E. de, and R. V. Dijk. 2012. *The Social Life of Connectivity in Africa.* New York: Palgrave Macmillan.

Bryceson, D. F., J. B. Jønsson, and H. Verbrugge. 2014. "For Richer, for Poorer: Marriage and Casualized Sex in East African Artisanal Mining Settlements." *Development and Change* 451: 79–104.

Bureau de la Mairie de Kikwit. 2016. "Rapport de recensement administratif de la population." Kikwit.

Burrell, J. 2009. "Could Connectivity Replace Mobility? An Analysis of Internet Cafe Use Patterns in Accra, Ghana." In M. de Bruijn, F. B. Nyamnjoh, and I. Brinkman, eds., *Mobile Phones: The New Talking Drums of Everyday Africa*, 151–69. Leiden: Brill.

Butler, J. 2004. *Precarious Life: The Powers of Mourning and Violence.* London: Verso.

Butler, J. 2009. *Frames of War: When Is Life Grievable?* New York: Verso.

Çankaya, S., and P. Mepschen. 2019. "Facing Racism: Discomfort, Innocence and the Liberal Peripheralisation of Race in the Netherlands." *Social Anthropology* 27.4: 626–40.

CDC-Investment Works. 2020. "What Is the Impact of Fibre Connectivity in the Democratic Republic of Congo? Practical Thinking on Investing for Development." Insight Portfolio Learning, CDC-Group, August 26. https://assets.cdcgroup.com

/wp-content/uploads/2020/08/26204824/What-is-the-impact-of-fibre-connectivity-in-the-DRC.pdf (accessed January 20, 2022).

Chalfin, B. 2017. "'Wastelandia': Infrastructure and the Commonwealth of Waste in Urban Ghana." *Ethnos* 82.4: 648–71.

Champaud, J. 1981. "L'espace commercial des bamiléké." *L'Espace Géographique* 3: 198–206. https://horizon.documentation.ird.fr/exl-doc/pleins_textes/pleins_textes_5/b_fdi_02-03/01491.pdf

Cheeseman, N., H. Matfess, and A. Amani. 2021. "Tanzania: The Roots of Repression." *Journal of Democracy* 32: 77–89.

Chevrillon-Guibert, R. 2013. "Des commerçants au coeur de l'expérience islamiste au Soudan: Rapports de/au pouvoir et recompositions des communautés darfouriennes zaghawa à l'aune des alliances du mouvement islamique soudanais 1950–2011." PhD dissertation, Auvergne University.

Choplin, A., and A. Franck. 2014. "Seeing Dubai in Khartoum and Nouakchott: 'Gulfication' on the Margins of the Arab World." In S. Wippel, K. Bromber, C. Steiner, and B. Krawietz, eds., *Under Construction: Logics of Urbanism in the Gulf Region*, 271–84. London: Ashgate.

Clapham, Christopher. *Africa and the International System: The Politics of State Survival.* no. 50. Cambridge: Cambridge University Press, 1996.

Commission Économique des Nations Unies pour l'Afrique. 2016. *Évaluation des données de l'urbanisation en Afrique.* Addis Ababa: Groupe de la Publication et de l'Impression de la CEA.

Crane, J. T. 2014. *Scrambling for Africa: AIDS, Expertise, and the Rise of American Global Health Science.* Ithaca, NY: Cornell University Press.

Cross, J. 2014. *Dream Zones: Anticipating Capitalism and Development in India.* London: Pluto Press.

Cuvelier, J. 2011. "Men, Mines and Masculinities: The Lives and Practices of Artisanal Miners in Lwambo (Katanga Province, DR Congo)." PhD dissertation, KU Leuven.

Daniels, J. 2009. "Rethinking Cyberfeminism(s): Race, Gender, and Embodiment." *Women's Studies Quarterly* 371.2: 101–24.

Datta, A. 2019. "Postcolonial Urban Futures: Imagining and Governing India's Smart Urban Age." *Environment and Planning D: Society and Space* 37.3: 393–410.

De Boeck, F. 1998. "Domesticating Diamonds and Dollars: Identity, Expenditure and Sharing in Southwestern Zaire 1984–1997." *Development and Change* 29.4: 777–810.

De Boeck, F. 2011. "Inhabiting Ocular Ground: Kinshasa's Future in the Light of Congo's Spectral Urban Politics." *Cultural Anthropology* 26.2: 263–86. https://doi.org/10.1111/j.1548-1360.2011.01099.x. https://dx.doi.org/10.1111/j.1548-1360.2011.01099.x

De Boeck, F., and M.-F. Plissart. 2004. *Kinshasa: Tales of the Invisible City.* Amsterdam: Ludion.

de Certeau, M. 1988. *The Practice of Everyday Life.* Translated by Steven Rendall. Berkeley: University of California Press.

Degani, M. 2017. "Modal Reasoning in Dar Es Salaam's Power Network." *American Ethnologist* 44.2: 300–314.

Degani, M. 2023. *The City Electric: Infrastructure and Ingenuity in Postsocialist Tanzania.* Durham, NC: Duke University Press.

Dehelean, D. 2009. "Environmental Friendly Welding—an Evolution from 3d (Dirty, Dusty, and Dangerous) to 3c (Cool, Clever, and Clean)." *Environmental Engineering & Management Journal* 8.4: 957–61.

Deleuze, G. 1988. *Spinoza: Practical Philosophy.* Translated by Robert Hurley. San Francisco: City Lights Books.

Demirdirek, M., B. Msallam, and C. Wilson. Forthcoming. "'My Phone Is Like My Office': Social Media Entrepreneurship Among Congolese Refugee Women in Dar es Salaam (Tanzania)." Under review for publication in *New Media and Society.*

Diaz Olvera, L., D. Plat, P. Pochet, and S. Maïdadi. 2002. "Étalement urbain, situations de pauvreté et accès à la ville en Afrique subsaharienne: L'exemple de Niamey." In Y. Bussiere and J.-L. Madre, eds., *Démographie et transport: Villes du Nord et villes du Sud,* 147–75. Paris: L'Harmattan.

Diaz Olvera, L., D. Plat, P. Pochet, and S. Maïdadi. 2012. "Motorbike Taxis in the 'Transport Crisis' of West and Central African Cities." *EchoGéo* 20. http://journals.openedition.org/echogeo/13080

Dilger, H., A. Kane, and S. Langwick, eds. 2012. *Medicine, Mobility, and Power in Global Africa: Transnational Health and Healing.* Bloomington: Indiana University Press.

Ding, Y., and C. L. Pang. 2018. "South–South Migrant Trajectories: African Traders in China as Guoke." In F. Hillmann, T. van Naerssen, and E. Spaan, eds., *Trajectories and Imaginaries in Migration,* 56–73. London: Routledge.

Di Nunzio, M. 2018. "Anthropology of Infrastructure." *LSE Cities, Governing Infrastructure Interfaces-Research Note* 1: 1–4.

Djouda Feudjio, Y. 2014. "Les jeunes bend-skineurs au Cameroun: Entre stratégie de survie et violence de l'état." *Autrepart* 3.3: 97–117. https://doi.org/10.3917/autr.071.0097

Dongala, E. 2005. *Les petits enfants naissent dans les étoiles.* Paris: Babelio.

Dongmo, J. L. 1981. *Le dynamisme bamileke.* Vol. 1: *La maitrise de l'espace agraire,* vol. 2: *La maitrise de l'espace urbain.* Yaoundé: CEPER.

Doughty, K. 2020. "Carceral Repair." *Cambridge Journal of Anthropology* 38.2. https://doi.org/10.3167/cja.2020.380203

Duffield, M. 2001. *Global Governance and the New Wars: The Merging of Development and Security.* London: Zed Books.

Duffield, M. 2007. *Development, Security, and Unending War.* Malden, MA: Polity Press.

Duffield, M. 2019. *Post-Humanitarianism: Governing Precarity in the Digital World.* Malden, MA: Polity Press.

Dufour, D.-R. 2011. *Baise ton prochain: Une histoire souterraine du capitalisme.* Paris: Denoël.

Dy, A. M., S. Marlow, and L. Martin. 2017. "A Web of Opportunity or the Same Old

Story? Women Digital Entrepreneurs and Intersectionality Theory." *Human Relations* 70.3: 286–311.

Dy, A. M., L. Martin, and S. Marlow 2018. "Emancipation Through Digital Entrepreneurship? A Critical Realist Analysis." *Organization* 25.5: 585–608. https://doi.org/10.1177/1350508418777891

Easton-Calabria, E. 2019. *Digital Livelihoods for People on the Move.* Report, United Nations Development Programme, December.

Eberhard, A., K. Gratwick, E. Morella, and P. Antmann. 2017. "Independent Power Projects in Sub-Saharan Africa: Investment Trends and Policy Lessons." *Energy Policy* 108: 390–424. https://doi.org/10.1016/j.enpol.2017.05.023

Eeuwijk, P. Van. 2014. "The Elderly Providing Care for the Elderly in Tanzania and Indonesia: Making 'Elder to Elder' Care Visible." *Sociologus* 64.1: 29–52.

Ekere, A. U., and R. C. Echem. 2013. "Complications of Fracture and Dislocation Treatment by Traditional Bone Setters: A Private Practice Experience." *Nigerian Health Journal* 11.2: 59–66.

Ela, J.-M. 1998. *Innovations sociales et renaissance de l'Afrique noire: Les défis du "monde d'en-bas."* Paris: L'Harmattan.

Elliott, K. 2020. *Young Men Navigating Contemporary Masculinities.* New York: Palgrave Macmillan.

Epstein, A. L. 1981. *Urbanisation and Kinship: The Domestic Domain on the Copperbelt of Zambia, 1950–1956.* London: Academic Press.

Fanon, F. 1961. *Les damnés de la terre.* Paris: Editions François Maspero.

Farmer, B. H., ed. 1977. *Green Revolution? Technology and Change in Rice-Growing Areas of Tamil Nadu and Sri Lanka.* Boulder, CO: Westview Press.

Fassin, D. 1992. *Pouvoir et maladie en Afrique.* Paris: Presses Universitaires de France.

Fassin, D. 2007. "Humanitarianism as a Politics of Life." *Public Culture* 19: 499–520.

Feierman, S., and J. M. Janzen, eds. 1992. *The Social Basis of Health and Healing in Africa.* Berkeley: University of California Press.

Ferguson, E. S. 1977. "The Mind's Eye: Nonverbal Thought in Technology." *Science* 197: 827–36.

Ferguson, J. 1999. *Expectations of Modernity: Myths and Meanings of Urban Life on the Zambian Copperbelt.* Berkeley: University of California Press.

Fischer, M. M. J. 2018. *Anthropology in the Meantime.* Durham, NC: Duke University Press.

Fischer, M. M. J. 2023a. *At the Pivot of East and West: Ethnographic, Literary and Filmic Arts.* Durham, NC: Duke University Press.

Fischer, M. M. J. 2023b. "Varieties of STS: Kenya: Techpreneur, Transnational Node, Kibera." *Engaging Science, Technology, and Society* 91: 173–82. https://n2t.net/ark:/81416/p4mg6j (accessed August 16, 2023).

Fischer, M. M. J. 2023c. "Kenya: Techpreneur, Transnational Node, Kibera." *Engaging Science, Technology, and Society.* STS Infrastructures (Platform for Experimental Collaborative Ethnography), 9(1): 173–82. https://n2t.net/ark:/81416/p4mg6j (accessed August 16 2023).

Fischer, M. M. J. 2025. "The Kigali Story, The Singapore Model, and Rights to the City." *JRAI, Journal of the Royal Anthropological Institute*. https://doi.org/10.1111/1467-9655.14308

Fischer, M. M. J. and A. Sadruddin. Forthcoming 2025. "Through the Artist's Eyes: Forms of Creative Life in Rwanda". *HAU, the Journal of Ethnographic Theory*.

Fontein, J. 2015. *Remaking Mutirikwi: Landscape, Water and Belonging in Southern Zimbabwe*. Woodbridge: Boydell and Brewer.

Fredericks, R. 2018. *Garbage Citizenship: Vital Infrastructures of Labor in Dakar, Senegal*. Durham, NC: Duke University Press.

Freedom House. 2017. "Sudan." https://freedomhouse.org/country/sudan/freedom-net /2017 (accessed February 2021).

Fritschi, J., and M. A. Wolf. 2012. "Mobile Learning for Teachers in North America: Exploring the Potential of Mobile Technologies to Support Teachers and Improve Practice." UNESCO Working Paper Series on Mobile Learning. https://eduq.info /xmlui/handle/11515/19074

gdckenya. 2021. "GDC Congratulates Nakuru on the Step to City Status." *Geo Blog*, June 4. https://www.gdc.co.ke/blog/gdc-md-ceo-congratulates-nakuru-on-the-step-to -city-status/

Geissler, P. W., and N. Tousignant. 2020. "Beyond Realism: Africa's Medical Dreams Introduction." *Africa* 90.1: 1–17.

Geissler, P. W., ed. 2015. *Para-States and Medical Science: Making African Global Health*. Durham, NC: Duke University Press.

Geissler, P. W., G. Lachenal, J. Manton, and N. Tousignant, eds. 2016. *Traces of the Future: An Archaeology of Medical Science in Africa*. Bristol: Intellect.

Geothermal Development Company. n.d. "Menengai Geothermal Project." https://www .gdc.co.ke/menengai.html (accessed April 3, 2025).

Geschiere, P. 2013. *Witchcraft, Intimacy, and Trust: Africa in Comparison*. Chicago: University of Chicago Press.

GoK (Government of the Republic of Kenya). 2018. *Kenya National Electrification Strategy: Key Highlights*. Edited by Ministry of Energy. Nairobi: Government of the Republic of Kenya.

Gondola, C. D. 1999. "'Bisengo ya la joie': Fêtes, sociabilité et politique dans les capitales congolaises." In Odile Goerg, ed., *Fêtes urbaines en Afrique: Espaces, identités et pouvoirs*, 87–111. Paris: Karthala.

Gondola, C. D. 2013. "Le culte du cowboy et les figures du masculin à Kinshasa dans les années." *Cahiers d'Études Africaines* 53.209–10: 173–99.

Gough, K. G., A. G. Tipple, and M. Napier. 2003. "Making a Living in African Cities: The Role of Home-Based Enterprises in Accra and Pretoria." *International Planning Studies* 8.4: 253–77.

Graeber, D., and D. Wengrow. 2021. *The Dawn of Everything: A New History of Humanity*. London: Penguin UK.

Graham, M., ed. 2019. *Digital Economies at Global Margins*. Cambridge, MA: MIT Press.

Graham, S., and S. Marvin. 1996. *Telecommunications and the City: Electronic Spaces, Urban Places*. London: Routledge.

Graham, S., and S. Marvin. 2001. *Splintering Urbanism: Networked Infrastructures, Technological Mobilities, and the Urban Condition*. London: Routledge.

Graham, S., and C. McFarlane, eds. 2015. *Infrastructural Lives: Urban Infrastructure in Context*. London: Routledge.

Guattari, F. 1979. *L'Inconscient machinique: Essais de schizo-analyse*. Paris: Éditions Recherches.

Guattari, F. 1996. *Chaosmosis: An Ethico-Aesthetic Paradigm*. Bloomington: Indiana University Press.

Guma, P. K. 2020. "Incompleteness of Urban Infrastructures in Transition: Scenarios from the Mobile Age in Nairobi." *Social Studies of Science* 50.5: 728–50. https://orcid.org/0000-0001-8511-5664

Guma, P. K., and J. Monstadt. 2021. "Smart City-Making? The Spread of ICT-Driven Plans and Infrastructures in Nairobi." *Urban Geography* 42.3: 360–81.

Günel, G. 2019. *Space Ship in the Desert: Energy, Climate Change and Urban Design*. Durham, NC: Duke University Press.

Gunn, W., T. Otto, and R. C. Smith, eds. 2013. *Design Anthropology: Theory and Practice*. New York: Bloomsbury Academic.

Hampshire, K. R., and S. A. Owusu. 2013. "Grandfathers, Google, and Dreams: Medical Pluralism, Globalization, and New Healing Encounters in Ghana." *Medical Anthropology: Cross Cultural Studies in Health and Illness* 32.3: 247–65.

Haraway, D. J. 2013. *When Species Meet*. Minneapolis: University of Minnesota Press.

Harms, E., S. Hussein, S. Newell, L. Schein, S. Shneiderman, T. S Turner, and J. Zhang. 2014. "Remote and Edgy: New Takes on Old Anthropological Themes." *HAU: Journal of Ethnographic Theory* 4.1: 361–81.

Hart, J. 2024. *Making an African City. Technopolitics and the Infrastructure of Everyday Life in Colonial Accra*. Bloomington, IN: Indiana University Press. https://publish.iu press.indiana.edu/projects/making-an-african-city

Hart, K. 1973. "Informal Income Opportunities and Urban Employment in Ghana." *Journal of Modern African Studies* 11.1: 61–89.

Harvey, D. 1996. "Cities or Urbanization?" *City* 1.1–2: 38–61.

Harvey, P., and H. Knox. 2012. "The Enchantments of Infrastructure." *Mobilities* 7.4: 521–36.

Harvey, P., and H. Knox. 2015. *Roads: An Anthropology of Infrastructure and Expertise*. Ithaca, NY: Cornell University Press.

Havard, J.-F. 2001. "Ethos 'bul faale' et nouvelles figures de la réussite au Sénégal." *Politique Africaine* 82.2: 63–77.

Hecht, G., ed. 2011. *Entangled Geographies: Empire and Technopolitics in the Global Cold War*. Cambridge, MA: MIT Press.

Hendriks, T. 2013. "Work in the Rainforest: Labour, Race and Desire in a Congolese Logging Camp." PhD dissertation, KU Leuven.

Hendriks, T. 2022. *Rainforest Capitalism: Power and Masculinity in a Congolese Timber Concession*. Durham, NC: Duke University Press.

Henriet, B. 2021. *Colonial Importance: Virtue and Violence in a Congolese Concession, 1911–1940*. Oldenbourg: de Gruyter.

Herbst, Jeffrey. 1990. "War and the State in Africa." *International Security* 14.4: 117–39.

Hilson, G., and S. M. Banchirigah. 2009. "Are Alternative Livelihood Projects Alleviating Poverty in Mining Communities? Experiences from Ghana." *Journal of Development Studies* 45.2: 172–96.

Horton, R. 1993. *Patterns of Thought in Africa and the West: Essays on Magic, Religion and Science*. Cambridge: Cambridge University Press.

Hountondji, P. 1990. "Scientific Dependence in Africa Today." *Research in African Literatures* 21.3: 5–15.

House-Midamba, B., and F. K. Ekechi, eds. 1995. *African Market Women and Economic Power: The Role of Women in African Economic Development*. Westport, CT: Greenwood Press.

Hug, P. 2003. "Noir pour blanc 'ethno-écolo-branché': Voyager virtuellement dans un restaurant africain reel." *Alinéa* 13: 143–62.

Hughes, T. P. 1993. *Networks of Power: Electrification in Western Society, 1880–1930*. Baltimore: Johns Hopkins University Press.

Hughes, T. P. 1998. *Rescuing Prometheus*. New York: Pantheon.

Hwang, B. 2013. "Panty-Slapped: Cyberactivism and African Feminism Join Forces." *Feminist Africa* 18: 140–44.

Ibrahim, B., and A. Bize. 2018. "Waiting Together: The Motorcycle Taxi Stand as Nairobi Infrastructure." *Africa Today* 65.2: 72–91.

Internet Live Statistics. 2020. https://www.internetlivestats.com/internet-users/sudan/ (accessed October 5, 2020).

Jackson, S. J. 2014. "Rethinking Repair." *Media Technologies*, January 17, 221–39.

Jappe, A. 2003. *Les aventures de la marchandise: Pour une nouvelle critique de la valeur*. Paris: Denoël.

Jasanoff, S., and K. Sang-Hyun. 2009. "Containing the Atom: Sociotechnical Imaginaries and Nuclear Power in the United States and South Korea." *Minerva* 47.2: 119–46.

Johanson, R. K., and A. V. Adams. 2004. *Skills Development in Sub-Saharan Africa*. New York: World Bank.

Jønsson, J. B., and D. F. Bryceson. 2009. "Rushing for Gold: Mobility and Small-Scale Mining in East Africa." *Development and Change* 40.2: 249–79.

Juma, C. 1989. *The Gene Hunters: Biotechnology and the Scramble for Seeds*. London: Zed Press; Princeton, NJ: Princeton University Press.

Juma, C. 2011. *The New Harvest: Agricultural Innovation in Africa*. New York: Oxford University Press.

Juma, C. 2023. *The University Drop-In: The Life of Calestous Juma in His Own Words.* Terra Alta, WV: Headline Books Publishing.

Juma, C., H. Monteith, H. Krugmann, T. Angura, H. Acquay, A. E. Akino, P. Wandera, and J. Mugabe. 1995. *Economic Policy Reforms and the Environment: African Experiences.* Geneva: United Nations Environment Programme.

Juma, C., and J. B. Objwang. 1989. *Innovation and Sovereignty: The Patent Debate in African Development.* Nairobi: African Centre for Technology Studies.

Kadoda, G., and S. Hale. 2015. "Contemporary Youth Movements and the Role of Social Media in Sudan." *Canadian Journal of African Studies* 49.1: 215–36.

Kaffo, C., P. Kamdem, and B. Tatsabong. 2012. "Le transport par moto entre satisfaction des besoins des 'cadets sociaux' et insécurité urbaine au Cameroun: Quelles conjugaisons?" In P. Kamdem and M. Kuete, eds., *L'insécurité au Cameroun: Mythes ou réalités*, 20–45. Yaoundé: Iresma.

Kaffo, C., P. Kamdem, B. Tatsabong, and L. M. Diebo. 2007. "L'intégration des 'mototaxi' dans le transport public au Cameroun ou l'état à la remorque de l'informel: Une solution d'avenir au problème d'emploi et de mobilité urbaine en Afrique subsaharienne." Presented to the conference "Le taxi, premier transport à la demande, solution d'avenir pour les mobilités urbaines," L'Institut pour la ville en mouvement, Fondation Calouste Gulbenkian, Lisbon, September 20–21. http://www.ville-en-mo uvement.com/

Kalieu, C. 2016. "Surgissement, prolifération et intégration des motos-taxis dans les villes camerounaises: Les exemples de Douala et Bafoussam." PhD dissertation, Université Bretagne Loire.

Keja, R. 2022. *Political Silence of Youth in Togo: Mobile Phones, Information, and Civic (Dis)Engagement.* Berlin: de Gruyter.

Kemp, S. 2020. "Digital 2020: Sudan." https://datareportal.com/reports/digital-2020 -sudan (accessed October 5, 2020).

Keutcheu, J. 2015. "Le fléau des motos-taxis." *Cahiers d'Études Africaines* 219. http://jour nals.openedition.org/etudesafricaines/18208

Kibari N'sanga, R., and L. Mulala. 2011. *Le virus Ebola à Kikwit: Mythe, mystère ou réalité. Et quinze ans après?* Kinshasa: Edition Akor Press.

Kitchin, R. 2014. "The Real-Time City? Big Data and Smart Urbanism." *GeoJournal* 79.1: 1–14.

Klein, H. K., and D. L. Kleinman. 2002. "The Social Construction of Technology: Structural Considerations." *Science, Technology, & Human Values* 27.1: 28–52.

Kummitha, R. K. R., and N. Crutzen. 2017. "How Do We Understand Smart Cities? An Evolutionary Perspective." *Cities* 67: 43–52.

Kusiak, P. 2010. "'Tubab' Technologies and 'African' Ways of Knowing: Nationalist Techno-Politics in Senegal." *History and Technology* 26.3: 225–49.

Kusimba, S. 2018. "Money, Mobile Money, and Ritual in Western Kenya: The Contingency Fund and the Thirteenth Cow." *African Studies Review* 61.2: 158–82.

Lahiri-Dutt, K. 2012. "Digging Women: Towards a New Agenda for Feminist Critiques of Mining." *Gender, Place and Culture* 192: 193–212.

Lambert, H. 2012. "Medical Pluralism and Medical Marginality: Bone Doctors and the Selective Legitimation of Therapeutic Expertise in India." *Social Science and Medicine* 74.7: 1029–36.

Langwick, S. 2007. "Devils, Parasites, and Fierce Needles: Healing and the Politics of Translation in Southern Tanzania." *Science, Technology & Human Values* 32.1: 88–117.

Langwick, S. 2011. *Bodies, Politics, and African Healing: The Matter of Maladies in Tanzania*. Bloomington: Indiana University Press.

Larkin, B. 2008. *Signal and Noise: Media, Infrastructure, and Urban Culture in Nigeria*. Durham, NC: Duke University Press.

Larkin, B. 2013. "The Politics and Poetics of Infrastructure." *Annual Review of Anthropology* 42: 327–43.

Larkin, B. 2018. "Promising Forms: The Political Aesthetics of Infrastructure." In N. Anand, A. Gupta, and H. Appel, eds., *The Promise of Infrastructure*, 175–202. Durham, NC: Duke University Press.

Lasch, C. 1979. *The Culture of Narcissims. American Life in an Age of Diminishing Expectations*. New York: W.W. Norton & Company.

Latour, B. 1984. *Les microbes, guerre et paix, suivi de irréductions*. Paris: Métailié, Pandore.

Latour, B. 1993. *"ARAMIS" ou l'amour des techniques*. Paris: La Découverte.

Latour, B. 1995. *Aramis: or, The Love of Technology*. Translated by Catherine Porter. Cambridge, MA: Harvard University Press.

Latour, B. 1999. *Pandora's Hope: Essays on the Reality of Science Studies*. Cambridge, MA: Harvard University Press.

Latour, B. 2004. "How to Talk About the Body? The Normative Dimension of Science Studies." *Body & Society* 10.2–3: 205–29.

Latour, B. 2006. *Changer de société, refaire de la sociologie*. Paris: Découverte.

Latour, B., and P. Weibel, eds. 2005. *Making Things Public: Atmospheres of Democracy*. Cambridge, MA: MIT Press.

Lecercle, J.-J. 2019. *De l'interpellation: Sujet, langue, idéologie*. Paris: Editions Amsterdam.

Lee, M. 2014. *Africa's World Trade: Informal Economies and Globalisation from Below*. London: Zed Books.

Lefebvre, H. 1968. *Le droit à la ville*. Paris: Éditions Anthropos.

Lehmann, K., and M. Söllner. 2014. "Theory-Driven Design of a Mobile-Learning Application to Support Different Interaction Types in large-Scale Lectures." Paper presented to the Twenty-Second European Conference on Information Systems (ECIS), Tel Aviv, Israel, June 9–14.

Liadi, O. F., and O. A. Olutayo. 2017. "Traditional Apprenticeship, Normative Expectations and Sustainability of Masonry Vocation in Ibadan, Nigeria." *International Journal of Sociology of Education* 6.2: 186–215.

Light, D. W. 2004. "From Migrant Enclaves to Mainstream: Reconceptualizing Informal Economic Behavior." *Theory and Society* 33.6: 705–37.

Lipovetsky, G., and J. Serroy. 2007. *L'écran global: Culture-médias et cinéma à l'âge hyper-moderne*. Paris: Éd. Le Seuil.

Livingston, J. 2012. *Improvising Medicine: An African Oncology Ward in an Emerging Cancer Epidemic*. Durham, NC: Duke University Press.

Löwy, M. 2006. "Le capitalisme comme religion: Walter Benjamin et Max Weber." *Raisons Politiques* 32.3: 203–19.

Luque-Ayala, A., and S. Marvin. 2015. "Developing a Critical Understanding of Smart Urbanism?" *Urban Studies* 52.12: 2105–16.

Madianou, M., and D. Miller. 2012. *Migration and New Media: Transnational Families and Polymedia*. London: Routledge.

Malaquais, D. 2001. "Arts de feyre au Cameroun." *Politique Africaine* 82.2: 101–18.

Malefakis, A., T. Grob, and C. Luginbühl. 2016. *Making a Living from Old Shoes: Tanzanian Street Vendors as Urban Experts*. Zurich: Benteli.

Malipula, M. 2014. "Depoliticised Ethnicity in Tanzania: A Structural and Historical Narrative." *Afrika Focus* 27: 49–70.

Malisa, Z. 2021. "Dk Mwigulu: Tozo ya miamala si michango ya kirafiki ni sheria ya Bunge." *Mwananchi*, August 20. https://www.mwananchi.co.tz/mw/habari/kitaifa/dk-mwigulu-tozo-ya-miamala-si-michango-ya-kirafiki-ni-sheria-ya-bunge-3518510 (accessed November 15, 2021).

Mangi, M. P. 2017. "Geothermal Exploration in Kenya—Status Report and Updates." In *Sustainable Development Goals (SDG) Short Course II on Exploration and Development of Geothermal Resources, Lake Bogoria and Naivasha, Kenya*. https://orkustofnun.is/gogn/unu-gtp-sc/UNUGTP-SC-25-0701.pdf (accessed September 30, 2019).

Manji, A. 2015. "Bulldozers, Homes and Highways: Nairobi and the Right to the City." *Review of African Political Economy* 42.144: 206–24. https://doi.org/10.1080/03056244.2014.988698

Marchais, G. 2009. "Règles publiques, règles privées: Les taxis-motos au Bénin." *L'Économie Politique* 1: 59–68. https://doi.org/10.3917/leco.041.0059

Marchand, T. H. J. 2008. "Muscles, Morals and Mind: Craft Apprenticeship and the Formation of Person." *British Journal of Educational Studies* 56.3: 245–71.

Margier, A., and L. Melgaço. 2016. "Introduction au dossier 'Whose right to the city? / Le droit à la ville, pour qui?'" *Environnement Urbain / Urban Environment* 10. http://journals.openedition.org/eue/1483

Marshall-Fratani, R. 2001. "Prospérité miraculeuse." *Politique Africaine* 82.2: 24–44.

Martinez-Alier, J. 2002. *The Environmentalism of the Poor: A Study of Ecological Conflicts and Valuation*. Cheltenham: Edward Elgar.

Marx, K. 1938. *Capital*. Vol. 1. London: Allen & Unwin.

Mavhunga, C. C. 2014. *Transient Workspaces: Technologies of Everyday Innovation in Zimbabwe*. Cambridge, MA: MIT Press.

Mavhunga, C. C. 2017a. "Introduction: What Do Science, Technology, and Innovation Mean from Africa?" In C. C. Mavhunga, ed., *What Do Science, Technology, and Innovation Mean from Africa?*, 1–27. Cambridge, MA: MIT Press.

Mavhunga, C. C., ed. 2017b. *What Do Science, Technology, and Innovation Mean from Africa?* Cambridge, MA: MIT Press.

Mavhunga, C. C., J. Cuvelier, and K. Pype. 2016. "Containers, Carriers, Vehicles." *Transfers* 62: 43–53.

Mbembe, A. 2001. *On the Postcolony.* Berkeley: University of California Press.

Mbembe, A. 2010. *Sortir de la grande nuit: Essais sur l'Afrique décolonisée.* Paris: Découverte.

Mbembe, A. 2016. "Future Knowledges." Abiola Lecture, presented the Annual Meetings of the African Studies Association, Washington, DC, December.

Mbembe, A. 2019. "Bodies as Borders." *From the European South* 4: 5–18.

McAdam, M., C. Crowley, and R. T. Harrison. 2020. "Digital Girl: Cyberfeminism and the Emancipatory Potential of Digital Entrepreneurship in Emerging Economies." *Small Business Economics* 55.2: 349–62.

McGranahan, G., A. Kyessi, S. M. Osman, G. Steel, M. H. Andreasen, G. M. Hamid, E. Ille, and W. J. Kombe. 2020. *Examining the Urban Land Nexus and Inclusive Urbanization in Dar es Salaam, Mwanza and Khartoum.* Brighton, UK: Institute of Development Studies and East African Research Fund.

McIntosh, J. 2010. "Mobile Phones and Mipoho's Prophecy: The Powers and Dangers of Flying Language." *American Ethnologist* 37.2: 337–53.

McKay, R. 2018a. "Conditions of Life in the City: Medicine and Gendered Relations in Maputo, Mozambique." *Journal of the Royal Anthropological Institute* 24: 1–18.

McKay, R. 2018b. *Medicine in the Meantime: The Work of Care in Mozambique.* Durham, NC: Duke University Press.

Meehan, K. M. 2014. "Tool-Power: Water Infrastructure as Wellsprings of State Power." *Geoforum* 57: 215–24.

Melchior-Bonnet, S. 1994. *Histoire du miroir.* Paris: Editions Imago.

Meli, V. M. 2011. "Transport routier rural et transhumance rurale-urbaine dans quelques localités des hautes terres de l'Ouest-Cameroun." *Revue des Hautes Terres* 1.1: 65–92.

Meli, V. M. 2014. "Le 'clando' rural à ciel ouvert: Là où la transgression est la norme." In S. Perseil and Y. Pesqueux, eds., *L'organisation de la transgression: Formaliser l'informel?*, 175–89. Paris: L'Harmattan.

Melly, C. 2017. *Bottleneck: Moving, Building, and Belonging in an African City.* Chicago: University of Chicago Press.

Meyer, B. 2001. "Prières, fusils et meurtre rituel." *Politique Africaine* 82.2: 45–62.

Meyer, B. 2015. *Sensational Movies: Video, Vision, and Christianity in Ghana.* Oakland: University of California Press.

Mibei, G., and J. Lagat. 2011. "Structural Controls in Menengai Geothermal Field." In *Proceedings of the Kenyatta International Conference Centre*, 21–22. Nairobi.

Miller, P. S. 2021. "Shifting Notions of Endogamy and Exogamy: Religion, Social Class and Race in Marriage Practices in the Upper-Middle Class Neighbourhood of Amarat." In A. Franck, B. Casciarri, and I. Salim El-Hassan, eds., *In-Betweenness in*

Greater Khartoum: Spaces, Temporalities, and Identities from Separation to Revolution, 282–309. New York: Berghahn Books.

Misser, F. 2013. *La saga d'Inga: L'histoire des barrages du fleuve Congo.* Tervuren: L'Harmattan.

Mitchell, T. 2009. "Carbon Democracy." *Economy and Society* 38.3: 399–432. https://doi.org/10.1080/03085140903020598

Mitchell, T. 2014. "Introduction: Life of Infrastructure." *Comparative Studies of South Asia, Africa and the Middle East* 34.3: 437–39. https://doi.org/10.1215/1089201x-2826013

Mol, A. 2002. *The Body Multiple: Ontology in Medical Practice.* Durham, NC: Duke University Press.

Monstadt, J., and S. Schramm. 2017. "Toward the Networked City? Translating Technological Ideals and Planning Models in Water and Sanitation Systems in Dar es Salaam." *International Journal of Urban and Regional Research* 41.1: 104–25.

Moriset, B. 2020. "The Geography of E-Commerce." In B. Warf, ed., *Geographies of the Internet*, 1–32. London: Routledge.

Msuya, E. 2021. "Rais Samia aagiza kufanyiwa kazi suala la tozo." *Mwananchi*, July 19. https://www.mwananchi.co.tz/mw/habari/kitaifa/rais-samia-aagiza-kufanyiwa-kazi-suala-la-tozo-3478426 (accessed April 1, 2025).

Mukolwe, E., and J. Korir. 2016. "Social Media and Entrepreneurship: Tools, Benefits, and Challenges. A Case Study of Women Online Entrepreneurs on Kilimani Mums Marketplace on Facebook." *International Journal of Humanities and Social Science* 6.8: 248–56.

Mulemi, B. A. 2010. *Coping with Cancer and Adversity: Hospital Ethnography in Kenya.* Leiden: African Studies Centre.

Murray, M. J. 2017. *The Urbanism of Exception: The Dynamics of Global City Building in the 21st Century.* Cambridge: Cambridge University Press.

Mutagwaba, W. K., R. Mwaipopo-Ako, and A. L. Mlaki. 1998. "The Impact of Technology on Poverty Alleviation: The Case of Artisanal Mining in Tanzania." Presented to the Third REPOA Research Workshop, Dar es Salaam, April 15–16. http://www.tzonline.org/pdf/technologyandpoverty.pdf

Mutongi, K. 2017. *Matatu: A History of Popular Transportation in Nairobi.* Chicago: University of Chicago Press.

Muyinda, P. B., J. T. Lubega, K. Lynch, and T. Van Der Weide. 2010. "Mobile Learning Objects Deployment and Utilization in Developing Countries." *International Journal of Computing and ICT Research* 4.1: 37–46.

Nading, A. M. 2014. *Mosquito Trails: Ecology, Health, and the Politics of Entanglement.* Oakland: University of California Press.

Nading, A. M. 2017. "Local Biologies, Leaky Things, and the Chemical Infrastructure of Global Health." *Medical Anthropology* 36.2: 141–56.

Nageeb, S. 2004. *New Spaces and Old Frontiers: Women, Social Space, and Islamization in Sudan.* Lanham, MD: Lexington Books.

Nagi, T., and H. Alkabir. n.d. "Shadow Labourers: Urbanisation, Displacement and Women Vendors in the Capital City of Sudan."

Nash, J. 1979. *We Eat the Mines and the Mines Eat Us*. New York: Columbia University Press.

Ndegwa, M. K., H. de Groote, and Z. M. Gitonga. 2015. "Evaluation of Artisan Training in Metal Silo Construction for Grain Storage in Africa: Impact on Uptake, Entrepreneurship and Income." *International Journal of Educational Development* 43: 12–21.

Ngoie, G., and D. Lelu. 2010. *Migration en République Démocratique du Congo: Profil national 2009*. Geneva: Organisation Internationale pour les Migrations.

Nguluma, A. T. 1990. "The Role of Law and Administrative Mechanisms in the Development of Science and Technology: Policies and Strategies in Post-Independence Tanzania." IDRC Manuscript Report no. 242.

Nouraie-Simone, F., ed. 2005. *On Shifting Ground: Muslim Women in the Global Era*. New York: Feminist Press.

Obrist, B. 2016. "Place Matters: The Home as a Key Site of Old-Age Care in Coastal Tanzania." In J. Hoffman and K. Pype, eds., *Ageing in Sub-Saharan Africa: Spaces and Practices of Care*, 95–114. Bristol: Policy Press.

Odumosu, T. B. 2017. "Making Mobiles African." In C. Mavhunga, ed., *What Do Science, Technology, and Innovation Mean from Africa?*, 137–50. Cambridge, MA: MIT Press.

Okoro, O. M. 2004. "Principles and Methods in Vocational and Technical Education in Nigeria." https://www.academia.edu/33801757/Vtetoprint

Olsen, W. C., and C. Sargent, eds. 2017. *African Medical Pluralism*. Bloomington: Indiana University Press.

Olutayo, L. 2010. "Engendering Rural Development Through Indigenous Productions Relations in Africa." In L. Heinecken and H. Prozesky, eds., *Society in Focus— Change, Challenge and Resistance: Reflections from South Africa and Beyond*, 106–19. Newcastle upon Tyne: Cambridge Scholars.

Omondi, C. 2011. "Borehole Geology and Hydrothermal Mineralisation of Wells MW-01 and MW-02, Menengai Geothermal Field, Central Kenya Rift Valley." United Nations University Geothermal Training Programme, Orkustofnun, Grensasvegur 9.

Onuminya, J. E. 2004. "The Role of the Traditional Bonesetter in Primary Fracture Care in Nigeria." *South African Medical Journal* 94.8: 652–58.

Orwell, G. 1950. *1984*. Paris: Gallimard.

Osborn, E. L. 2009. "Casting Aluminium Cooking Pots: Labour, Migration and Artisan Production in West Africa's Informal Sector, 1945–2005." *African Identities* 7.3: 373–86.

Owen, J. 2015. *Congolese Social Networks: Living on the Margins in Muizenberg, Cape Town*. London: Lexington Books.

Paget, D. 2021. "Tanzania: The Authoritarian Landslide." *Journal of Democracy* 32: 61–76.

Pain, M. 1984. "Le dynamisme bamiléké." *Annales de Géographie* 93.519: 590–95. https://www.persee.fr/doc/geo_0003-4010_1984_num_93_519_20293

Peters, R. 2020. "Motorbike-Taxi-Drivers as Infrastructure in the Indonesian City." *Ethnos* 85.3: 471–90.

Pfaffenberger, B. 1988. "Fetishised Objects and Humanised Nature: Towards an Anthropology of Technology." *Man* 23.2: 236–52.

Phippard, T. 2023. "Urban Fractures: Mobility, Risk, and the Accidenté in Kikwit, DR Congo." *Africa: Journal of the International African Institute* 93.1: 140–58.

Pierskalla, J. H., and F. M. Hollenbach. 2013. "Technology and Collective Action: The Effect of Cell Phone Coverage on Political Violence in Africa." *American Political Science Review* 107.2: 207–24.

Pignare, P., and I. Stengers. 2007. *La sorcellerie capitaliste: Pratiques de désenvoutement.* Paris: Découverte.

Pillay, D. 2007. "Introduction to Special Issue: Globalization and the Challenges to Labour and Development." *Labour, Capital and Society / Travail, Capital et Société* 40.1–2: 2–16.

Pinch, T. J., and W. E. Bijker. 1984. "The Social Construction of Facts and Artefacts: or How the Sociology of Science and the Sociology of Technology Might Benefit Each Other." *Social Studies of Science* 14.3: 399–441.

Plat, D. 2003. "Mobilités quotidiennes en Afrique subsaharienne: Économies et finances." Habilitation à diriger des recherches, Université Lumière, Lyon II.

Plummer, A. 2019. "Kenya and China's Labour Relations: Infrastructural Development for Whom, by Whom?" *Africa: Journal of the International African Institute* 89.4: 680–95.

Portelli, S. 2023. "Spirits of Displacement: Gnawa Rituals and Gentrification in Casablanca." *Focaal: Journal of Global and Historical Anthropology* 1: 1–15. https://www.berghahnjournals.com/view/journals/focaal/aop/fcl042001/fcl042001.xml

Prag, E. 2013. "Mama Benz in Trouble: Networks, the State, and Fashion Wars in the Beninese Textile Market." *African Studies Review* 56.3: 101–21.

Preci, A. 2024. "On the Banks of the Pilcomayo River: Wichí Fishery in the Age of Motorcycles." *Cultural Geographies* 31.2: 231–48. https://orcid.org/0000-0002-1411-5138

Pype, K. 2007. "Fighting Boys, Strong Men and Gorillas: Notes on the Imagination of Masculinities in Kinshasa." *Africa: Journal of the International African Institute* 77.2: 250–71.

Pype, K. 2011. "Dreaming the Apocalypse: Mimesis and the Pentecostal Imagination in Kinshasa." *Paideuma* 57: 81–96.

Pype, K. 2012. *The Making of the Pentecostal Melodrama: Media, Religion, and Gender in Kinshasa.* New York: Berghahn Books.

Pype, K. 2016a. "(Not) Talking Like a Motorola: Politics of Masking and Unmasking in Kinshasa's Mobile Phone Culture." *Journal of the Royal Anthropological Institute* 22.3: 633–52.

Pype, K. 2016b. "On Interference and Hotspots: Ethnographic Explorations of Rural-

Urban Connectivity in and Around Kinshasa's Phonie Cabins." *Académie Royale des Sciences d'Outre-Mer* 62.2: 229–60.

Pype, K. 2017a. "Smartness from Below: Variations on Technology and Creativity in Contemporary Kinshasa." In C. C. Mavhunga, ed., *What Do Science, Technology and Innovation Mean from Africa?*, 97–115. Cambridge, MA: MIT Press.

Pype, K. 2017b. "Branhamist Kindoki: Ethnographic Notes on Connectivity, Technology, and Urban Witchcraft in Contemporary Kinshasa." In K. Rio, M. MacCarthy, and R. Blanes, eds., *Pentecostalism and Witchcraft*, 115–44. Cham: Springer.

Pype, K. 2018. "Of Masters and Machines: Anthropological Reflections on Invention and Intelligence." *JJ Bachofen Lecture Series: Basic Questions of Anthropology* 4: 1–20.

Pype, K. 2019. "(Not) in Sync—Digital Time and Forms of (Dis-)connecting: Ethnographic Notes from Kinshasa (DR Congo)." *Media, Culture Society* 43.7: 1197–212.

Pype, K. 2021. "Digital Creativity and Urban Entrapment in Kinshasa: Experiments in Solving Precarity." *City and Society* 33.2: 324–45.

Pype, K. 2022a. "Coding the City: Mapping Eco-Systems and Zones of Opportunity in Kinshasa's Emerging Tech Scene." In G. Musila, ed., *Routledge Handbook of African Popular Culture*, 323–45. New York: Routledge.

Pype, K. 2022b. "Fishing Nets, Kabila's Eyes and Voter's Cards: Citizen-State Mediations in DR Congo." In W. Adebanwi, ed., *Everyday State and Democracy in Africa: Ethnographic Encounters*, 259–80. Athens: Ohio University Press.

Raheem, H. O. 2011. "Indigenous Knowledge and Rural Housing Development in Ona-Ara Local Government Area of Oyo State, Nigeria." Sc. Project. Department of Urban and Regional Planning, University of Ibadan.

Rahier, N. 2021. "Overheated Stomachs: Notes on Urban Life and Toxicity in Nakuru, Kenya." *Africa: Journal of the International African Institute* 91.3: 453–72.

Rahier, N., Devos, E., DeBlock, H., and Stroeken, K. (2025). "A Questionable Account of Ethnographic Validity: Sukuma Dandies in Katavi, Tanzania." *Journal of Organizational Ethnography* 14.1: 125–38.

Renault, E. 2014. "10 Critique du marché." In E. Renault, *Marx et la philosophie*, 186–99. Paris: Presses Universitaires de France.

Roberts, L. 2016. "Deep Mapping and Spatial Anthropology." *Humanities* 5.1: 5. https://www.mdpi.com/2076-0787/5/1/5

Rodgers, D., and B. O'Neill. 2012. "Infrastructural Violence: Introduction to the Special Issue." *Ethnography* 13.4: 401–12.

Rodina, L., and L. M. Harris. 2016. "Water Services, Lived Citizenship, and Notions of the State in Marginalised Urban Spaces: The Case of Khayelitsha, South Africa." *Water Alternatives* 9.2: 336–55. https://doi.org/10.14288/1.0363016

Root, A. 2012. "Beyond the Soapbox: Facebook and the Public Sphere in Egypt." *Online Journal of the Virtual Middle East* 61. http://www.cyberorient.net/article.do?articleId=7751 (accessed July 29, 2015).

Rutten, M., and M. Mwangi. 2012. "Mobile Cash for Nomadic Livestock Keepers: The Impact of the Mobile Phone Innovation (M-Pesa) on Maasai Pastoralists in Kenya."

In J.-B. Gewald, A. Leliveld, and I. Pesa, eds., *Transforming Innovations in Africa: Explorative Studies on Appropriation in African Societies*, 79–101. Leiden: Brill.

Sahabana, M., and X. Godard, eds. 2003. "Les transports et la ville en Afrique au sud du Sahara, le temps de la débrouille et du désordre inventif, 2002." *Les Annales de la Recherche Urbaine* 93.1: 182–83.

Sassen, S. 1991. *The Global City: New York, London, Tokyo.* Princeton, NJ: Princeton University Press.

Schipani, A. 2021. "Special Report: Sudan After the Revolution." *Financial Times*, January 26.

Schon, D. A. 1967. *Technology and Change.* New York: Delacorte Press.

Sharkey, H. J. 2008. "Arab Identity and Ideology in Sudan: The Politics of Language, Ethnicity and Race." *African Affairs* 107.426: 21–43.

Sharp, L. 1991. *The Possessed and the Dispossessed: Spirits, Identity, and Power in a Madagascar Migrant Town.* Berkeley: University of California Press.

Shaw, R. 2002. *Memories of the Slave Trade: Rituals and the Historical Imagination in Sierra Leone.* Chicago: University of Chicago Press.

Sheller, M., and J. Urry. 2006. "Introduction: Mobile Cities, Urban Mobilities." In M. Sheller and J. Urry, eds., *Mobile Technologies of the City*, 1–17. New York: Routledge Taylor & Francis e-Library.

Showers, K. B. 2011. "Beyond Mega on a Mega Continent: Grand Inga on Central Africa's Congo River." In S. D. Brunn, ed., *Engineering Earth: The Impacts of Megaengineering Projects*, 1651–79. Dordrecht: Springer.

Siemens, G. 2014. "Connectivism: A Learning Theory for the Digital Age." *International Journal of Instructional Technology and Distance Learning* 2.1: 3–10.

Sierra, A., and J. Tadié. 2008. "Introduction: La ville face à ses marges." *Autrepart* 1.45: 3–13.

Sietchiping, R., M. J. Permezel, and C. Ngomsi. 2012. "Transport and Mobility in Sub-Saharan African Cities: An Overview of Practices, Lessons and Options for Improvements." *Cities* 29.3: 183–89.

Simmel, G. 1950. *The Sociology of Georg Simmel.* London: Collier Macmillan.

Simone, A. 2013. "Cities of Uncertainty: Jakarta, the Urban Majority, and Inventive Political Technologies." *Theory, Culture & Society* 30.7–8: 243–63.

Slavova, M., and E. Okwechime. 2016. "African Smart Cities Strategies for Agenda 2063." *Africa Journal of Management* 22: 210–29.

Smith, C. 2017. "'Our Changes'? Visions of the Future in Nairobi." *Urban Planning* 2.1: 31–40.

Smith, É. 2013. "Retour historique sur les 'printemps démocratiques' en Afrique subsaharienne." *Afrique Contemporaine* 1: 100–101. https://doi-org.kuleuven.ezproxy.kuleuven.be/10.3917/afco.245.0100

Solomon, H. 2021. "Death Traps: Holes in Urban India." *Society and Space* 39.3: 423–40.

Sonny, P., and Y. Pesqueux. 2013. *L'organisation de la transgression: Formaliser l'informel?* Paris: L'Harmattan.

Sopranzetti, C. 2018. *Owners of the Map: Motorcycle Taxi Drivers, Mobility, and Politics in Bangkok*. Oakland: University of California Press.

Star, S. 1999. "The Ethnography of Infrastructure." *American Behavioral Scientist* 43.3: 377–39.

Steel, G. 2017. "Navigating (Im)mobility: Female Entrepreneurship and Social Media in Khartoum." *Africa: Journal of the International Africa Institute* 87.2: 233–52.

Steel, G. 2021. "Going Global—Going Digital: Diaspora Networks and Female Online Entrepreneurship in Khartoum, Sudan." *Geoforum* 120: 22–29.

Steel, G., I. Cottyn, and P. Van Lindert. 2017. "New Connections—New Dependencies Spatial and Digital Flows in Sub-Saharan African Livelihoods." In L. De Haan, ed., *Livelihoods and Development: New Perspectives*, 148–67. Boston: Brill.

Stefanelli, A. 2021. "'Excesses' of Modernity: Mundane Mobilities, Politics and the Remaking of the Urban." *Social Anthropology / Anthropologie Sociale* 29.4: 1049–63.

Stiegler, B. 1998. *Technics and Time: The Fault of Epimetheus*. Stanford, CA: Stanford University Press.

Stiegler, B. 2012. *Uncontrollable Societies of Disaffected Individuals*. London: Polity Press.

Street, A. 2014. *Biomedicine in an Unstable Place: Infrastructure and Personhood in a Papua New Guinean Hospital*. Durham, NC: Duke University Press.

Stroeken, K. 2005. "Immunising Strategies: Hip Hop and Critique in Tanzania." *Africa: Journal of the International Africa Institute* 75.4: 488–509.

Stroeken, K. 2011. "Resident Violence: Miner Mwanga Magic as a War-Technology Anthropology." In K. Stroeken, *War Technology Anthropology*, 120–34. Oxford: Berghahn.

Stroeken, K., A. Verdoolaege, M. Versichele, F. de Backere, D. Devos, S. Verstichel, and N. Van De Weghe. 2015. "Zone-it Before IT Zones You: A Location-Based App for Building Community While Preserving Privacy." *Journal of Location-Based Services* 9.1: 16–32.

Sylvanus, N. 2013. "Chinese Devils, the Global Market, and the Declining Power of Togo's Nana-Benzes." *African Studies Review* 56.1: 65–80.

Taee, J. 2017. *The Patient Multiple: An Ethnography of Healthcare and Decision-Making in Bhutan*. New York: Berghahn Books.

Tastevin, Y. P. 2011. "Panne de transmission: Une chronique mécanique de la diffusion de l'autorickshaw." In F. Wateau, C. Perles, and P. Soulier, eds., *Profils d'objets: Approches d'anthropologues et d'archéologues*, 231–42. Paris: Éditions de Boccard.

Taura, N. D., E. Bolat, and N. O. Madichie, eds. 2019. *Digital Entrepreneurship in Sub-Saharan Africa: Challenges, Opportunities and Prospects*. Cham: Palgrave Macmillan.

Taussig, M. T. 1980. *The Devil and Commodity Fetishism in South America*. Chapel Hill: University of North Carolina Press.

Taussig, M. T. 1999. *Defacement: Public Secrecy and the Labor of the Negative*. Stanford, CA: Stanford University Press.

Thacker, E. 2004. *Biomedia*. Minneapolis: University of Minnesota Press.

Thrift, N. 2004. "Intensities of Feeling: Towards a Spatial Politics of Affect." *Geografiska Annaler: Series B, Human Geography* 86.1: 57–78.

Ticktin, M. 2006. "Where Ethics and Politics Meet: The Violence of Humanitarianism in France." *American Ethnologist* 33: 33–49.

Tole, M. P. 1996. "Geothermal Energy Research in Kenya: A Review." *Journal of African Earth Sciences* 23.4: 565–75.

Tonda, J. 2005. *Le souverain moderne: Le corps du pouvoir en Afrique centrale (Congo, Gabon).* Paris: Karthala.

Tonda, J. 2006. *Tuée Tuée mon amour.* Rungis, France: La Doxa Editions.

Tonda, J. 2008. "La violence de l'imaginaire des enfants sorciers." *Cahiers d'Études Africaines* 1–2.189–90: 325–43.

Tonda, J. 2021. *Afrodystopie: La vie dans le rêve d'autrui.* Paris: Karthala.

Toulabor, C. 2012. "Les Nana Benz de Lomé." *Afrique Contemporaine* 4.244: 69–80.

Traxler, J., and A. Kukulska-Hulme. 2016. *Mobile Learning: The Next Generation.* New York: Routledge.

Trovalla, E., and U. Trovalla. 2015. "Infrastructure as a Divination Tool: Whispers from the Grids in a Nigerian City." *City* 19.2–3: 332–43.

Tsing, A. L. 2003. "Natural Resources and Capitalist Frontiers." *Economic and Political Weekly* 38.48: 5100–106.

Tublu, K. N. F. 2010. *Le mototaxi: Un nouveau mode dans la mobilité urbaine au Togo pour quelle qualité de vie?* Porto Novo: EPA.

Turner, V. 1969. *The Ritual Process: Structure and Anti-Structure.* Ithaca, NY: Cornell University Press.

Vachhani, S. J. 2013. "(Re)creating Objects from the Past: Affect, Tactility and Everyday Creativity." *Management and Organizational History* 8.1: 91–104.

van der Geest, S., and K. Finkler. 2004. "Hospital Ethnography: Introduction." *Social Science and Medicine* 59.10: 1995–2001.

Van de Walle, Nicholas. 2001. *African Economies and the Politics of Permanent Crisis, 1979–1999.* Cambridge: Cambridge University Press.

von Schnitzler, A. 2016. *Democracy's Infrastructure: Techno-Politics and Protest After Apartheid.* Princeton, NJ: Princeton University Press.

Waage, T. 2006. "Coping with Unpredictability: Preparing for Life in Ngaoundere, Cameroon." In C. M. Utas and H. Vigh, eds., *Navigating Youth, Generating Adulthood: Social Becoming in an African Context,* 61–87. Uppsala: Nordic African Institute.

Wamanji, E. 2010a. "Drilling the National Dream." *Steam,* September, 14–15.

Wamanji, E. 2010b. "How Menengai Will Light Kenya." *Steam,* January, 18–19.

Watts, M. J. 2004. "Antinomies of Community: Some Thoughts on Geography, Resources and Empire." *Transactions of the Institute of British Geographers* 29.2: 195–216.

Watts, M. J. 2007. "Petro-Insurgency or Criminal Syndicate? Conflict and Violence in the Niger Delta." *Review of African Political Economy* 34.114: 637–60.

Weber, M. 1992. *The Protestant Ethic and the Spirit of Capitalism.* Translated by Talcott Parsons. New York: Routledge.

Weber, M. 1998. *Citizenship in Ancient and Medieval Cities*. Minneapolis: University of Minnesota Press.

Weman, K. 2003. "Metal Arc Welding with Coated Electrodes." In *Welding Processes Handbook*, 63–67. Oxford: Woodhead Publishing.

Wendland, C. L. 2010. *A Heart for the Work*. Chicago: University of Chicago Press.

White, L., Jr. 1967. "The Historical Roots of Our Ecologic Crisis." *Science* 155: 1203–7.

Whyte, S. R. 1997. *Questioning Misfortune: The Pragmatics of Uncertainty in Eastern Uganda*. Cambridge: Cambridge University Press.

Whyte, S. R., S. Van Der Geest, and A. Hardon. 2002. *Social Lives of Medicines*. New York: Cambridge University Press.

Willame, J.-C. 1986. *Zaïre: L'épopée d'Inga, chronique d'une prédation industrielle*. Paris: Editions L'Harmattan.

Willemse, K. 2001. "'One Foot in Heaven': Narratives on Gender and Islam in Darfur, West Sudan." PhD dissertation, Leiden University.

Winner, L. 1977. *Autonomous Technology: Technics-Out-of-Control as a Theme in Political Thought*. Cambridge, MA: MIT Press.

Wittfogel, K. A. 1957. *Oriental Despotism: A Comparative Study of Total Power*. New Haven CT: Yale University Press.

Woolgar, S., and J. Lezaun. 2013. "The Wrong Bin Bag: A Turn to Ontology in Science and Technology Studies?" *Social Studies of Science* 43.3: 321–40.

Yemmafouo, A. 2017. "Pratiques foncières et dynamiques des paysages périurbains de Mbouda: Une contribution à l'étude des mutations spatiales autour des villes moyennes de l'Ouest-Cameroun." PhD dissertation, Université de Dschang.

Zaman, S. 2005. *Broken Limbs, Broken Lives: Ethnography of a Hospital Ward in Bangladesh*. Amsterdam: Het Spinhuis.